New Worlds from Fragments

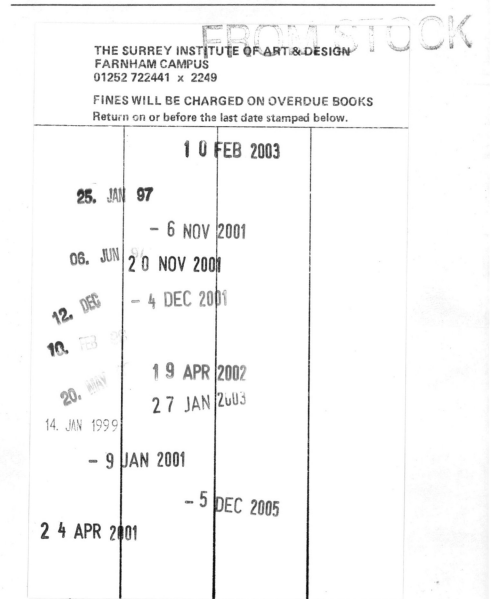

Studies in the Ethnographic Imagination

John Comaroff, Pierre Bourdieu, and Maurice Bloch, *Series Editors*

Reluctant Socialists, Rural Entrepreneurs: Class, Culture, and the Polish State   Carole Nagengast

The Power of Sentiment: Love, Hierarchy, and the Jamaican Family Elite   Lisa Douglass

Ethnography and the Historical Imagination   John and Jean Comaroff

Knowing Practice: The Clinical Encounter of Chinese Medicine   Judith Farquhar

New Worlds from Fragments: Film, Ethnography, and the Representation of Northwest Coast Cultures   Rosalind C. Morris

FORTHCOMING

Siva and Her Sisters: Gender, Caste, and Class in Rural South India   Karin Kapadia

New Worlds from Fragments

*Film, Ethnography,
and the Representation
of Northwest Coast Cultures*

ROSALIND C. MORRIS

WESTVIEW PRESS

Boulder • San Francisco • Oxford

Studies in the Ethnographic Imagination

The cover photograph, showing a Hamatsa initiate of the Kwakiutl Indians, was taken about 1902 by George Hunt, a Kwakiutl ethnographer and photographer who worked closely with Franz Boas. Neg. No. 22866, courtesy of the Department of Library Services, American Museum of Natural History.

Published in 1994 in the United States of America by Westview Press, Inc., 5500 Central Avenue, Boulder, Colorado 80301-2877, and in the United Kingdom by Westview Press, 36 Lonsdale Road, Summertown, Oxford OX2 7EW

Library of Congress Cataloging-in-Publication Data
Morris, Rosalind C.
  New worlds from fragments : film, ethnography, and the
representation of Northwest Coast cultures / Rosalind C. Morris.
     p.   cm.—(Studies in the ethnographic imagination)
  Includes bibliographical references and index.
  ISBN 0-8133-8574-1.—ISBN 0-8133-8783-3 (if published as a paperback)
  1. Indians of North America—Northwest Coast of North America—
Pictorial works.   2. Motion pictures in ethnology—Northwest Coast
of North America.   I. Title.   II. Series.
E78.N78M665   1994   93-47668
979.5'00497—dc20   CIP

Printed and bound in the United States of America

The paper used in this publication meets the requirements
of the American National Standard for Permanence of Paper
for Printed Library Materials Z39.48-1984.

10   9   8   7   6   5   4   3   2   1

Contents

Still Life with Vanishing Natives, 168
Last Words, 175

Preface and Acknowledgments

THIS BOOK BEGAN IN 1989 while I was a student in the Social Anthropology Department at York University in Toronto, Canada. Like all points of origin, this one is tenuous, and the book's beginnings undoubtedly lie somewhere further back, in time and space, and in the life of my scholarly imagination. Nonetheless, the research and the writing were undertaken during the academic year of 1988–1989, under the supervision of Ian Jarvie and Margaret Rodman.

The present work is a revised version of the original manuscript, written in the light of subsequent readings and thinking on the matter. However, the object of that analysis—namely, the ethnographic film of the Northwest Coast—remains the same. I have not done further archival research since 1989 and the films discussed here are those discussed in the original text, although both the introductory and the concluding chapters engage more recent material. The exclusion of ethnographic films produced since 1989 is in part a function of logistics. The revisions that ultimately informed the present work were made while I was conducting fieldwork in Northern Thailand, where access to North American documentary film is minimal, to say the least. But regardless of access, and despite the temptation to pursue an always impossible comprehensiveness, I believe the materials explored here are sufficient for my purposes. In any case, the films under consideration were screened at York University's own Film Library, the Sound and Moving Image Division of the Canadian National Archives, the Canadian Museum of Civilization in Ottawa, and the archives of the British Columbia Provincial Museum in Victoria. At various times, I received the expert assistance of curators and staff members at each of these institutions. All of their contributions are gratefully acknowledged here.

Like all intellectual endeavors, this one is indebted to the work of others. Formal recognition of those who directly influenced my thinking appears in the citations and references. But this book also grows out of discussions and engagements with colleagues, friends, and teachers. In particular, I want to recognize the contributions of Jean Comaroff and John Comaroff, both of whom read the manuscript and provided critical commentary. I am deeply— and differently—indebted to both of them for their incisive readings and enlightening suggestions. Ian Jarvie and Margaret Rodman may find the present work considerably changed from the original thesis, although I believe it is an extension of rather than a departure from its earliest formulation. I remain thankful for their patient advice, their intellectual guidance, and their abiding enthusiasm for the original project.

Others who should be thanked for less immediate assistance are Lorie Carr, who not only surrendered her dining room so that I might have a place in which to write but then tolerated my occasionally obsessive writing with patience and support, and Corrine Hunt, who first introduced me to the lives and hopes of Kwakiutl people.

Kellie Masterson of Westview Press has been a generous mentor and editor, and I am grateful for her intellectual comradeship and her personal friendship. Both have sustained me through the months of editing and revision. Michael M.J. Fischer, who read the manuscript as an outside reviewer for Westview Press, provided invaluable commentary on the original text and helped me to grapple with questions that remained unasked at that point. Others who deserve editorial credit are my parents, Pat and Hugh Morris. Like many academic writers, I must acknowledge my parents for both material and emotional support. However, my appreciation extends well beyond the justly deserved thanks for encouragement. At several points during the writing process, I sought and received editorial advice from my parents, who insisted that the value of scholarship depended upon both its intelligence and its accessibility. It is, in large part, to them that I owe my particular understanding of, and commitment to, responsible writing. And it is my hope that this book approaches their standards for a scholarship that is at once respectful of its audience and committed to its own originality.

Insofar as this book differs from the thesis from which it grew, I owe a special debt to Susan Turner. Through the many conversations that we shared on the issues raised here, an unwieldy manuscript matured into a book. I am most appreciative for her intellectual stimulation and literate criticisms, and for her good but gentle humor.

Of course, none of the people mentioned above can be burdened with any faults that appear in this book. Regrettably, I have been unable to accommodate or address all of the critical input received from readers and friends. Perhaps a later work will permit me to do justice to the lessons of this first book. In the meantime, I accept full and unqualified responsibility for all that follows.

Rosalind C. Morris

1

Preview: "Persistence of Vision"

There can be no aesthetics of the cinema, not even a purely technological one, which would not include the sociology of the cinema.
—T. W. Adorno

IN SEPTEMBER 1991, *Time* magazine ran a cover story with the flamboyant title "Lost Tribes, Lost Knowledge." Written by Eugene Linden and illustrated with William Couper's deeply textured photographs of aboriginal individuals—from places as diverse as highland Papua New Guinea and Bayanga of the Central African Republic—the *Time* essay is a tribute to the tenacity of a narrative in which Native peoples are imaged and imagined as beings on the verge of extinction. Linden's text is written in the apocalyptic tenor of medieval millenarianism:

> One horrible day, 1,600 years ago, the wisdom of many centuries went up in flames. The great library of Alexandria burned down. . . .
> Today, with little notice, more vast archives of knowledge and expertise are spilling into oblivion, leaving humanity in danger of losing its past and perhaps jeopardizing its future as well. . . .
> [T]he world's tribes are dying out or being absorbed into modern civilization. As they vanish so does their irreplaceable knowledge. (Linden 1991:40)

Thus does Linden begin his call to salvage arms. But in this tirade of anticipatory lamentation, Couper's images sit awkwardly, their dark cynicism providing bitter antidote to romantic sentimentality. It is as though the story as a whole were caught between the desire for instantiation and the temptation to irony. "Lost Tribes" is woven around a series of portraits, images of those very people whose existence, we are told, is now in question. The poses are not all frontal, as would have been required by an earlier documentary tradition aimed at the surveillance of bourgeois society's margins: the criminal, the insane, and the poor (Tagg 1988:34–59). Nonetheless, the eyes of the

1

pictured all return the look of the camera, asserting aboriginal presence in the very act of submitting to the camera's—and our own—"look." Yet it is not continuity that speaks here. Pictured thus, these people do not assert their ongoing lives, their survival, their possible futures. They do not refute the notion that they are dead or vanishing, as, for example, does Gloria Cranmer-Webster in her personal discussion of Kwakiutl history. In *Box of Treasures* (1983), the Kwakiutl answer to salvage ethnography, Cranmer-Webster can say with pride and defiance, "When you look at museum exhibits in a lot of places, it's as if we were gone. There's no reference to us still being alive. *And we are.*" Those portrayed in *Time* say nothing at all. They are absences, the reader's silent "others."[1] Effaced in the moment that they are rendered *as* faces, they become the currency of a global commodity economy in which portraits are circulated as the signs of social status (Tagg 1988:37–40) and where the simulacrum reigns supreme (Baudrillard 1983).

As in all salvage ethnographic narratives, Linden's tale of vanishing authenticity is ultimately countered by one of recuperation from without. The ironies of Couper's portraits and their potential refusal to signify loss are undermined and overcome by Linden's description of aboriginal cultures as being out of touch with their own knowledge, caught in the "voluntary" pursuit of cash and commodities (Linden 1991:42). Accordingly, it becomes the task of Western scholars and Western-educated Natives to seek and to preserve the vast repertoire of skills now slipping into oblivion.

Physically inset in the magazine, this other tale of heroic rescue is accompanied by a quite different set of images. Unlike the invasively close-up photographs of "traditionally" clad Natives, the scientists are featured in longshot, their facial blemishes and idiosyncrasies too distant to be visible or embarrassing. Embodiments of authority, the salvagers are seated in practical and eminently powerful contexts, either in laboratories or field situations. These detailed settings give to the images of science a sense of completeness and functionality, as well as particularity. In contrast, the neutral canvas backdrops of the Native portraits (in all but one case) create something akin to a museological space. Without context, without place (and Linden does not provide biographies for the Natives, as he does for the scientists), these faces appear as *objets d'art,* to be appreciated on purely aesthetic terms. The aesthetic tradition being evoked here is peculiarly modern in its cynical extremity, and the accompanying response is one of fascination. Susan Sontag (1977:42) has had the perspicacity to observe that fascination is boredom's underside. In making that connection, she facilitates an understanding of how the fetishism of alterity (whether in surrealism's violence or primitivism's romanticism) is related to a cultural and political fatigue that emerges in the whirlwind of modernity's consumerist orgy (Baudrillard 1983:88; Blau 1990:86).

William Couper's images are as alien as the grotesqueries of Diane Arbus's carnival series, and in their grinning faces and exaggerated deformities he, like Arbus, evokes a representational tradition of dramatic "othering." In their shadows one glimpses (because one is shown) the pathetic creatures whom early modern explorers imagined as the inhabitants of a still uncharted hemisphere (Boon 1982:3–26). Hence it is not the people but their knowledge—now commodified as something with exchange-value—that we are urged to pursue. Let us not mistake this valorization of Native "value" as an emancipatory gesture. Linden's plea is as bluntly consumerist as anything we might hear from *Wall Street*'s Gordon Gecko. Writes Linden (1991:56): "An indigenous culture can in itself be a marketable commodity if handled with respect and sensitivity." The photographs themselves position us as voyeurs. We gaze at them as at the freaks of a carnival sideshow, and in doing so, we experience the full power of an ideology that valorizes the exotic by creating otherness as the contradictory object of both horror and desire (Bhabha 1983). It goes without saying, though it should be remarked nonetheless, that the assumed "we," the viewing and reading subjects of Linden's article, is *not* aboriginal. Although the story is featured in an internationally distributed format with circulation throughout Asia, Africa, and the Pacific, readers are identified with, and interpolated as, Euro-Americans of the middle and upper-middle classes. These tribal peoples are unequivocally other. They are "they," primitive object to "our" (the presumed readers') metropolitan subject.

Anthropologists who read Eugene Linden's article might well wonder whether it is not a hoax, whether *Time* had not unearthed the story in the previous century's archives. Hence the title of this chapter. Originally, the phrase "persistence of vision" was used—incorrectly, as it turns out—to describe the physical (ocular and neurological) process by which a series of still pictures could be perceived as a single continuous but moving image (Jarvie 1987:148–149; Anderson and Anderson 1980). Persistence of vision was invoked as the biological and phenomenological ground of film *qua* "movies." I use it here in an ironic vein, both to foreshadow the discussion of film and to indicate the stubborn continuity (which is not to say identity) of the "vanishing Natives" trope in both academic and popular representations of Native peoples. The *Time* cover story is strikingly similar to the tales of vanishing Natives that were used a century and more ago to justify exploratory journeys, salvage expeditions, and, more insidiously, the traffic in human beings for museological purposes (Gilman 1985; Comaroff and Comaroff 1991:104). But perhaps more vexing for the contemporary anthropologist, the *Time* magazine piece echoes a kind of mythic charter that fueled the discipline's own salvage project during the first half of this century and, beyond that, into the structuralist heyday of the 1970s (Malinowski 1984; Levi-Strauss 1955). Thus it is with a certain shock of recognition that anthropologists must inevitably encounter this story, a relic of the discipline's own history now recuperated by one of the most widely disseminated magazines in the world.

Recognition and horror. For if anthropology was founded on, and in-scribed within, narratives of loss and alienation, the past few decades have seen a considerable amount of critical ink spilled in the effort to deconstruct those self-same myths. Coming from both within and outside the discipline, and with varying prognoses for the field itself, such criticism has laid bare the ideological underpinnings of the discipline's constructs: of notions like "primitiveness" and "modernity" (though much analysis remains to be done of the latter), "simple" and "complex," "tribal" and "civilized." And despite a lingering romanticism, it is no longer tenable to speak of tradi-tional worlds isolated from global, historical processes—if ever it was (Asad 1973; Clifford 1988a; de Certeau 1988; Fabian 1983). Such tropes now appear as the media for constituting rather than analyzing otherness, as the currency of an ideology that naturalizes differences in the metaphors of time and space (Fabian 1983). Those of us who identify as anthropologists per-haps flatter ourselves with newfound worldliness, a postmodern conscious-ness of *differance* and historicity. Such flattery, and the satisfaction it gener-ates, is some consolation for the humility required by the surrender of the discipline's more epic myths and the accompanying role of "hero" (Sontag 1966). But, if *Time* magazine is any indication, critical anthropology's les-sons have not yet made their way beyond the polished ivory walls of the academy, and self-congratulation is premature at best (Comaroff and Comaroff 1992).

The failure of our critical efforts to reach other ears should not, however, be taken as grounds for abandoning them. To the contrary, it is reason to repeat them—if need be, in new and more broadly intelligible languages. Although this book focuses on film and offers little explicit commentary on photography as such, Linden and Couper's "cover story" raises all of the issues to which I shall direct my attention in the following chapters: how aboriginal peoples are imaged, how their histories are narrated, and how representational strategies are related to the institutional structures in which they emerge. It raises still other questions about how the experience of loss and the perception of history are differently constructed at different times. And, implicitly, it poses the question of how "images" work as combinations of pictures and words, woven together as rhetorical and iconological wholes that exceed both forms in their communicative as well as affective aspects (Mitchell 1986).

All of these matters could, of course, be raised without recourse to *Time*. And one might well ask whether I have not erected a rather misshapen straw figure as a foil for my own project. To the contrary, however, my purpose here is not merely to deconstruct this particular essay and this particular set of images but, rather, to see them as cultural artifacts that are determined within a specific and specifiable moment of production. As such, they can also be made to reveal something about that moment, which is to say, about the present moment: our moment. "Lost Tribes, Lost Knowledge" is a document, if not a documentary, a mirror as well as a projection, and, hence, we may use it to pose reflexive questions. It is, as the structuralists have said of totems, "good to think." The most obvious of those questions is, quite simply, "Why now?" Why, in a year marked by political revolutions in the Baltics, the former Soviet Union, and Southeast Asia, and in the year of the Gulf War, did *Time* choose to run "Lost Tribes" as its cover story? I offer no easy answers to that question, and any conclusions that I draw in this book will inevitably seem oblique to such a pointed but necessary inquiry. Nonetheless, a few explanatory remarks are in order. These were foreshadowed a few pages earlier when I suggested that the fetishism of alterity—so potently exhibited in Couper's photographs—is meaningful precisely because our own subjectivities have been blunted by the onslaught of history, a history conceived and represented as cataclysmic, accelerating, and uncontrolled change.

One discerns here the symptoms of that direct but complex relationship between the experience of modernity *as* change and the desire for authenticity and purity, invariably understood as stasis (cf. Williams 1973; Fabian 1983). Indeed, these two temporal orientations imply each other. The pursuit of authenticity emerges from the experience of loss, of incoherence, even of progress. It is to this painful contradiction of the modern predicament that Walter Benjamin refers when he warns that "when newness [becomes] a fetish, history itself [becomes] a manifestation of the commodity form" (Buck-Morss 1989:82). Benjamin was prompted to make this remark while considering the display and sale of curios and antiques in the Paris Arcades. It was not, however, simply the revaluation and commodification of old things that struck Benjamin as symptomatic of the times but also the fact that this exchange of antiquities was taking place beneath the vaulted glass and steel of France's most severely modern edifice. What must be added to Benjamin's evocative meditation is an awareness of the degree to which antiquity, authenticity, and tradition were themselves located in categories of cultural otherness, whether these were understood along the axes of the rural and the urban or those of the primitive and the civilized. The traffic in antiques developed alongside the traffic in ethnographic objects, both of which were imagined as ciphers of lost origins. And it is for this reason that I think Benjamin's (1977) remarks and his never-completed exploration of nostalgia (Buck-Morss 1989) have relevance here in a consideration of Couper's ethnographic curiosities and Linden's discourse on the value of vanishing wisdom.

Nonetheless, it is insufficient to reduce Euro–North American representations of otherness to a bland and all-encompassing nostalgia, powerful though that impulse may be. To do so is to conflate a vast array of ideas and

images that, while related to one another, are historically specific and distinct in a number of important ways. In the end, the reductionist critique
only repeats orientalist binarisms in the act of naming them. To take the
lessons of recent historical and cultural criticism seriously, one must ask how
different narratives are employed in different contexts, for what purposes,
and with what results. And to this more specific task the following chapters
are devoted.

For now, one wants to ask once more why *Time* magazine would run
"Lost Tribes" as a cover story in these eminently troubled times. One must
acknowledge first the profound anxiety and even the sincerity (however des-
perate, however self-satisfied) with which Linden writes when he prophesies
the doom of Native lifeways. Ultimately, he is resigned to such disaster and
his story belies a concern with knowledge as commodity, rather than with
people as living beings. Thus he calls for a vast archive of indigenous wisdom, and virtually ignores the political struggles for self-determination that
are occurring the world over.[2] But what purpose is being served by the tex-
tualization of these Natives in such a manner? Of what are they a sign? It
behooves us to understand what "structures of feeling" (Williams 1973)
Linden is addressing, what great political unconscious he and *Time* magazine are invoking, and what powers they are soliciting with such a glossy
rendition of the vanishing Indian tale.

The nostalgia that operates here does not assume simply that these Native
peoples are a part of the reader's own past, that they are the residue of her or
his own evolution in its last visible stages. Such crude evolutionism may be
at work on some level but it is insufficient to guarantee sales, and, in the
end, *Time* chooses its stories for their salability. It seems to me that there is a
far more complex kind of regret at issue here. For the "Lost Tribes" of
whom Linden writes and as photographed by Couper are construed not as a
literal part of the reader's own past but as somehow equivalent to it. The
salvage operation is therefore a mediating gesture in which Western scientists save an "other" future past from vanishing irretrievably on the basis of
their own personal/collective experience of what such loss may entail. The
motivating assumption of such a liberal act is, of course, that Native peoples
do not and cannot anticipate their own loss. To be ahistorical in the postmodern world is to be without an adequate sense of a future past, without a
fear of loss. The displaced and displacing nostalgia that Linden voices is utterly amoebic. By rendering the histories of tribal peoples as proxy pasts for a
too-modern/postmodern commodity culture, the new rescuers encompass
difference while maintaining the irremediable gap of history. And as they do
so, they assuage both the disempowering panic that a rapidly transmuting
world order can induce and the liberal guilt that emerges in the recognition
of that order's destructive consequences. And it is this therapeutic value
which largely explains the cover story status of "Lost Tribes." If fascination

is boredom's ironic underbelly, then "Lost Tribes" is truly an article for the times, though it is perhaps not boredom so much as the dazed numbness of sensory overload that lies beneath the renewed desire for exotica.

What I am trying to achieve here is an understanding of the specificities of nostalgia and a comprehension of the political implications that particular representations entail. In this regard, I take John Tagg's (1988) provocative discussion of photography as a starting point. Writing in response to Roland Barthes's final work—to which I, myself, shall return in the conclusion to this book—Tagg (1988:3) asserts, "The photograph is not a magical 'emanation' but a material product of a material apparatus, set to work in specific contexts, by specific forces, for more or less defined purposes. It requires, therefore, not an alchemy but a history." Tagg himself goes further to describe the kind of history he has in mind, a history not of discoveries and technological innovations but of institutions and ideologies, of ways of seeing and modes of representation. His is an updated version of what T. W. Adorno was advocating in his call for a "sociology of the cinema," cited at the head of this chapter.

It is common for philosophers of art to erect categorical boundaries between film and photography, but as I have intimated in the preceding passages, my interest is not with the ontological status of either film or photography. Rather, I am concerned with the ways in which either and both have been employed in the representation of cultural others—and selves. Indeed, the specific insights developed in studies of one can fruitfully be applied to the other. This is especially true in considerations of documentary film, which—as a discipline—shares with photography a particular ideology of transparency and immediacy. As shall become apparent, that ideology has concealed and effaced the strategies and tropes of historically and institutionally relative narratives, all of which are saturated with moral and political implication.

At any given time, particular narratives, particular visions and versions of history, achieve hegemonic status. This is not to say that other, contesting narratives do not exist—they do; but it is important to realize the degree to which empowered narratives are experienced as real and true within a particular moment. In this book, I treat the history of ethnographic film on the Northwest Coast as a history of reigning narratives. Although the material considered here is almost exclusively filmic, I situate it within anthropology as a whole and attempt to trace the institutional forces that shaped it throughout this century. Such an approach entails a discursive analysis in the sense that it attends to the implicit subject position (which is not reducible to the personal subject) of representation (Tagg 1988:23). It is important to note, however, that in advocating a discursive analysis—that is, an analysis of institutions and representational strategies—I do not, in any way, intend to abandon "the real." Here again, Tagg's (1988:24) own grapplings with the subject are instructive: "What is denied is not the 'non-discursive' but the conception of it as a unitary category with general attributes, knowable through a 'non-discursive experience,' yielding general criteria of epistemological validity." What this means for a history of *changing* representations is that one does not look to "the real" for a critique of dominant narratives. Rather, different renditions of history all circulate within a given discursive formation, and emerge there to be authorized or discredited within particular institutional structures. Accordingly, there can be tensions and contradictions between various representations and different institutions at any particular time.

This is the case within anthropology itself, and not only between national and theoretical schools but in and between *genres*—especially between filmic and nonfilmic anthropology. One of the reasons for looking at filmic ethnography in its relationship to other representations is to understand how and why these genres are different. As such analysis is possible only within limited parameters, I have chosen to focus my attention on films about the Northwest Coast. It should be noted at the outset, however, that my primary concern in this book is with Canadian materials. Partly, this makes the field manageable; but, mainly, it is in keeping with my original project, which was to write an ideological history of Canadian visual anthropology. However, as the project has expanded, I have tried to broaden my considerations and conclusions to address the currents and trends that bind Canadian thought with its American counterpart. Wherever possible, then, the text refers to developments in American anthropology as well, but the focus of analysis is marked by the use of the terms "Euro-Canadian" and "Euro–North American."

The choice of a field is always problematic, and this is especially true here, where the connotations of sight ("field of vision") and culture area (as well as its homonym "field-site") have such profound consequence. Since the days of Boasian anthropology, the Northwest Coast has been a disciplinary fascination, central to all discussions of "culture area." The term itself encompasses a massive, international stretch of coastline and several distinct languages, as well as innumerable dialects. Member-cultures certainly traded and warred with one another, but the notion that they belonged to a single cultural complex, or that others did not, is a highly dubious and arbitrary one (see Chapter 2). It is, nonetheless, the vision on which a large subfield of early Canadian and American anthropology was founded, and it is that reified and environmentally deterministic vision that interests me here. For if the notion of culture area framed the filmmaker's gaze, filmmakers then reinscribed that category in their own narratives, thereby completing the circle of seeing and believing. This is not, then, a history of the Northwest Coast, as reflected by anthropological filmmakers, but a history of anthropology's imagination of the Northwest Coast. Included within that category of the anthropological are recent efforts at Native self-representation: the films of reclamation produced by and for Band councils. If, in the end, there is a response to Linden and Couper's tragic and condescending romanticism, it lies here, in this refusal to be silenced, to be reduced to the object of an aestheticizing gaze. Without denying all loss, without effacing the brute and often brutal effects of our particular global order, one can yet say, contra Linden and Couper, "All is not lost."

Notes

1. Regarding the use of "other" versus "Other" throughout this book, the point of my distinction is to separate general statements about cultural differences, specifically antihistorical (usually colonial) representations of singular cultural difference. The former is designated with the lower case, the latter with the upper case. In the former, differences are not totalized to create a monolithic image of unchanging otherness. In the latter, this reification is precisely the intended effect. My own text tries to reflect the nuances of usage and ideological implication in the discourse under discussion. It is intended as textual echo.

2. The most bitter irony is, of course, that the creation of a library makes knowledge vulnerable to destruction—both because knowledge abstracted and extracted from everyday usage is no longer functional or adaptable, and because it is literally and physically subject to damage. Witness the case of the Alexandrian library that introduces Linden's story.

2

Through a Glass Darkly: Terms and Problems for Analysis

A film is always a document—a documentary—of film and cinema, never in any immediacy of people.
—Stephen Heath

No Innocent Eye: Basic Terms and Concepts

LET ME RETURN, THEN, to the beginning. The title of this book, *New Worlds from Fragments*, is drawn from an article penned by Franz Boas in 1898. There, in a now-famous passage, Boas discusses the emergence of new myths and narratives among the people of the Thompson River: "It would seem that mythological worlds have been built up, only to be shattered again, and that new worlds were built from the fragments" (1898:18). The marvelling tone expresses a sentiment rarely attributed to Boas, the obsessive and often clinical surveyor. But it is also a marvelling tempered by wistfulness. The *bricolage* to which Boas refers was the product of cultural disintegration and was, for him, a sign of the endless historical processes by which cultures respond to their environment, undergo transformation, and, ultimately, cease to be. The sense of imminent demise, which Boas shared with virtually all of his contemporaries, lingers on. And it is this anticipatory nostalgia which aligns him with the authors of the *Time* magazine article and makes him important to the present analysis—despite the fact that he wrote almost a century ago and in circumstances very different from our own.

Boas's central preoccupation in the passage cited is also my own, to the extent that his narrative is an object for analysis. The representation of cultures in history—and the history of that representation—is one of this book's main areas of inquiry. The terms of Boas's lament, the concepts of

11

fragmentation and resurgence, recur throughout this text as the focal metaphors for anthropology's discourses on Native North Americans, and it is
my purpose to examine the specific deployment of those terms in various
narratives throughout the twentieth century. This book, then, is an attempt
to formulate an historicized theory of ethnographic film.

In the briefest and most general terms, such a theory begins with the
notion that ethnographic film can be conceived as a genre of anthropological representation and that its narrative form and content both manifest
and reveal the institutional structures in which it was, and continues to be,
produced. Given the hegemony of the museum during most of anthropology's history, this means that ethnographic film must be understood in
relation to museology. In the early part of this century, the influence of the
museum ensured that a concern with the representation of cultural forms
and relations would become an obsession with material culture and object
forms. Thus, I treat early ethnographic filmmaking as the instantiation of
anthropology's political and moral economy of collection and preservation.
Only in the last two decades have the developments in Native museology
called the salvage ethos into question and recast the problem of ethnographic inscription in terms of voice and expression rather than object and
representation. Such issues emerge toward the end of this book in an
analysis of indigenous filmmaking and its implications for a discipline no
longer defined in the acquisitive mode. Nonetheless, most of the analysis in
this book attests to a deeply rooted and deeply influential vision of ethnographic film as a mode of cultural reification.

The present chapter is devoted to a consideration of the many theoretical
questions that such a theory entails, whereas later chapters explore particular
narratives and the teleological ideologies that they imply in their relationship
to anthropology as a whole. This chapter ranges widely—some may feel too
widely—over issues of epistemology, the film's claim to indexicality, the history of the documentary concept, and the nature of ethnographic narrative.
But in its admittedly audacious attempt to negotiate the vast terrain of film
theory and anthropological poetics, this book aims to stimulate the further
development of an historicized ethnographic film theory. To this end, it explores some of the more extreme positions in ethnographic film and stages
them against one another in intertextual conflict, while preserving what I
feel is their legitimate element in the construction of an alternative vision.
Such a strategy, utilized in place of a literature survey, may seem overly eclec-
tic, and, to be sure, many of the writers on whom I draw would be uncomfortable with their placement alongside theoretical foes. With apologies to
those who insist upon the purity of their position, I nonetheless feel that
such theoretical "hunting and gathering" is justified in the endeavor to pro-
voke a rethinking of ethnographic film theory.

Historical Scenes and Theoretical Backdrops

It has been estimated that more than two hundred films about Northwest Coast Natives were made prior to the 1940s.[1] Many of these were simply short newsreels of topical interest, some were produced for police and/or military purposes, and still others were travelogues made to titillate the adventure-seeking but racist sensibilities of filmgoers in the early part of this century. Films in which Native peoples and their institutions constituted the primary or exclusive subject matter were few and far between. Nonetheless, these are precisely the films that I have identified as being "ethnographic."

In this respect, I take a rather different position than Karl Heider, who, in *Ethnographic Film* (1976), elaborates a pseudo-quantitative concept of "ethnographicness" based on a relationship of similarity between the image track and the objective world, as well as on the explanatory value of the filmic and extrafilmic narration. Now more than fifteen years old, Heider's book retains a position of authority within visual anthropological circles, despite the critical efforts of Faye Ginsberg (1988), Bill Nichols (1976, 1981), Jay Ruby (1982, 1983, 1988), and many of the contributors to the journal *Visual Anthropology*. For this reason, if for no other, it is worthy of serious critical attention. But I use it here as an instance of a more widely and frequently less bluntly articulated position. Because of its representativeness rather than its ubiquity, I want to clarify my own disagreements with the position taken in *Ethnographic Film* and to use that discussion as a starting point for a more general consideration of documentary film.

Vexed with the problem of adjudication—What makes a documentary film good or bad?—Heider has developed an "attribute dimension grid," which defines certain substantive and stylistic characteristics as more or less crucial to the ethnographic film. At the top of this scale is "ethnographic basis," meaning the degree to which the film is informed by "ethnographic understanding," while at the bottom and in direct opposition is "intentional distortion of behavior" (Heider 1976:112–113). Writing with the classroom in mind, Heider rates the presence of accompanying nonfilmic materials (number 2 of 14) more important than considerations of the ethnographer's/filmmaker's presence (number 9).

Clearly, ethnographic film is secondary to literary ethnography for Heider, and is intrinsically incapable of the kind of analytic abstraction that marks the written text. (See Hockings 1988 for a more recent statement of the same position.) One is reminded here of Rudolph Arnheim's immediately anachronistic tract, *Film as Art* (1958), which asserts that film's aesthetic value consists in its lack—its lack of sound, color, and three-dimensionality. But Heider's assumption of representational limits is not idiosyncratic. To the contrary, it derives from a pervasive concept of the visual as something that excludes language. The fundamental dichotomy between body and voice is so deeply entrenched in Western aesthetics that, despite decades of experimentation in the plastic arts, it is still commonplace to speak of the opposition between image and text. Endeavors to theorize a language or "rhetoric" of images, though promising, have tended to reduce the latter to latent structure and grammar, and have not, in general, fully explored the ideology of perception upon which these constructs rest (cf. Barthes 1985; Berger 1982; Crary 1990).

W.J.T. Mitchell has, however, pointed the way with a deconstruction of that opposition in his inspired book, *Iconology* (1986). In a broad exploration of the metaphors of representation, and paying particular attention to the *camera obscura* as the incarnation of mimetic poetics, Mitchell shows us how texts operate as total signifying systems in which the aural and the visual perform in a single sphere of signification. He thereby undermines the hegemony of the picture as the basis for an understanding of the image. The fecundity of his argument for a consideration of film should not be overlooked for it permits the reconsideration of all ontologically oriented film theory that, beginning with Arnheim, assumes the primacy of the pictorial and denigrates the aural as a compromised sign of reality.

Ethnographic film, and visual anthropology in general, takes up that visually oriented bias with apologetic vengeance, and thereby blinds itself to an analysis of the various ways in which films can and do signify. At once diminishing the visual text in comparison to the written, and claiming (if only tacitly) that the image-track (really picture-track) is the only unmediated instance of the real, visual anthropology resigns itself to a grossly confined project. But it is legitimate to ask why the representational capacity of the film should be reduced to its visual dimension. Why, indeed, is *Visual Anthropology* not titled "Ethnographic Film and Photography"? Why is voice the mere supplement of vision? And why is voice deemed aural even in its visualization as titles? There is a clear, if tacit, ideology of perception embedded in the construction of film as a visual text, and it has to do with the commitment both to "seeing is believing" and to the sense that the "visual" artifact has greater materiality than does its auditory counterpart.

Let me return to Karl Heider and his particular rendition of the visual/aural opposition. By a generous reading, Heider's argument seems relevant and plausible if we limit our considerations to early silent documentaries and the homemade films of ethnographers who went into the field without the possibility of synchronous sound recording. But even then, the subtitle provided the possibility of voice. To say that subtitles are not real voices but mere representations of voice and therefore less real than the image-track (a not uncommon response) is, of course, to demand an investigation of the image's claim to immediacy. For Heider, as for many—if not most—documentary theorists, the immediacy of the image-track is not in question. It only becomes an issue at an ethical level when one considers the possibility of "intentional distortion." Otherwise, we are to presume that films and photographs *present* to us what Stanley Cavell (1973) calls "the world viewed." As though the film were merely a frame through whose absent center one could observe the world in all its metamorphoses. But film is more than its frame, and even framing is a moment of semantic construction, a way of imbuing "the seen" with meaning.

Documentary film's claim to immediacy is the claim of photographic indexicality, the sense that the photograph is materially imprinted with reality. To be sure, photographs and films are imprinted with something, but the question of what we see when we look at either photographs or films remains to be answered. John Tagg provides a succinct and powerful counterpoint to the naturalist commitment when he claims that "*every* photograph is the result of specific and, in every sense, significant distortions which render its relation to any prior reality deeply problematic. . . .

"The indexical nature of the photograph—the causative link between the pre-photographic referent and the sign—is therefore highly complex, irreversible, and can guarantee nothing at the level of meaning" (1988:2–3). Thus, the question is not How is the world transformed into its image? but, as Maureen Turin asks, "How does meaning enter the image?" (1985:7). The answer, so enormous in its implications as to sound absurd, must be: through processes of coding and analogy (Eco 1976), and through the operations of a technological apparatus that emerges in a specific representational and ideological tradition extending back (at least) to Renaissance perspectival painting (Baudry 1974–1975; Pleynet 1978).[2]

Insofar as naturalist photography is concerned, the image reproduces the *appearance* of reality. What this means is that, in viewing the photograph, the subject enacts a specific history of representation that includes particular notions about the nature of reality: its categories, organization, significance. It is therefore as a trialogic relationship among the viewer, the photographer, and the historical context of both the photograph and the viewer that the act of reading imbues the image with its power to signify. More than this, the image mobilizes an entire perceptual structure that permits the viewer to translate certain phenomena into signs of a structured reality. When we say that the image presents or even represents the world (or a part of it), we are saying that we have learned to recognize certain qualities of line, density, and spatial orientation, certain principles of color and proportion, as the basis of a system that evokes the three-dimensional and temporally extended domain of (culturally mediated) experience. The ability to recognize the subject matter of a photograph depends entirely upon its conformity to the structures and cardinal measures of a socially situated perception. When the principles of everyday vision are undermined by the photograph (as in the work of, say, Moholy-Nagy), then it appears to us as abstraction, as something unnatural, or as a symbolic representation of something ephemeral and beyond empirical actuality. Given these issues, it is difficult to imagine a more complex or highly mediated process than that of viewing a photograph. And there are times when one is tempted to see such an act of visual translation as being utterly miraculous. For in what sense can the flat sheet of paper marked by myriad black dots be identical with reality?

And yet, we experience it as such. We learn to experience the apprehension of a photograph as being analogous to the apprehension of the world. The act of viewing itself performs that mimesis which is then located in the image itself. Accordingly, the investigation of a photograph (or a film) can provide us with the means of critically analyzing our own vision of reality and, indeed, our own construction of reality. This applies on aesthetic and ideological levels to an equal degree. I will return to this problem below; but for now, Heider's problem, of what constitutes a good and valid ethnographic film, remains. If the film does not, in its very being, partake of the reality about which its maker wishes to speak (as Bazinian theorists would argue), how does it represent that phenomenon? On some level, Heider's evaluative scheme acknowledges this problem, but it does so only by displacing the question of reference onto the written text. The pursuit of proximity between the image track and the "objective world" already suggests the inevitability of what Tagg calls "significant distortion." Heider's solution is to call for secondary materials that will contextualize and verify the filmic text—that will compensate for its inherent lack. In doing so he assumes that the visible world exists independent of a socialized vision and that its status and accessibility are not in question. In an ironic way, then, Heider admits to the poverty of visual hermeneutics when he suggests that the obvious mediations of the literary text provide a better ground for anthropological understanding than does the photograph, with its seeming transparency and supposed lack of conceptual structuring. In Heider's analysis, language is indicative and hence capable of explanation, whereas the photographic record, being indexical, is demonstrative—perhaps even performative—and is therefore of little use in social analysis, except as data. On this basis, Heider calls for a naive realism, elevating an aesthetic position into a question of veracity.

At the other end of the theoretical spectrum is Sol Worth, who counters Heider's pursuit of transparency with a definition located in the invisible, the incipient, and the unconscious. Worth (1969, 1972) defines all films, from the Hollywood thriller to the voice-over documentary, as having ethnographic potential, since all are cultural artifacts. For Worth, the ethnographic dimension of film is something akin to a use-value that is realized by the receiver (audience) according to the purposes for which a film is screened. But if this formulation escapes the intentionalist fallacy—the notion that a message means what its sender intends it to mean—it errs in the direction of solipsism, and by ignoring the material structures and aesthetic/ideological traditions within which a film is produced, it accords the individual viewer's idiosyncratic reading far too much authority (Brunette 1988). In essence, a film becomes ethnographic for Worth when its viewer treats it ethnographically, irrespective of the stated or implicit objectives of the filmmaker, the structures of reception to which it is directed, and the institutional context of its production. In response, one needs to ask about the status of the viewer and the kinds of relationships that are possible between filmmakers and their audiences. Those relationships are constituted through specific conventions and communicative codes, and operate within specific interpretive communities, sometimes dispersed, as in the cross-continental audience of Spike Lee fans, and sometimes more intimate, as in the classrooms of film schools.

The recognition of filmic codes—and of a filmmaker's transcendence of those codes—is, I would argue, the basis of everyday film-viewing experience. This is not to suggest a perfect unity of artistic intention and audience experience; interpretive communities and possible readings are many and various, though perhaps not as infinite as some may suggest. Nor do I mean to reduce film to its most banal communicative level. There is always a "surplus" of meaning, a beyond of expression that exceeds the film's translatability to different subject positions. Nonetheless, there is a sense in which films are always purposefully communicative. Even films that self-consciously defy the conventional rules of composition and genre expectation[3] succeed in communicating something, if only an awareness of themselves as artifice and of the conventions that must be violated in order to effect that rupture of understanding which marks them as avant-garde.

But to return, Sol Worth's claim for the immanence of "ethnographicness" might appear less obviously tenable if applied to literary documents. All books and literary productions are cultural artifacts, but they are ethnographies only in the most general and trivial sense, even when being used by ethnographers for research purposes. There is, of course, an extent to which a Kafka novel or an Atget photograph has ethnographic value, but though both may reveal something about the cultural forms of a particular moment in a particular place (where place connotes class, race, and gender as well as location), they do so incidentally. Ethnography is as much an institutionally sanctioned and structured discipline, in the sense ascribed to psychoanalysis by de Certeau (1986) and to clinical medicine by Foucault (1975), as it is the representation or interpretation of cultures, as Geertz (1973b) has argued. While all books and films may contain ethnographic information, they are not all ethnographies in the specific sense; they do not share the formal—genre—conventions and historical traditions of ethnography as a discipline. But these institutional frameworks and politico-economic contexts are crucial (if not total) determinants of any discourse. Thus, one wants a more precise and specific notion of the ethnographic film, one that defines the text, as it were, contextually.

Ethnographic Film as Genre

If not a spectrum of "ethnographicness" nor a potentiality of the filmic text, then what is "ethnographic film"? I prefer to conceive of ethnographic film as an institutionally situated genre defined by its subject matter and its objectives: namely, as the representation and/or evocation of cultural groups and the "explicitation" (not necessarily the explanation) of sociocultural institutions and/or practices. Needless to say, those parameters entail aesthetic considerations (Pryluck 1988:256). But such a definition locates ethnographic film within the discipline of anthropology in general and, while leaving room for normative judgments, it does not equate aesthetic value (or style, for that matter) with ethnography.

Traditionally, genre criticism has categorized films on the basis of a particular set of shared themes and iconography (Nichols 1976:107). More than that, however, genre types are defined on the basis of films' relationships to an external, which is to say an extrafilmic, world (Nichols 1976). That world is not, it must be remembered, nondiscursive (Tagg 1988:23). We are speaking here of a set of representations, a culturally ordered world, and not of some pure and absolutely prior level of bodily "experience" or unconsciousness. Thus, it may be argued that Western films narrate the frontier ethic and its expansionist project, or that road movies articulate the radical individualism of a mobile and atomistic society. In either case, the films are "about" a kind of *experience* and an ideology of that experience which transcends the dramatic narrative in which they are produced. Genre criticism is thus a kind of anthropological criticism insofar as it considers films in terms of their relationship to an *ordered world*.

David MacDougall (1978:405) seems to overstate the matter when he claims that "ethnographic film cannot be said to constitute a genre, nor is ethnographic film a discipline with unified origins and an established methodology." MacDougall's assertion addresses both the analysis of ethnographic films and the filmmaking itself, and this duality may account for some of its confusion. He would have been more accurate had he claimed that there is no anthropological genre criticism. Indeed, there has been relatively little theorization of film in anthropology generally, and even less that deals with film as a mode of representation in which the ideology of the discipline is played out. Increasingly, anthropologists are drawing attention to this lacuna in the literature and in the discipline's self-analysis (Ginsberg

1988; Rosenthal 1988; Ruby 1983; Young 1988), but as late as 1988, Marcus Banks could decry the state of the theoretical art, noting that anthropologists have barely been even cognizant of the "issue of realism" in ethnographic film (1988:2–3). Bill Nichols, acknowledging the "generally ill-defined nature of [the] entire enterprise," supports a genre criticism (1981:238) and I take my belated cue from him.

Like the term "ethnography," "genre" indicates a methodological orientation as much as anything; genre criticism establishes the kinds of questions to be asked and defines the set of films to be considered. My concern in this book is with a rather narrowly defined group of films, films that constitute a quite coherent and intertextually referenced set. Their subject matter is the "Northwest Coast," and they represent the entire span of ethnographic film history. By selecting films in this manner I do not mean to valorize the culture area concept, nor to reify that vast stretch of culturally diverse and historically divergent human existence. I choose and use "Northwest Coast" because it has been utterly central to the anthropological imagination and because it was in the descriptive elaboration of that particular culture area that so many of the discipline's now-commonplace tropes were developed. Andrew Sarris has remarked that "film history is both films *in* history and the history of films" (1976:242). In a similar fashion, a visual anthropology must be concerned with films in their dual aspect: as symbolic statements about foreign cultures, but also as embodiments of our own culture's system of representation. Our "visual" anthropology must be films *in* anthropology and an anthropology *of* films.

The Ethnographic Gaze and the Spectacle of Culture Area

The notion of a Northwest Coast culture area was first articulated by Alfred Kroeber in 1923 and later refined by Boas and Sapir (McFeat 1966:vii–viii). Early assumptions about homogeneity have more recently been challenged on methodological grounds (Szathmary and Ossenberg 1978) and on the basis of a reexamination of coastal languages (Jorgenson 1980). In response to that critique some have attempted to recuperate the concept through a structuralist vision of layered history in which a basic identity is overlaid with ephemeral diversity (Adams 1981:362–363). But here the problem of difference is merely displaced, brushed off, if you will, like so much topsoil. What is perhaps most unacceptable about the culture area approach is that it completely fails to account for its own subject position. It cannot raise the question of what constitutes similarity, analogy, or difference, except as statistical relationships between already-selected objects. And such utter blindness to the act of representation, and hence to the act of ethnography, needs now to be addressed and redressed. One wants to know why some differences are deemed to *make a difference* and why others are not so authorized.

The assumption behind the culture area concept is, of course, that cultural differentiation is determined by a preexistent environment to which people adapt themselves and which they may modify either materially or symbolically, but which always remains prior. Thus it becomes possible to map the practices and the formal arrangements of social groups onto a landscape whose contours provide the limits of identity and difference. To be sure, many people of this so-called Northwest Coast themselves profess beliefs in the essential relationship between place and human identity (humanness—specifically Kwakiutl, Heiltsuk, or Tsimshian humanness— being correlate with settlement), but for the most part these are highly particularized relationships. More important for our purposes is the culturally relative nature of that landscape, the degree to which it is imbued with meaning and symbolically mapped by its inhabitants, who are themselves internally differentiated in ways that may be quite different from the representations of the ethnographer.

In much recent museological and ethnographic work done by Native individuals and institutions, the question of particularity is accorded primary significance. The sense of uniqueness that once manifested itself in intertribal warfare, competitive trade, and even political alliance now finds itself expressed in Native-produced and other Nativist films wherein the matter of being Heiltsuk or Kwakiutl takes priority over any generalized experience of pan-Indianness (though this latter is not completely excluded). Indeed, most of the films of the late 1970s and 1980s are specific to single linguistic groups, with little, if any, attention paid to questions of cross-cultural comparison. It is only in contrast to a political and cultural (Euro–North American) Other, in relation to whom all Native groups share a similar structural-historical position, that a Native identity emerges. That identity is, of course, of great political significance and forms the basis of alliance (as real as the alliance of social and political entities against which it defines itself) in legal contests with provincial, state, and federal governments (Clifford 1988b).

Like much postcolonial political theory, recent filmmaking is a product of political particularism, which differs significantly from precontact separateness and implicitly rejects the undifferentiated identity imposed by colonial representations. That is, it responds to the fact of a history in which "contact" led to the encompassment and subsequent insertion of various Native communities into the colonial state. Only within the context of that colonial state did these various groups acquire a single and collective identity; only beneath its structure of domination did they become "Indians." This is perhaps a less extreme particularism than that discussed by Radhakrishnan, who refers to the demise of "totalizing narratives" (Lyotard 1984) and their reified categories of Other as the "'post-historical' politics of radical indeterminacy" (Radhakrishnan 1987:199; see also Jameson 1984). But it is an assault on modernist colonial representations nonetheless, and may therefore qualify for the label "postmodern" if not "poststructuralist" (in Radhakrishnan's sense). The "post" of "post-historical," as well as the "post" of "postmodern" that it implies, indicates both a temporal situation and a particular orientation toward the colonial state and its discourses. In both cases, the "post" is a sign of subsequence and negation. It refuses the "antecedent [and dominating] practice that laid claim to a certain exclusivity of insight" (Appiah 1991:341–342) and that denied local subjectivities in the process of its own self-constitution.

In the case of Native filmmaking, the postcolonial position defines itself largely as a rejection of the categories of colonial "Self" and "Other" by which Tsimshian, Kwakiutl, and Haida or Bella Coola people were defined as Indians and thereby made subject to wardship. But the concern with localized identity has been expressed more directly and more intelligibly (for anyone—i.e., most people—not conversant in the dialect of academic postmodernity) by individuals such as Margaret Seguin (1985:23) cites: "I'm not an Indian, I'm a Tsimshian." In the end, these few words are as eloquent a refusal of gross "totalization" as any theoretical critique, though they inevitably fall far short of the kind of completely indeterminant politics which Lyotard or Radhakrishnan might advocate.

In a severely postmodernist reading, of course, Seguin's informant merely substitutes one essentialism for another. Yet it seems to me that there is good cause to privilege the Tsimshian assertion over the ethnographer's abstraction, even if the word "Tsimshian" itself requires further analysis in terms of the local hierarchies and differences (class, ethnicity, gender, etc.) that it covers over. Identities are always contingent. And for all the raucous debate about fractured subjectivity in the postmodern world, the self-essentializing gesture, strategic or not, grounds agency and thereby enables moral and political action. If the narrative of emancipation from colonial oppression is, as Lyotard calls it, "totalized," if it imposes a false closure even in this more contained sense of ethnicity, then so be it. Postmodern theory has yet to account for the strange and perhaps dubious fact that the denigration of totalized narratives and the rejection of their presumed "unified subject" occur precisely as those people who were previously denied any subjectivity (who were created as Other by the displacement of modernity's own internal difference) have managed to grab hold of the means to represent themselves—in admittedly totalized terms.

I do not want to take on all of postmodern theory here (or anywhere else! and I am sympathetic to much of it), but I do want to raise a number of questions that will be addressed, both implicitly and overtly, in later chapters. Foreshadowing those discussions, it may be noted here that the Tsimshian or Kwakiutl or Heiltsuk assertion of essential identity is part of a continuing commitment to the realist, though not necessarily the modernist, project. What we see in the later "Native" productions is not a "dissolution of linear narrative . . . and a 'revolutionary' break with the (repressive) ideology of storytelling" (Jameson 1984:54) but a "renarration," to use Mas'ud Zavarzadeh's (1991:21–26) term, of particular histories. What these renarrations reject, then, is not the possibility of a teleologically coherent narrative but the specific *telos* assigned by evolutionism and the modernist vision of vanishing Indians. In this context I want to pause, to "cut" and shift scenes, in order to explore the debate over narrative and representation as it has taken shape within anthropology, before considering how it has affected ethnographic film.

Revisions: Ethnographic Film and Anthropological Poetics

Upon reading Rilke's *Letters on Cézanne* and Hofmannsthal's letters on color, Richard Exner was prompted to remark that "the poets have learned how to see" (Rilke 1991:xvii). Later on, after the euphoric discovery of postimpressionist color, cinema would provide the metaphors and the fantastic ground for a new literature that existed in the thrall of space and motion (Caws 1981). And with that new literature—the literature of Artaud, Bachelard, Bréton, and Leiris, to name but a few—came the endeavor to theorize the visual in its relation to textuality, and also to understand the materiality of the text itself. Most prominent among these endeavors, surrealism offered up the possibility of a radical new vision and, more than that, the methodology for a reorientation of vision: montage, collage, the artificial text identifying itself as artifice. In the usurpation of realism, surrealism dared to suggest that realist perception itself was distorted, and in that assault it attempted to destabilize the place of the viewing subject. How timid and etymologically myopic in comparison is Clifford Geertz's (1973b) realization that ethnographic texts are "fictions" in the sense of being things made. And yet the relevance of the surrealist project for ethnographic representation has recently been explored—though somewhat belatedly, and still inadequately, in direct response to Geertz's modest discovery (Clifford and Marcus 1986; Clifford 1988a, 1988b; Marcus and Fischer 1986). But if the poets of the late nineteenth and early twentieth centuries found guidance and inspiration for a rejuvenated poetics in the plastic arts and in cinema, ethnographic film must now turn to its literate counterpart for direction. Having forsaken its origins in Méliès's phantasmagoria (the tradition of the magic lantern and the *faérie*) and having identified itself with the empiricism of the Lumière brothers (de Brigade 1975), documentary film has yet to elaborate its own poetics (Nichols 1981).

And what of anthropological poetics more generally? Most of the energies of the "interpretive turn" in anthropology have been devoted to an analysis of the ways in which textual—rhetorical and narrative—conventions circumscribe cultural representation (Clifford 1988b; Marcus and Cushman 1982; Pratt 1986; Rosaldo 1986). Though it is perhaps unfair to consider the interpretivists *in toto* (Clifford's appreciation of Michel Leiris is hardly comparable to Marcus and Fischer's exuberant but anemic tour of surrealism, the Frankfurt School, and postmodern politics), all of them share an attempt to deconstruct ethnographic transparency. They are all equally intent upon unveiling the "central eye"[4] of the ethnographic subject as a position with specific epistemological and political implications.

In its simplest form, the interpretivist argument goes something like this: Ethnographic realism is a mode of representation that is conventional, socially constructed (not natural), and ideologically determined or over-determined (not neutral). Thus, Mary Louise Pratt (1986:27) stresses the continuity of narrative forms between travelogues and self-identified ethnographies. Similarly, James Clifford (1986b) argues that ethnography is organized through allegory and Renato Rosaldo (1986:96–97) draws attention to the use of the pastoral as a mode of ethnographic representation, all of them pointing to the literary genre conventions underlying anthropological knowledge and its inscriptions. Although there is disagreement between these writers as to where ethnography and fiction intersect, all agree that the dichotomy between form and content is a false one, based on shaky epistemological foundations.

This confrontation with realism has led some, Marcus and Fischer most notable among them, to advocate a new kind of ethnography, one that would juxtapose simultaneous sites (or, rather, their representations) as a means of understanding the locality of transnational processes. Ideally, such a strategy provides the reader with a sense of how global processes are appropriated and manipulated, localized and internalized in particular ways. However, it does not then posit causal or historical priority but instead generates an image of co-existence and thus co-evality. The result is that the ethnographer's own subject position is also decentered. Unlike the surrealists of the 1920s and 1930s (such as Roussel or Leiris), who kept their aesthetic and scholarly practices quite separate, Marcus and Fischer want to bring aesthetic modernism into the anthropological arena. Doing so would force the reader into a direct confrontation with difference, a difference unresolved by authoritarian (voice-over?) commentary. Rather than rendering otherness transparent to a singular vision, juxtaposition is said to affirm the opacity, the impenetrable otherness of those whom anthropologists study.

However, this otherness is not a projection or displacement of Western society's internal differences. It is an acknowledgment of independence and
integrity. In this regard, surrealist juxtaposition is fundamentally at odds
with the technologies of surveillance and the logic of insight upon which it
rests. Its modernism is antimodern, at least if we understand modernity in
terms of the disciplinary technologies that Foucault has outlined. Indeed, its
greatest promise lies in its capacity to bear witness to the ways in which other
cultures refuse to be seen through.

As a literary strategy and aesthetic ideal, the new ethnographic surrealism
has much to commend it. Nonetheless, it would be wrong to see this new
strategy as a complete break with realist aspirations. In advocating juxtaposition as a means of reorienting the ethnographic gaze, the new surrealists
often justify it as a form of representation that is appropriate to the times—
times that are characterized by dislocation, large-scale migrations, the fragmentation of nation-states, and so on. In this respect, strategies of juxtaposition enact the apotheosis of mimetic poetics. A new empiricism parading as
antirealism, juxtaposition runs the risk of effacing the vision/authority that
perceives resonances between elements and then stages them in montage. In
this way it repeats the supposed sins of older representational strategies that
effaced the place of the interlocutor through the construction of an omniscient voice. In anthropology, at least, there is a profound continuity between older realists and contemporary antirealists. Although there are some,
such as Stephen Tyler (1987) who would prefer that anthropologists abandon the ethnographic ship altogether, recent interventions in critical anthropology are understandable as a simple if rather loud insistence upon the
reflexivity of the writer/ethnographer.

Of course, mere self-identification is inadequate to the demands of reflexivity and, more important, to political critique. A preface, a flamboyant an-
nouncement of self, or a more literate oscillation between the interior life of
the ethnographer and the exterior field scene can never suffice as a solution
to the problem of transparency. And one must be wary of the narcissistic
impulse by which Locke's pure perceiving self is smuggled back into the
text. In its most banal forms, interpretivist reflexivity simply shores up its "I"
as the locus of a knowledge that is always defined through opposition to an
ethnographic object. Without actually surrendering the rest of the empiricist
paradigm, it also reifies that object as Other.

Obviously, the more radical poststructuralist writers (Derrida, Lyotard,
Bataille et al.) do not accept self-reference as an adequate subversion of
modernist realism. For the interventions of these writers are precisely a refusal of the unity of the self—that "self-same self" whom moderate interpretivists are indexing. In their readings, the modern subject is a product of
imperial expansion whereby the West encompasses all the rest, making the
colonial Other its twin while at the same time projecting or displacing its

own internal differences onto that categorical opponent. This Other then becomes the object of a renewed desire for extension and encompassment, and thus, via the consumptive logic of late capitalism, it spins itself out in a "widening gyre" of homogenization (Clastres 1980; Foucault 1973; Jameson 1984; Pefanis 1991:9–20, 25). Philosophical poststructuralism finds its literary counterparts and expressions in a wide variety of texts, many of which give the reader an impression of severe dislocation because the narrator is dispersed and the narrative lacks temporal linearity. Thus, texts like Bessie Head's *A Question of Power* or even Salman Rushdie's *Midnight's Children* disarm the reader because the possibilities of identification are so thoroughly and constantly deferred. But the demands for a fixed subject-position are somewhat different for texts that claim to have access to the real, and this includes anthropological texts.

Within anthropology itself, the actual practice of postmodern ethnography is still in its infant stages. Nor has it produced a single or unified strategy, and perhaps this lack of a recognizable representational project is what many identify as the basis of the discipline's current identity crisis. Yet there are affinities, even between works as diverse as Vincent Crapanzano's *Tuhami* (1980) and Michael Fischer and Mehdi Abedi's *Debating Muslims* (1990). These points of convergence focus on the status of the representing subject and the assertion of difference as the basis for dialogue. Both *Tuhami* and *Debating Muslims* construct themselves around the principle of dialogue and underscore the centrality of negotiation in the construction of anthropological knowledge. In the former, the text reproduces a series of exchanges between ethnographer and informant as a way of laying bare the very process of knowledge production. Crapanzano's introduction of the interlocutor into the life history undermines the assumed stability and fixity of both ethnographic and informant identity. It then draws attention to the ethnographic subject as something that emerges in the dialogic encounter. *Debating Muslims* takes this problem of knowledge construction one step further by playing with the problem of voice in such a way as to threaten the very notion of separate and autonomous selves in dialogue. Moving from autobiographical accounts of a boyhood in Iran to essays on the *Qur'an* and the politics of culture during revolutionary upheavals, Fischer and Abedi use a variety of voicing techniques. At times, the textual voice separates and indicates the distinct visions of the North American scholar and the Iranian student-turned-fieldworker. At times the voices blur in what the authors call a "bifocal" vision. The resulting text is not so much a series of juxtapositions in the surrealist mode as an oscillation of perspectives around a single event, namely the Iranian revolution. It might be argued that the use of autobiography in *Debating Muslims* does not call attention to the dialogue of fieldwork as does *Tuhami* but, rather, provides the means for accessing that old Geertzian ideal, the "Native's point of view." Indeed, there appears to be a tension between the rhetorical strategies and the philosophical objectives of the book. This tension may be a function of the fact that *Debating Muslims* uses dialogue on two distinct levels. On the first it is a vehicle of textual organization; on the second it is an allegory for a particular way of cultural being in which debate itself is a central organizing principle. Despite such tension, however, the book pursues an important goal, which is intellectual parity and empowered conversation between members of vastly, though not completely, different cultures. Accordingly, it rejects the anthropological claim to representational authority while pointing the way for a discipline that wants to abandon its imperial roots.

Such paths are not yet as apparent in visual anthropology. Still constricted by its presumption of photographic indexicality, ethnographic film has yet to fully enact its own aesthetics of dialogue. Until very recently, its appropriation of the postmodern critique has consisted not in the deconstruction of the representing subject but in its foregrounding (Asch and Asch 1988; Pryluck 1988; Ruby 1988). Such a centering of the authorial subject is most apparent in the recent rehabilitation of that hyperrealism that Frederick Wiseman and Jean Rouch advocated with *cinéma vérité.* The ultimately self-conscious film style, *cinéma vérité* arose in the 1960s to give absolute primacy to the objective event. The camera was supposed to capture the unadulterated and unchoreographed reality of everyday existence. Of course, the camera itself was an intrusion and directly influenced the actions of the persons being filmed. However, as *vérité* matured, the fact of the camera's presence became an additional object of filmmaking: Confrontations between the camera(person) and the "actor" (in the sense both of agent and of *dramatis personae*) were included in the edited footage as a means of signifying the filmmaker's presence and self-consciousness. Warren Bass has termed this style of filmmaking "superobjectivity," rather than subjectivism, in his analysis of film style (1982:140–141), thereby exposing the fact that the acknowledgment of a subject position does not necessarily alter the status of subject-object relations.

It is important to realize that the hyperrealism of *cinéma vérité* has by now been largely abandoned and its major practitioner, Frederick Wiseman, has returned to the stylistic conventions of the movement's earlier days. In films like *Hospital* he seeks the "found" moment, when the subjects "perform naturally," *as though* the camera were not there. Clearly, this eminently staged "found" moment requires an exceptional rapport between the actors and the filmmaker, a rapport dependent upon great familiarity and trust. Indeed, what appears most natural and most innocent is often most knowing. The "naturalness" of the profilmic event is cultivated; it reenacts an original moment that precedes the camera's arrival and that must always remain imaginary insofar as the filmmaker is concerned. In this regard, it is something akin to the seemingly self-contradictory "rehearsed theatrical improvisation" described by Richard Schechner (1985). That paradoxical quality—which expresses the documentary filmmaker's insatiable desire for invisibility, for pure neutral observation—is singled out by Bill Nichols as a definitive characteristic of the ethnographic film (1981:241). And this despite the fact that such neutrality, as Nichols himself emphasizes, remains ever beyond the grasp of the filmmaker. There is, to put matters bluntly, always a camera.

And what of Walker Evans and the invisible (because hidden) mechanical eye, the concealed weapon of surveillance or the voyeur's desirous lens? To be sure, it is possible to avoid direct and knowing confrontation between the camera, as a technical object, and its filmed subjects—through duplicity and dissimulation. Few would condone such ethics of invasion, and certainly I do not. But, in any case, the point is secondary in many ways. For the camera is not an eye, though even the latter optical device is socialized, and it is not a neutral receiving surface. This is true on two levels. First, quite simply, the camera is always directed, and the object of its focus is always framed by and for someone. Second, as a technological apparatus the camera produces a kind of image that operates according to codes of emphatically Western realist perspective, a perspective that revolves around a single and unified point of view (Baudry 1974–1975; Crary 1990; Pleynet 1978). In realist cinema this basic ideological structure of the technological apparatus is reproduced and ramified through the use of "suture" and seamless editing to reproduce a "centered" vision. The object and the measure of that vision is, as Bonnitzer points out, typically the body (Lellis 1982:82). Thus the language of shots, both close-up and long-shot, and the fragmentation they may signify assume a notion of wholeness whose paradigm is the human form. It is perhaps unnecessary to belabor the specificity of that paradigm. But if the technological and aesthetic ground of film is rooted in a renaissance vision (though not reducible to it), the endeavor to represent cultural others and to depict social institutions must always be a problem of mediation, or even of double-mediation, as the Schutzian phenomenologists would argue.

Yet, despite these technological considerations, despite the fact that one always sees in a historically particular way and that cameras manifest this way of seeing as much as editing does, there remains the problem of what Bill Nichols calls "What to do with people?" Limited vision need not entail blindness, and, given the parameters of this representational history, there is still space for an ethnographic film project. At least as much space as there is for any representational project. Within these horizons, Richard Schechner and Frederick Wiseman (among others) offer the staged improvisation and cultivated spontaneity in answer to the impossibility of what would ultimately be a purely voyeuristic, though not purely objective, cinema. In essence, these are compensatory strategies, carried out in cinema's own existentialist world—the world of "as though." Despite reservations, Nichols also endorses this modus operandi and cites *Kenya Boran* (1974) as one of its most exemplary instances. Here the filmmakers use prompting to generate the profilmic event; discussions are initiated by an interviewer or director and then allowed to take their own course as the camera rolls (Nichols 1981:279–284). Such strategies are employed in many of the films that will be discussed later in this book, films such as *Bella Bella* (1975) and *Box of Treasures* (1983), to name but two. Like *Kenya Boran*, their primary objective is to have subjects explicitly articulate ideas and beliefs that would otherwise remain tacit, thereby overcoming the thorny problem of attributing thoughts to otherwise silent actors.

Although this strategy is among the more sincere and sophisticated attempts to grapple with the ethical conundrum of representing others and of giving space to other voices, it is, I think, the ultimate ethnographic *trompe l'oeil*. It encourages the viewer to assume that the events depicted are "natural" or "found" because the fact of construction and the power of the filmmaker to textualize and manipulate those events are effaced. Here the confluence of strategies in ethnographic filmmaking and in interpretive (literary) ethnography ought to give one pause. The kind of innocence that Wiseman or the makers of *Kenya Boran* pursue is entirely artificial and the acknowledgment of this fact does not, in the end, mitigate it. As Bass (1982) has suggested, such gestures of self-reference can be, and often are, used to further buttress the claim to objectivity. And one occasionally feels that it is there, in the encompassment of the viewing subject, and in the exposure of its own making, that documentary cinema imagines its ultimate achievement: not so much a panoptic vision, which would always be blind to its own point of reference, but a pure objectivity unrestrained by the limits of any eye.

Objectivity is, of course, the very cornerstone of ethnographic authority. The *rhetoric of immediacy* and the stylistic devices of realism form a means of authenticating that objectivity and are employed in the film's claim to representational authority. In ethnographic realism (as much a feature of written as filmic ethnography), the rhetoric of immediacy is the means by which the film validates its claim to objectivity and even omniscience (Clifford and Marcus 1986). In a film like *The Axe Fight,* where immediacy is foregrounded through the inclusion of shots and a sound recording of frightened and confused anthropologists, the self-reflexive gesture becomes a way of signifying not the constructedness and hence the limitations of the text, but the hubris of fieldwork and the pure presentational capacities of film. Ethnographic films of even the most self-conscious filmmakers have, in general, not yet abandoned this realism. And doing so would inevitably entail the surrender of documentary's greatest source of legitimacy. Perhaps for this reason, one has yet to see much in the way of sustained abstraction in ethnographic film. Nor have there been many attempts to develop something comparable to literary criticism's *écriture*, writing in which the "regimes of truth" are eschewed in favor of a "performance" that, in its transgressive form, assaults the omniscient vision and its canonization in realism (Pefanis 1991:5). Trinh T. Minh-ha's films and Julie Dash's recent *Daughters of the Dust* stand as remarkable exceptions to this general conservatism, but their status as extraordinary achievements also affirms the rule of realist filmmaking.[5]

Yet if one were serious about enacting the surrealist project or any one of its poststructuralist permutations, such departures from realism would be necessary. The subjectivism of surrealism was not the acknowledgment of the creative act, of the fact that an object was "made," for such acknowledgment was taken for granted. Rather, subjectivism lay in the full articulation of an interior (that is, viscerally experiential) vision and in the pursuit of that shock of insight which might be attained in the experience of disorientation. Achieved in the refusal of aesthetic expectation, in the valorization of alterity, and in the often violent juxtapositions of dissimilars, surrealism offered a totally antirealist position. To reduce surrealism to the niceties of montage and/or collage is to seriously underestimate the power of that aesthetic and perhaps the degree to which it is an aesthetic of power—certainly an aesthetic of violation.

It remains to be seen whether this is a viable alternative for ethnographic film, however. I do not mean to rehabilitate the reflexivity that is carried out within empiricist parameters, but I think that anthropologists need to seriously question whether a radically postmodern position—such as Bataille or Lyotard would advocate—is compatible with ethnography. This stance may seem ironic, given "the importance of anthropological thought for the critique of totality" (Pefanis 1991:2). Yet my hesitation does not stem from the fact that anthropology in its evolutionist formulation was a primary source of humanism's totalizing discourse. It is both possible and necessary to expunge crass evolutionism from anthropology. Nor do I think that anthropology should distance itself from postmodernism's ethical project, which is to say, the critique of Western expansionism. That tradition also has deep roots in the discipline. But there is a sense in which the unrestrained revelry in violent excess, in parodic assault and ridiculing laughter, threatens to displace critical analysis. The ethical project of postmodernism needs to materialize itself in a comprehension of the structures—ideological, institutional, and economic—by which a given regime of power/knowledge operates. There is definitely a place for *écriture*, for ludic interventions and transgressive performance. I do not dispute that. But critical, and therefore explanatory, discourse also has a place, or places, and one of those places is anthropology. The "playful" (but ever so serious) rejection of totalitarianism requires this other, in some ways more mundane, analysis for its ground, and we should not permit the aesthetic pleasures of formal experimentation to negate the analytic project.

And so we have returned, via a rather long detour, to Nichols's cynical and aphoristic question: What to do with people? At times, in anthropological analyses of representation and textual production, the world is bracketed to the point that it becomes a palpable absence. As Paul Rabinow (1985) and Bob Scholte (1986) have observed, the "interpretive turn" in anthropology sometimes seems to entail an abdication of the social realm. The irony of such a betrayal should not be lost. For, if anything, the recent awareness of anthropology's own narrative forms as powerful and ideologically committed structures comes from an engagement with "others," the people who are its subject (object). It might even be argued that the "interpretive turn" is a necessary response to those resisting voices, to the emergence of other anthropologies, and to the irrepressible assertion of subjectivity in subaltern studies.

It would be difficult to chart the rise of subaltern voices during the past two decades. The names of Said, Spivak, Trinh, Chatterjee, and Bhabha come to mind as some of the major antitheorists of otherness.[6] Their writings are diverse and often at odds with one another: Spivak draws primarily from Derrida in a critique of Western metaphysics, Bhabha does so in the lineage of Lacan, and Trinh brings together the critiques of both a poststructuralist and a postcolonial orientation. But as members of what might be called, following Kwame Anthony Appiah (1991:348), "a *comprador* intelligentsia," they have been unified by a common project: the refusal to be represented as absence in the discourses of colonialism. This book is not, however, a history of subaltern studies. Rather, after considering the disciplinary tradition of ethnographic filmmaking, it looks at the response of Native peoples outside of the academy who have taken hold of its representational apparatus in order to speak and to make themselves heard. And it aims to explore the implications of that gesture for anthropology in general. For it is during the confrontation—Bruner (1986) gently calls it a dialogic encounter—between these two that the narrative of salvage is forced to give way to one of renewal.

On the Nature of Narrative

Having spoken at such length about narrative conventions, I must now perhaps pause and clarify just what is meant by narrative. It should be noted at the outset that I do not intend to follow in Lyotard's (1984) or Jameson's (1984) footsteps and denigrate narrative by rendering it as the master strategy of oppression. Whereas the Victorian metanarrative of progress may indeed be the pernicious embodiment of imperial ideology, that of Native or any other emancipation cannot be so construed. The argument for an immanent (totalitarian) politics rings hollow in the face of those narratives of liberation which guide Native and other struggles for self-determination. Lyotard's assertion that narrative and meaningfulness are correlate in the modern world, and that we now inhabit the meaningless and exhausted time at the end of narrative, already assumes the complete homogenization of the world (hence there is no need to narrate progress through encompassment). But anthropology belies this assertion; if we have learned anything in the last decade it is that, despite the universalization of commodity economies and consumerist logic, transnational processes are always domesticated in culturally particular ways. Differences are constantly emerging in response to the possibility of homogenization.

Somewhat unexpectedly, there is an ironic sense in which postmodernism shares the nostalgia of salvage anthropology, although its nostalgia seeks difference rather than original unity. To be sure, its abandonment of loss (the loss of totalitarian representation) is celebratory, but the sense that meaning is either total or nonexistent, narrative or nonlinear, must inevitably show up a vestigial binarism, a lingering commitment to that very Aristotelean logic whose ghost we are now so relentlessly trying to exorcise. There is an implicit story, a teleologically coherent narrative, informing these lamentations and one that is not so far removed from Levi-Strauss's own romantic grieving at the end of *Tristes Tropiques* (1984). From the point of view of this text, those structures of intelligibility are of great interest in and of themselves. But leaving Lyotard and Jameson aside for the moment, I return to the question of narrative.

There are two levels on which I invoke the concept of narrativity. The first of these has to do with temporality as it applies to the events narrated, and to the sequential organization of those events as they are abstracted and textualized (Bruner 1986:145). The second has to do with representational form and is a principle of structuration (one opposed to poetic and expository principles), which gives the text its shape and determines the kinds of readings that will be available to an audience. These two levels, the one a substantive dimension of the story-as-text and the other a formal principle of textuality, can be reconciled if they are conceived in hierarchical terms. Gerard Genette (1982:133) confronts this very problem when he writes that "every narrative in fact comprises two kinds of representations, which however are closely intermingled and in variable proportions: on the one hand, those actions and events which constitute the narration in the strict sense and on the other hand, those objects or characters that are the result of what we now call *description*." Following this passage, Genette goes on to discuss the relationship between description and narrative, arguing that the former, like narrative in the narrow sense, has diegetic, explanatory, and symbolic functions (Genette 1982:134–135). He claims that even in the work of someone like Robbe-Grillet, who worked in both the cinematic and the literary media to liberate pure description from the shadow of narrative, description is ultimately a vehicle of narrative. From there, Genette concludes that description cannot be categorically opposed to narrative, but must instead be considered "one of its aspects" (Genette 1982:137). As a shorthand, I propose to differentiate these levels of narrativity by referring to the broader, temporally based concept as a "paradigmatic narrative" and the narrower structural principle as simple narrative.

Paradigmatic narratives, the term I shall use to denote the broader concept in avoidance of the debate over "metanarratives," are construed through a variety of rhetorical means. The exposition so characteristic of ethnographic film is not opposed to narrative in its broad sense but, to the contrary, has narrative functions. Admittedly, this rather neat resolution leaves us with theoretical problems still unassailed, not the least of which has to do with the truth or falsity of narrative statements. In structuralist terms—and most narratology is at least vaguely structuralist in orientation—the question of truth in narrative is an issue of content or reference, and therefore belongs outside of the semiotic realm. The truth-value of any statement is independent of its narrativity. Thus, to accept the structuralist position and at the same time to maintain the possibility of critique, one is required to carry out two distinct modes of analysis: first, on the formal or semiotic level, which includes the actual signifying practices and codes that ethnographers and filmmakers employ; and, second, on the substantive level, which is composed of the ethnography's content and its relationship to a social world. And yet such a vision, which ultimately reifies the Platonic opposition between representation and represented, between the image and its original presence, cannot ultimately provide the grounds for a genuinely historicized analysis. In the place of a doubled analysis forever caught in the form-content dichotomy, we need a theory that is capable of exploring the very relationship between these levels, one that speaks to the fact that, ultimately, "the world" represented in the film frame is also the context of that film's production. We need, therefore, "to map out the productivity and effectivity of successive, coexistent, contradictory or conflictual languages; to plot the limits governing what they can articulate and how far they can remain convincing by recruiting the identification of their speakers and channelling the convictions of those they address" (Tagg 1988:23).

"After Such Knowledge":
Rethinking the Real and the Reel

This book, too, has a context and speaks within a tradition of film theory—most especially documentary film theory—whose primary concern has been with questions of truth. We live, as Susan Sontag says, "unregenerately in

Plato's cave" (1977:3). Earlier, I indicated that I would use the word "ethnographic" to denote a genre of films. Defined primarily in terms of subject matter, these ethnographic representations are also to be understood as narrative constructions that, quite emphatically, are not mere slices of reality, nor windows onto the world. Let me then pause to reconsider the question of documentary realism, and to briefly trace the contours of its history in film theory generally.

According to Brian Henderson, film theory can be divided into two types: "part-whole theories and theories of the relations to the real" (1976:390). These two schools are exemplified in the opposed theories of Sergei Eisenstein (1949) and André Bazin (1967), with Eisenstein's notion of montage being representative of the former whereas Bazin's concern with film's relationship to the "Being" of the world represents the latter. Henderson points out the important fact that both kinds of theories, despite their vastly different ontological and metaphysical assumptions, are essentially concerned with the real and begin from there. It is sufficient here to note that, for all their differences, both Eisenstein and Bazin saw the cinematic image as an unmediated fragment of reality. Eisenstein then argued for aesthetic transformation through montage, whereas Bazin argued for fidelity in a realist aesthetic.

The problem that Eisenstein and Bazin raise and problematize for us is the relationship between a picture and the pictured, or, in semiotic terms, between a photographic or cinematic sign and its referent. But the reference to photograph as sign suggests that the realism which posits a natural identity between the image and the world is a naive one. Its desire for the perfect testimonial can never be realized in the photograph, and not even Barthes's (1982) nostalgic plea for the analogic grounds of the photograph can mitigate such a conclusion. Even on the most banal level, photographs are two-dimensional images that (usually) evoke a three-dimensional presence. Films, in most cases, also entail the construction of a temporal plane, a diegetic line, that signifies but does not correspond to lived time. One must therefore speak of films in terms of resemblance, where resemblance itself is understood as a culturally determined process of selection and recognition (Nichols 1981:11). Photographs use iconic and indexical signs to generate meaning, and film adds to these the unmotivated signs of graphic and aural language. Everyday perception is also governed by these semiotic codes, and it is the conventional correspondence between these two conventional codes—those of viewing film and those of more quotidian perception—that gives films the aura of the natural (Nichols 1981:11–12; Eco 1976).

On this basis, realism comes to signify not merely style but a whole ideology of perception: a particular way of organizing signs and meaning. Thus Roemer (1971:103) writes that, "while the screen exceeds all other media in verisimilitude, its reality is nevertheless a *mode*." When we watch ethnographic films, we generally recognize the objects pictured and we invariably expect such recognition to be a part of the spectator experience. This recognition "installs us into a place of knowledge and slips us in place as subject to this meaning. The place seems given, seems ready-made, available due to the image's recourse to the codes of realism" (Nichols 1981:38). Instead of seeing a framed image, we see or we think we see the world. What is key in this imagined totality (which never appears to us in its fullness) is the generation of a sense that the imaged world extends beyond the screen. Not in any literal sense—people are fully aware that the film is indeed a film and that the careening train will not burst into the viewing space (Jarvie 1987)— but in the sense that the viewed world is infinitely accessible, and that the truncated quality and "distortions" of any film are merely a function of the camera's inability to capture it all. Filmic realism is possible only in the admission of this supposed limit, and in the assumption of a beyond that it entails. Realist film works by providing a corresponding subjectivity in the camera's position to match that of the viewer. The recognition of the film's codes is thus a kind of identification. Pascal Bonnitzer, writing in *Cinéthique*, states the matter in its most extreme voice when he describes the notion of an analogic cinema as follows:

> What is hidden here is the ideological/symbolic reality of the "spontaneous" effect of recognition instigated by the mechanical production of a certain type of figuration, the apparatus of production "disappearing in what it has produced," the *eye* of the subject/spectator coming then to substitute itself for it, thus closing the imaginary scene. (cited in Lellis 1982:82)

For all its verbal convolution, Bonitzer's statement does, nonetheless, underestimate the degree to which films manipulate that recognition factor. They do so through ironic contradiction and deferral. Moreover, it is the relationship between the familiar and the enigmatic, between recognition and its betrayal, that drives the film's narrative and enchants the viewer (cf. Nichols 1981:38–39) or, as some theorists would have it, annuls the viewer's critical capacity (e.g., Zavarzadeh 1991).

What does this mean for a theory of documentary? The commonsensical and still beloved distinction between so-called art films and documentaries is that the latter are true and factual while the former are imaginary and fictional. Such a formulation, in all its intuitive obviousness and simplicity, immediately becomes problematic when we consider such things as docudramas or fictional films that use news footage to establish a mood or historical context (witness the recent production of *JFK*). And it is rendered completely untenable if one refuses the ideology of indexicality, as I do here.

While the first use of the term "documentary" is usually attributed to Grierson in reference to Robert Flaherty's film, *Moana*, the concept of filmic documentation had already been used by Edward Curtis in the first decade of the century (Pierre Stevens 1988, personal communication).

Nonetheless, it is Rotha's definition of documentary, inspired by Grierson, that was adopted by the World Union of Documentary Filmmakers in 1948:

> All methods of recording on celluloid any aspect of reality interpreted either by factual shooting or by sincere and justifiable reconstruction, so as to appeal either to reason or emotion, for the purpose of stimulating the desire for, and the widening of, human knowledge and understanding, and of truthfully posing problems and their solutions in the sphere of economics, culture and human relations. (cited in Edmonds 1971:12–13)

One is astonished at the breadth of this definition, which, by embracing both invention and re-creation, is leagues from the turgid insistence on pure actuality that characterizes so much recent documentary theory. Both broader and narrower than the commonsense definition, the Union's statement is an overtly political one, advocating both a pedagogic and a problem-solving role for filmmakers. The debate between proponents of documentary neutrality and the Griersonian propagandists has been continuous throughout the history of documentary film. I have no intention of pursuing it further here, save to repeat my earlier assertion that there is no innocent eye.

Even so, it is possible to maintain distinctions between film genres, of which ethnographic films are one instance. However, these distinctions are rhetorical and not ontological. Documentary films are not self-contained as the ideology of Hollywood claims for its films; they do not require the conscious suspension of disbelief, but insist upon their own reality. They refer to a presumed world, tacitly claiming the possibility of verification. Documentary films claim correspondence, whereas narrative (in the narrow sense) films claim resemblance. Where narrative films begin with the unspoken preface "as if," documentary films begin with a tacit "this is."

Remembering that the conventions for depicting reality change over time, one wants to ask how it is that ethnographic narratives develop and change as well. In the following chapters, I attempt to read films in a doubled manner, decoding the logic and the references of individual texts and then reading along the grain to decipher the paradigmatic narratives that operate in them. As suggested earlier, the representation of Northwest Coast cultures has gone through several stages, with various narratives reigning at different times. Thus, films produced in the early part of the century (such as *Saving the Sagas, The Kwakiutl of British Columbia,* or *The Tsimshian Indians of British Columbia*) narrate the disappearance of aboriginal groups. Films of the immediate postwar years continue this tradition with significant innovations, but in the late 1960s another narrative appears, one that speaks of revival, renewal, and cultural continuity. We are therefore left with the matter of how these conventions and narratives change. Where do these innovations originate? Bertolt Brecht claimed simply that "reality changes; in order to represent it, modes of representation must change" (1974:51). But even if we were content to agree that the experienced world changed inexorably with the passage of time, it would be necessary to explain the changes in representational strategies. For changes are uneven and fragmented, representations multiple and conflicting. One wants to know where and how the differences emerge.

This is the sociological dimension of film aesthetics to which Adorno refers (as cited at the head of Chapter 1). What is the relationship between the various sites of society's order and the forms of its representation? How do ethnographic films mediate between filmmakers and their subjects, between their subjects and their audiences, between Native and non-Native selves and others? And further: How does the history of ethnographic film relate to the history of ethnography on the Northwest Coast? Or to that of anthropology in general?

In his own consideration of American ethnography, Edward Bruner was prompted to remark the dramatic transformation of dominant narratives: "In the 1930s and 1940s the dominant story constructed about Native American culture change saw the present as disorganization, the past as glorious, and the future as assimilation. Now, however, we have a new narrative: the present is viewed as a resistance movement, the past as exploitation and the future as ethnic resurgence" (Bruner 1986:139). Similar shifts occurred during the history of ethnographic filmmaking, but often in tension with those in literary ethnography. The transitions were complex and highly ambiguous, not merely a turning over of narrative leaves. They were contested and the legacy of that contest is a still-unresolved ambivalence in contemporary filmmakers' visions of Native history, and of Native future history.

The implication is that, at any one time, there is always more than one narrative, always more than one representation of the real. Yet different narratives are more or less authorized as true during different eras, and one or another always dominates. To the extent that it seems—and is made to seem—utterly natural, historically true, or universal, such a narrative may be termed hegemonic in Gramsci's sense (1971:348). But, as Jean and John Comaroff (1991:25) have asserted, hegemony "exists in reciprocal interdependence with ideology: it is that part of a dominant worldview which has been naturalized and, having hidden itself in orthodoxy, no more appears as ideology at all." It is not merely the ruling classes who are possessed of ideology. It is not merely the ruling classes who are possessed of a "will-to-power" and who can articulate that will in the form of a narrative history that extends into the future. If there exists orthodoxy, then there exists the possibility of heterodoxy. Those subordinated groups who inhabit the devalued spaces of gender, class, race, and ethnicity, and who know themselves as groups, also have ideologies (Comaroff and Comaroff 1991:24). The pursuit of Native self-representation in North America is precisely an attempt to legitimate these potentially subversive narratives. Insofar as Native North Americans are concerned, the stories and the practices of resistance have been in existence for as long as Natives and Euro–North Americans have been in conflict. But it is only recently that they have begun to acquire a sufficiently natural aura as to become powerful legal tools in battles to repatriate artifacts and to reclaim land or to demand recompense for collective suffering.

At what point do the fissures emerge? Where does hegemony's edifice crack and open itself up to the wedge of other representations? Bruner's answer, which is rather at odds with the suggested unity of the story-text-telling he elaborates, is derived from Geertz's (1973a:93) distinction between "models for" and "models of" reality; the disjuncture lies between representation and experiential reality, the latter always escaping complete encompassment (Bruner 1986:143). But lest we retreat too far into Plato's cave, it may be useful to recall Tagg's careful deconstruction of that fallacious opposition between representation and nondiscursive experience (1988:23–24). If there is a conflict between representations, it emerges not in the contradiction of one narrative by a not-yet-narrativized experience but in the contradiction of one narrative by another. The nondiscursive is not a unitary and ordered entity that can be accessed *as* narrative, and as a foil for hegemony. What we experience as natural, as habit's silent universe, is already ordered even if it cannot be articulated as a rule (Bourdieu 1977:94). Thus, the potential rupture of hegemony exists in its always tenuous relationship with ideological representations (Gramsci 1971:333; Comaroff and Comaroff 1991:26), and with other (Other) narratives.

It follows that these narratives, the vehicles of various ideological visions, are not merely interpretive; they are constitutive of selves and social relations. The point is acutely relevant for any consideration of film and the imaging of Native cultures, both by Native and non-Native filmmakers. Film is a form, and a forum, of enactment. One may therefore ask, What is being acted out in the films that prophesied assimilation and extinction? And what is being acted out in the films that tell of revival and cultural rebirth? To answer these questions is to comprehend the ways in which a history is constructed, the ways in which the past is made intelligible through its incorporation in the present moment. Ethnographic films are media in which, according to a Sartrean conception of history, "each generation reinteriorizes the past, assumes responsibility for it and in doing so, recreates it as well" (Jameson 1971:292). That re-creation of the past is simultaneously a creation of the future.

The destiny of Native peoples narrated by salvage ethnography was translated into policies such as wardship and the criminalization of ritual practice; it legitimated the confiscation of ritual paraphernalia and the wholesale plundering of aboriginal communities. While it was dominant, the narrative of assimilation made the political apparatus of assimilation possible. Having been partially replaced or displaced by an alternative, assimilation has now given way to the possibility of reconstruction. To borrow from Richard Schechner (and with apologies for an admitted infidelity to his intentions), "The movie is what we have of the past" (1985:65). It is also what we have of the future. I do not mean to aggrandize ethnographic film, but I do want to emphasize the relationship between representation's political and aesthetic aspects. For it is there that histories are made.

Notes

1. This estimate was made by Pierre Stevens, curator of the Sound and Moving Image Division of the National Archives in Ottawa. Stevens himself has been preparing a filmography of the Northwest Coast and generously shared his research with me. I gratefully acknowledge his assistance.

2. For an excellent overview of the developments of film theory that led to this conclusion, see Turin 1985:7–27.

3. Examples here range from Resnais and Robbe-Grillet's *L'année dernière à Marienbad* to Michael Snow's *Presents*.

4. I borrow the term "central eye" from Mary Anne Caws's provocative history of mannerist and modernist perception, *The Eye in the Text* (1981:174).

5. Both Trinh and Dash have received the prestigious Maya Deren award, Trinh in 1991 and Dash in 1993. The award, which is given to independent film and video artists, signals both the excellence of the work and its marginality relative to mainstream circles.

6. This term—"antitheorists of otherness"—is John Comaroff's (1991, personal communication).

3

Celluloid Savages:
Salvage Ethnography and the
Narration of Disappearance

All photographs are of the past, yet in them an instant of the past is arrested so that,
unlike a lived past, it can never lead to the present. Every photograph presents us with
two messages: a message concerning the event photographed and another concerning a shock of discontinuity.
  —John Berger

[T]he persistent and repetitious "disappearance" of social forms at the moment of their
ethnographic representation demands analysis as a narrative structure.
  —James Clifford

Backdrop: People, Places, and Positions

IN THE OPENING SEQUENCE OF Edward Curtis's epic melodrama, *In the Land
of the Head Hunters* (1914), we see a Native man standing in the bow of a
massive cedar canoe. He gesticulates excitedly as the canoe approaches the
shore, but it is not his manner that draws attention as much as the fact that
he is completely feathered. Liminal, he seems to be neither fully human nor
animal, partaking of two worlds in an embodiment of totemic principles. He
is an image of himself, and that image is fleshed out in a narrative featuring
all the supposedly essential elements of aboriginality as it was defined at the
time of the film's making: head-hunting and warfare as the manifestation of
barbarism; discipline, loyalty, and perseverance (not to mention physical
beauty) as the expression of nobility.

The representations of the eighteenth and nineteenth centuries frequently
combined these two contradictory qualities—savagery and nobility—in a

single construct that popularized and perverted Rousseau's original vision (Pearce 1965). Indeed, this unity of extremes is among the predominant tropes of ethnographic representation. What is now, in the discourses of postmodernity, termed "othering," the essentializing of difference, is not unique to modern or bourgeois Western cultures. But this particular construction of otherness—of a paradoxical and historically prior noble savagery—emerges most clearly in Enlightenment and post-Enlightenment thought. It incorporates those qualities which seemed most antithetical to the imagined collective self of utopian rationalists and of their less philosophically oriented heirs, the colonial administrators. "Perhaps," as James Boon (1982:6) suggests (though I invoke him less cynically than he himself might appreciate), "anthropology in any society necessarily produces only what that society's internal conditions require it to conceptualize as *other* than itself."

In this context, it is important to remember that this era of nascent filmmaking was also an era of Western expansionism in North America, when the "West" signified empty space, abundant resources, and endless opportunity. Anachronistically, perhaps, it remained the North American counterpart to the "dark continent," a still unknown land in need of cartographic illumination and administrative discipline (cf. Brantlinger 1985). In both Canada and the United States, "the West" (specifically, the Northwest for Americans) had come to occupy the place that North America had previously occupied for Europeans. And we would do well to remind ourselves that the designation of local inhabitants as Indians was more than just a nominal quirk of history. These autochthonous peoples were, in many ways, the shadow-people of a triangular continent (India) on whose enormous wealth Britain had built and staked its empire. Though cities like Seattle, Vancouver, and Victoria were burgeoning by the turn of the century, the Northwest Coast continued to evoke for easterners the contradictory images of pristine beauty and unruly savagery (this latter becoming, as we shall see, instrumental in the criminalization of aboriginal ritual). Curtis's production, the first major attempt to film aboriginal peoples (Kwakiutl) on the Northwest Coast, is exemplary in many respects. Although as a love story its primary purpose is dramatic rather than anthropological, the problems to be addressed and variously solved by all ethnographic filmmaking on the coast are present here in embryo. These are the problems of authenticity, of historical reconstruction, and of the means by which one is to present ethnographic information within a narrative frame. For Curtis, authenticity was either endangered or had vanished and was in need of reconstruction. *In the Land of the Head Hunters* initiated a tradition of historical reconstruction that was to become central to all ethnographic filmmaking of the era.

In the Land of the Head Hunters is clearly an allegorical narrative in the sense given that term by James Clifford (1986b); it very explicitly and self-consciously tells a story whose structure is one of conflict and closure. The (melo)dramatic value of the film is privileged in the extreme, and there is virtually no effort to provide an ethnographic context for the events that unfold on screen. A completely particularized narrative, it offers no sustained attempt to analyze or explain social or cultural institutions and practices. There is, in short, no generalizing exposition. Other filmmakers/ethnographers, including B. E. Norrish, Franz Boas, and Harlan Smith, did make films that can be more properly considered a part of the ethnographic genre, and they will be examined more carefully in the following pages. As for Curtis, it is difficult to estimate how much, if at all, *In the Land of the Head Hunters* influenced later ethnographic filmmaking on the coast, but it is certain that Curtis's ethnography (he wrote four volumes on coastal cultures) was known to other anthropologists concerned with the area. The film itself is significant as a point of origin and of departure; it inaugurated a new era of representation on the Northwest Coast in which ethnography would have a viscerally romantic aesthetic sensibility.

In the Land of the Head Hunters was produced about a decade and a half after British Columbia's first film, itself made only two years after the first movies were screened in Victoria (Browne 1979:1). The province quickly became a favorite site for cinematographers, and by the 1920s travelogues and educational shorts about the province were being produced in large numbers both by private individuals and as tourism promotionals (Browne 1979:4). The B.C. provincial government had intervened in filmmaking in 1908, and in 1920 an amendment to the British Columbia Motion Picture Act created the British Columbia Patriotic and Educational Picture Service,[1] mainly to assuage fears that cinema represented a morally corrupting force. But, in addition, it is likely that provincial authorities recognized an enormous potential for political and commercial propaganda. By this time, the newsreel had become a regular feature of cinema programs. Spurred by the information needs of World War I, and the sheer novelty of a supposedly immediate access to world events, the newsreel had gained immense popularity and would later provide the basis for a Canadian documentary tradition.

And yet, despite the relatively high level of filmmaking activity on the Northwest Coast, there was little in the way of what we might now term visual anthropology. After Curtis's epic melodrama in 1914, virtually no filmmaking was devoted to the Native population on the coast until the 1920s, when it became the subject and site of intense activity. During this period, Fox Movietonews and Associated Screen News (ASN) together produced only seven films about Native peoples on the coast (Browne 1979). For the most part, the Fox productions are inferior in every way: trite and poorly filmed versions of the rudest stereotypes. The ASN, however, did produce three significant if somewhat formulaic films about coastal Natives, including *Fish and Medicine Men* (1928), *Saving the Sagas* (1927), and *Totem Land* (1930). All of the ASN's films were produced by B. E. Norrish; *Fish and Medicine Men* and *Saving the Sagas,* in particular, were directed and shot by J. B. Scott. At least one of them benefited from the cooperation of Marius Barbeau, anthropologist and folklorist *extraordinaire* at Canada's National Museum of Man.[2] Like all newsreels of the time, they aimed both to entertain and to edify, with the result being a rather uncomfortable exaggeration and dramatization of indigenous attributes.

The newsreel shorts about Native cultures had guaranteed audiences thanks to a 1920 law requiring that all movie presentations be preceded by fifteen minutes of government-produced or -approved material (Browne 1979:14). However, the newsreel did not remain dominant in the visual anthropology that grew up in the postwar years, and it was quickly eclipsed by museum productions in the 1920s. Between 1920 and 1935, the National Museum of Man was responsible for at least twelve full-scale productions about Native cultures of the Northwest Coast, all but one directed and filmed by Harlan I. Smith. Other government productions were made under the auspices of the Department of Trade and Commerce Exhibits Publicity Bureau in Ottawa, the Canadian Government Motion Picture Bureau (forerunner to the National Film Board), and the British Columbia Forestry Service. A few films, including those of Edward Curtis and Franz Boas, were made privately, though still in keeping with the conventions established by these larger institutions.[3]

Ethnographic Auteurs of the Early Years

In selecting the Norrish, Boas, and Smith films for analysis, I have attempted to assemble a representative body of films, one that reveals the various filmmaking strategies dominant during this period. The inclusion of ASN productions in the realm of ethnographic film may be questionable if the institutional funding and personal biographies of filmmakers are considered to be adequate or exclusive criteria for the classification of films. Undoubtedly, my choice will be irksome to some. However, it must be remembered that, in the early 1900s, anthropology was not yet thoroughly established as a discipline and was only beginning to entrench itself within the structures provided by the museum. Indeed, institutional anthropology in Canada did not begin until 1910, when Edward Sapir arrived at the National Museum of Man (McFeat 1976:149). Of course, the Northwest Coast had been the subject of anthropological investigation since 1896, when Boas first did fieldwork there, but it was some time before a clearly demarcated ethnology of the Northwest Coast was established. More important (Boas's contempt for dilettantism aside), the news documentaries embodied many of the same assumptions about Native cultures as did the anthropologically more professional productions of Boas and Smith. In terms of filmmaking, Boas himself was an amateur, not in Flaherty's sense of the impassioned nonacademic (Rouch 1988:233) but quite simply as a man without technical expertise.

Even so, it might be argued that B. E. Norrish does not deserve to be honored with recognition as an exemplary figure in the history of ethnographic filmmaking, and that his neat narration of disappearance was nothing more than a crass journalistic attempt to mobilize the emotions of his viewers. Certainly, *Saving the Sagas* and *Totem Land* were geared to a commercial audience, but it was an erudite audience, one who would recognize concepts such as potlatch and for whom a Canadian opera singer (Juliet Gaultier de la Verndrye) would be a familiar face. In fact, Norrish addressed the same audience as did Harlan Smith, and if his anthropology was ruder, it nonetheless partook of the same narrative tropes and ideological assumptions. And for that reason, I include it here.

The footage for Boas's *The Kwakiutl of British Columbia* (1930) was shot at the end of his long and prolific career, although the postproduction editing was posthumously finalized (by Bill Holm) in 1973. Without wanting to endorse Antonio Marazzi's (1988:117) distinction between ethnographic and anthropological film as that between the pure inscription of field-experience and the subsequently theorized narrative, we must nonetheless acknowledge the problems of authorship that accompany a film such as Boas's. In analyzing *The Kwakiutl,* I consider the film in terms of its content at the level of the shot and theme, and devote less attention to the question of narrative structuration. In part, my inclusion of the film stems from Boas's involvement with Harlan Smith, but also from a sense that Boas's failure to edit the film himself may reveal something about his own orientation toward film as an anthropological tool. Though time may simply have run out for Boas, the footage of *The Kwakiutl* is formally and substantively so much apiece with his written work that the parallels demand serious attention. For much of Boas's written ethnography reads like the footage for the Kwakiutl: numerous sequences of detailed images strung together one after the other with only minimal overt theorization. Moreover, while he occasionally discussed anthropological uses for the footage, these did not include the production of an edited "film." Finally, and perhaps most important, I include *The Kwakiutl* here because of the sheer magnitude of Boas's influence over Northwest Coast ethnography generally. One wants to know how his ethnographic sensibility may have translated itself into film and how its trajectory in that media might have differed or paralleled the tradition to which it gave rise in the written medium.

It is now recognized that, although Boas produced little in the way of filmic anthropology, he had plans for much more work in the area (Jacknis 1988). Indeed, film may have seemed to him to offer the ultimate instrument for his own historical particularist project: the accumulation of sufficient detailed material to begin theorizing the relationship between history and culture. One need not belabor Boas's contributions to ethnology; George Stocking has provided a comprehensive account of his singular career (1968, 1974). But Boas's influence in ethnographic filmmaking is less definitive. The channels of his possible influence were twofold: first, through his association with Harlan Smith, whom he accompanied on the Jessup North Pacific Expedition (Stocking 1974:112–114); and, second, through his student, Edward Sapir, who directed activities at Canada's National Museum of Man.

As for Harlan Smith, the most prolific and cinematographically accomplished filmmaker of this trio, he was an archaeologist by training. However, his collaboration with Boas on the Jessup expedition extended into all areas of the American quadrilateral anthropology, excepting linguistics. Meticulously organized, Smith's films are miniature explorations of the visible in culture. It has long been assumed that much of Smith's work was destroyed in the 1967 fire at the National Museum (Browne 1979; Zimmerly 1974). A supplement to Colin Browne's filmography (1979), which appears in a companion book by Dennis Duffy (1986), includes one additional Smith reference, but it does not undercut the claim that almost half of the archaeologist's work went up in flames during the unintended fireworks of Canada's centennial celebrations in Ottawa. However, the lamentations of visual anthropologists seem to have been unnecessary. With the exception of two or three films, which most likely never existed but were identified with more than one title and therefore mistaken for separate productions, prints of all the Smith films are extant in the Sound and Moving Image Division of Canada's National Archives.[4] Though many of the original negatives were indeed lost, at least one print of each remains.

An Archaeology of Canadian Anthropology: Institutional and Intellectual Contexts for Ethnographic Filmmaking

These are the characters in this not always dramatic history of ethnographic filmmaking. Having sketched their biographical background, let us now consider their place—both the place in which they filmed and the place of their filming in constituting that space as such. The well-documented transition from evolutionism to historicism and culturalism in American anthropology was largely effected through the work of Franz Boas (Bidney 1953; Leaf 1979). From the beginning, the Northwest Coast was at the center of Boasian anthropology. Although its cultures had been the subject of observation by missionaries and explorers for well over two hundred years, it was not until the early twentieth century that extensive and intensive fieldwork was carried out. Most of this was conducted with the financial assistance of museums in the United States and Canada, and, from 1910 onward, the

National Museum of Man played an increasingly important role as the institutional framework for both research and the dissemination of a Boasian paradigm in Northwest Coast studies and Canadian anthropology generally.

As Tom McFeat points out, museum-based anthropology in Canada was allied with geology (until the late 1950s) and this alliance solidified a natural history orientation within the discipline: "[W]ith the Geological Survey, anthropology seemed principally to be a kind of natural history which is the stamp Boas had put on all reconstructive ethnography, making it consistent with archaeology and physical anthropology" (1976:151). George Stocking has pointed out the ideological implications of such institutional organization, noting that a natural history mode of anthropology tends to produce an "object orientation" in which cultures are analogous to the artifacts unearthed by archaeologists: They are, in short, objectified and reified. I would argue, more strongly than Stocking, that the object orientation of anthropology did not merely result from its dependence on museums but, rather, that the museum-based political economy of anthropology was itself the result of an ideology in which aboriginal cultures were commodified for acquisitive purposes. In the end, the articulation of that object orientation with the narratives of disappearance, and more, with a vision of Native culture as a vanishing *authenticity*, was almost perfect.

Anthropology at the turn of the century assumed the inevitable extinction of Native cultures and drew much of its legitimacy from its claim to be salvaging what little remained of doomed peoples (Marcus and Fischer 1986:24). It is in this context that we must view the films of Norrish, Boas, and Smith. But rather than simply impose this structure upon the films as an analytic *fait accompli*, let us consider them each in turn, attending to their organization and the iconographic traditions they deploy, as well as what they say, substantively, about the cultures of the Northwest Coast.

Canned Culture: B. E. Norrish, Popular Anthropology, and the Narrative of Salvation

In B. E. Norrish's production, *Saving the Sagas*, we have a film that narrates transformation and assimilation, while also narrating the effort to arrest that process through preservation. The axes of meaning in the film are death and redemption, cultural transformation and anthropological rescue. In the synopsis and titles that follow, an overall structure of meaning becomes apparent. That narrative expresses what Raymond Williams (in a different context) has termed a "structure of feeling" (1973:12), by which assimilation is experienced and conceived as loss. What follows here is both a semantic analysis, a distillation of the film's symbolic, thematic, and ideological content, and an analysis of the film's techniques, its operations as a system of

signs. In writing the synopses, I have attempted to be as sparing as possible
in description, and have kept strictly to the frame provided by the titles
where these exist, as well as to the chronology of the film (and not the
events depicted elsewhere). The result of this policy is a rather lengthy summary and, I fear, a laborious reading experience. However, while acknowledging the irremediable chasm between a film and its literary description, I
think these lengthy synopses offer the most satisfactory opportunity for a
thickly described interpretation. Ideally, they will also permit readers to engage the material critically and to read against the grain of my own text, if
such is deemed necessary or desirable.

Where the Norrish film is concerned, my reading is dual; I assume that its
narrative operates on at least two distinct planes. On the first, Norrish tells
of two anthropologists recording the cultural ways of a vanishing people.
The Natives are depicted as liminal. Caught in the transitional space in
which they still retain some of their traditional forms, they are also adopting
foreign lifeways and converting to Protestant Christianity. This explicit narrative is underlaid by another, whose assumptions are sometimes in complicity with the overt story, and sometimes ironically at odds with it. My
object here, and in subsequent analyses, is to understand how these various
levels of meaning operate, interact, and create coherence or instability in the
filmic text.

Synopsis: *Saving the Sagas* (1927)

The opening title of *Saving the Sagas* reads: "A screen recording of the
vanishing culture, the rites and songs and dances of the Indians along the
Canadian Pacific Coast, north of Vancouver." This is immediately followed
by a shot of the water, presumably the Pacific Ocean. Entering on the right
of the screen is a canoe in which three passengers are seated. Slowly, the
boat crosses the screen and vanishes to the left.

A second title introduces Marius Barbeau and Ernest MacMillan, who
"set out with camera and phonograph." Following is a shot of a low barge
on which a table is located. At the table are two men, one with a movie
camera mounted on a tripod, the other with a phonograph bearing a large,
fluted trumpet.

The next intertitle reads: "The ways of the white-man—and radio-jazz—
are sweeping away the old color of Indian life of British Columbia." And
following this, a man, probably Dr. MacMillan, is shown adjusting the
phonograph.

We are told that "our explorers" simply come upon an old village of the
"Wolf Tribe," called Angeda. The camera pans along the shoreline, revealing a spine of totem poles and, in the foreground, a canoe on smooth
waters. The film then cuts to a close-up of one totem pole, which appears
to be weathered and cracked. In a long-range shot, which follows a
title identifying the place as Guticks, "still the home of the Eagle people,"
houses made of long planks rise above small bluffs and hills.

Next we are told that the maker of the poles and the craft of carving "survive here." And we see in close-up a hand using an adze to carve a mask, the chips of cedar wood falling away regularly from the emerging face.

In the subsequent sequence, the film introduces the Eagle Chief, who is supposedly holding to old rites and "chanting his glories on the site for his grave" as a way of ensuring that his funeral sermon is properly carried out. Accompanying this narration is a series of shots, one depicting an elderly man in cape standing adjacent to a small totem, and one of the same man shaking a rattle. These are intercut with images of a mallet striking a drum and of an eagle sculpture.

At this point, the film introduces new Native characters, "the Eagle squaws" who "still know the measure of the old potlatch dances." The image-track that accompanies these titles features the women dancing amid driftwood on an otherwise empty beach. The dance is specified as a kind of lullaby in which an infant is rocked to sleep. The camera cuts from a close-up of a woman's arms bent at the elbows (rocking?) to one in which a young woman gestures with her hand toward her mouth. Her movement is interpreted in the intervening title: "And if we know Indians—and we do—this little beauty is signalling for a kiss—or maybe a drink."

Returning to the anthropological team of Barbeau and MacMillan, the title describes their work together as an endeavor to "record the songs and chants, fading away with the advance of the white man." Here the two suited men are featured at work over a desk, surrounded by onlooking Natives as they scribble in notebooks. "The cannery cans the salmon, the camera cans the dances and now the phonograph cans the songs—everything canned but the Indians." A shot of the Indians speaking and/or singing into the phonograph trumpet follows, as those watching exchange glances with one another.

In the following sequences the viewer sees a group of men throwing stones or dice, and we are told that this is a gambling game. The film continues with additional shots of other games, including one involving sleight of hand described as "just the Indian version of the white man's old shell game."

The final sequences are devoted to religious and ethical issues. We are told of the "Church Army's" missionary activities on the Northwest Coast, after which we view two men—one with a drum, the other with a book (a Christian Bible?). In concluding, the film narrates the conversion of the last "pagan Chief" and his forced adoption of monogamy. Having "devoutly puzzled" over the choice he would have to make among his three aging wives, the Chief opts for a previously unseen young woman, who enters from the right and parades herself before him. The Chief ponders the choices, looking back and forth between the three women seated on a log and the single woman standing at his side. He accepts the latter eagerly. And here the film ends.

Saving the Sagas identifies itself in its first title as a screen recording of the ceremonial practices of a vanishing people. That it is also a screen recording of the activities of two anthropologists becomes apparent shortly afterward.

The trope of the two explorers in fact becomes a vehicle for the filmmaker's insinuation into the scene. We are told first that the film is a recording and, second, that two anthropologists are also engaged in a recording process. Their disappearance from the narrative during the middle sequences permits the director or narrator to assume their role, and to tacitly claim a point of view which appears identical with that of Barbeau and MacMillan. In this way, they lay claim to scientific authority—an authority that is reaffirmed in the statement that the narrators "know Indians"—and that buttresses the film's claim to veracity. Not incidentally, this image of the recorder, a kind of dopplegänger for the filmmaker, becomes a commonplace in popular ethnographic films. In Norrish's later production, *Totem Land* (1930), for example, there is an almost identical scene in which traditional songs and chants are being recorded; but rather than an ethnographer, the musicologist in that film is Juliet Gaultier de la Verndrye, the somewhat eccentric Canadian opera star.

But let us return to the beginning of the film. The first scene reveals a canoe entering and then exiting the frame, moving smoothly over quiet waters. Occupied by unidentified Natives, this canoe comes to signify passage, and around its burgeoning symbolism the broader narrative is woven. The threesome simply vanishes from our view, identified in terms of neither origin (What lies beyond the frame? Whence did they come?) nor identities. In two of the first three intertitles, there is reference to the disappearance of aboriginal lifeways and the encroachment of white (Anglo-Canadian) culture. Yet this allusion to, and visualization of, disappearance is juxtaposed against a statement of persistence. The village is *still* home to the "Wolf Tribe" (never mind that totems were associated with clans and/or moieties and not tribes) and totem-carving *survives* here. In this initial juxtaposition the film sets up a contradiction whose resolution must then occupy the rest of the filmic narrative. How can disappearance and survival be reconciled within a single temporal frame? In this case, the trope of reconciliation is one of redemption.

In its final sequences, the film centers on conversion to Christianity. A shot of two men, one with a drum and the other with a book that we are to assume is a Bible (although we cannot be certain), epitomizes a conflict between two modes of religious experience and social order. The relationship between the drum and traditional religious practice had been established earlier in the film when the drum appeared in the dancing scenes as backdrop, and in a separate shot following the title "The Eagle Chief holds to the old rites." There, the arrangement of images and narration through contrast and parallel establishes a relationship of identity, with the old rites physically manifest in the totem pole and the mallet striking the drum's taut surface.

One of the more striking aspects of the film's movement between disappearance and redemption is the visual parallel between the first and last scenes. In the final sequence, the Chief must decide among three women, choosing one for his permanent bride as part of his acceptance of Christian values and its valorization of the nuclear family. The shot is framed so that we see the Chief standing to the right of three seated women who, in turn, occupy the left half of our screen. Yet, as we wonder how the Chief will resolve his dilemma, the script introduces a new element, with the unexpected appearance of a fourth female character. Entering from the right is the young woman whom he will choose over all three. In his preference for the young woman, the Chief excludes the others who together symbolize Native traditions. Earlier, these three women had been pictured dancing on the beach and were identified as the guardians of the potlatch tradition. In place of polygamy, the Chief accepts monogamy. Instead of shamanic ritual, he endorses Christian theology. The three women, seated on the left of our screen, occupy the same position as the canoe (with its three unidentified passengers) after it has moved into the space of departure from the screen at the film's beginning.

Crystallized in this scene of absurd choices and ironically undercut moralizing is a set of deeply rooted assumptions about the nature of "savagery" and "sexuality." It is necessary to recall here that the audience for this film would have been an urban, bourgeois audience. But though it is common to superimpose the liberal mores of Left Bank cafés or a Bohemian underground onto the urban North American scene when thinking about the 1920s and 1930s, the Anglo-Canadian context was far more akin to Victorian England than to the New York, Paris, or Vienna of that time. Its population was decidedly puritan. And in the prurient but prudish imagination of Victorian and Edwardian culture, tribal peoples were thought to be sexually promiscuous, and the perversion of polygyny (pictured in *Saving the Sagas*), though morally superior to polyandry, was singled out as an example of Native people's moral incapacity (Stocking 1987:202). Thus, conversion to Christianity would necessarily have to be accompanied by a similar conversion to monogamy. In the film, the rejection of the three women, and through them, the rejection of traditional lifeways, indicates the triumph of Christianity's moral and political economy. But if conversion is so partial, and if morality resides so stubbornly in the blood, culture itself must be relegated to the realm of epiphenomenon, where it becomes an elaborate but superficial system resting upon more basic biological foundations (Boon 1972). In some regards, then, conversion becomes impossible and, in the eyes of the filmmaker, is forever mocked by Nativeness itself. This is the implicit ideological message of *Saving the Sagas,* where extinction is the necessary *telos* of Native cultures even when the explicit narration extols the process of moral and cultural transformation.

In this respect, *Saving the Sagas* is decidedly Victorian, despite its production date. Victorian anthropologists would have positioned Native societies beneath an undifferentiated Western Civilization (with bourgeois ideology

naturalized), not merely because such societies were presumed to be culturally stunted, or somehow truncated in their development—which would
have implied the possibility of change and development—but because tribal
peoples were thought to be "racially incapable" (Stocking 1987:237).
Hence the cultural and moral recidivism evoked in the last scene.

Saving the Sagas paid lip service to the new ideas of an anthropology that
denied the evolutionism of its predecessors, but it also reiterated Victorian
racialism. The film occupies an uneasy and ambiguous point of transition
that is itself largely the result of Franz Boas's work. Where Victorian anthropology had naturalized the ideological functions of religion in a doctrine of
"evolutionary racialism," Boasian anthropology had replaced evolutionism
with historicism, thus restoring culture to the center of anthropological
inquiry. At the same time, it denied the possibility of a normative cross-
cultural comparison in evolutionary terms. In the final analysis, then, *Saving
the Sagas* is torn between the two conflicting notions of cultural identity
offered by Victorian racialism and Boasian historicism, of culture as a product of biological identity and as a historically contingent set of forms.

In Norrish's film, these two concepts are in some sense positioned as the
ideal and the real, respectively. The ideal or normative bias of Norrish's film
sees assimilation through conversion as the only acceptable future for coastal
Natives. But *Saving the Sagas* also casts doubt on the possibility of civilization, its savage ridicule of the Chief and its patronizing commentary on
the seductive young "squaw" contributing to an ironic, if incomplete, negation of its dominant story, namely the story of metamorphosis.

Like all texts, *Saving the Sagas* contains the possibility of other readings.
Its narrative grain may be followed or resisted, and, depending upon the
position of its audience, its voice may be facile and didactic or ironic and
cynical. Yet, despite this potential plurality of readings, the film's construction of a story is highly consistent and carefully realized. We have seen that
Norrish constructed his story around a set of binary oppositions that occupy
the beginning and the end of the film, but we have inadequately considered
the narrative movement that transforms the initial condition of disappearance into one of resubstantiation. In the middle of the narrative, at the
center of the filmic text, is the image of death, which is manifested in the
haunting shots of the Chief's incantation over his own grave-site. The image of an elderly man securing his well-being and his future remembrance,
through an acknowledgment of his own death's imminence, occupies a crucial position in the narrative. Not only does it appear close to the middle of
the film's running time, but it also provides the transition point in the
passage from disappearance to redemption: disappearance as the literal and
metaphoric death of a culture, and redemption in the form of individual
Christian conversion. The two poles are reconciled in the concept of assimilation, which, for the Christian viewer and exegete, embodies both. This

point of transition is the liminal moment of Van Gennep's (1966) *rites de passage*, the juncture of transformation in which all that has gone before is wiped clean and replaced with a new order and a new position in the world. Salvation, it must be remembered, also entails renunciation, and although the renunciation of the old ways is not completed until the last scene of the film (and then dubiously), it is foreshadowed in this middle image. In the same manner that salvage anthropology assumes the inevitable homogenization of cultures, and so makes ethnography an exercise in the cultivation of memory, the Chief's address to his grave-site embodies the acknowledgment of his own mortality and, with that, the end of aboriginal power.

For the film to work as allegory, there remains only the task (though by no means a minor one) of equating the Chief with his entire culture, in order that his death can truly be said to symbolize cultural extinction. But the film has already constructed an identity between the Chief and Native culture writ large. He is the only Native character to receive sustained attention and to be consistently associated, through explicit narration, with the old ways and rites. It is the Chief who, in the final instance, eschews the polygyny of tribal social mores and adopts instead the stringent monogamy of Christianity.

This raises for us the related issue of how power was organized within Native Northwest Coast societies. Of course, the obfuscation of power relations within Band societies was common in the anthropology of the day. Boas himself has been criticized for his "neglect of commoners" (Ray 1966). And the question of slavery has been one of the thorniest problems in Northwest Coast studies. Rarely does the ethnographic literature of this early period point to the possibility of difference and conflict within so-called simple societies. Veiled by the flattening concept of "subsistence" and elided by a utopian desire to find equality in the "primitive," much early ethnography tacitly valorized the indigenous aristocratic ideal. Frequently, the main interlocutors and most trusted informants were people (usually men) of high status, of exceptional education or ritual knowledge, and it is their somewhat extraordinary point of view that comes to represent, in the work of the ethnographer, a conflated "native point of view" (Geertz 1983). The early ethnography of the Northwest Coast (until the mid-1930s) relied heavily on an incipient structural-functionalist paradigm in which unity and a corresponding assumption of completely shared ideational systems was the rule. The possibility that other cultures were also subject to internal division, to power politics, or to the workings of hegemonic processes did not generally cross the minds of those early ethnographers, for whom a Native was a Native was a Native. The object of their investigations—in addition to pure documentation—was an understanding of cultural logic and functional necessity. They were not concerned with the means by which order could be maintained in the very face of the potential for disorder and resistance.

Norrish's film is typical of the contemporary ethnography in this respect. It constructs a single point of view and attributes to Native persons a singular collective consciousness as their counterpart. For this reason, a "native point of view" can be taken for granted. It is not an object for interpretive investigation, as it would become for the humanist ethnography of a Geertzian mold, nor one for deconstruction, as in later more radical exercises (either Derridian or Marxian in origin). Rather, it is a totalized and singular perspective embodied and contained within a specific character who can then stand for—symbolize—the culture as a whole.

Even so, that point of view, unitary and unequivocal though it may be, remains a blank spot in the narrative. It is the underside of the Archimedean point, the dark abode of alterior vision. We never see the world as the Chief might, and the camera movements identify the narrator's point of view only with that of the anthropologists, although here the identification is neither consistent nor continuous. Native exegesis, here as elsewhere at the time, is entirely absent. Later, when we turn to an analysis of more recent films, this problem of point of view and Native exegesis will acquire new texture and dimension. For now, I merely want to raise a few issues in regard to the effacement of subjectivities that is so blatantly part of the newsreel format.

It is perhaps necessary to begin with a specification and differentiation of silence. There are many silences here: not just that of the Chief, even though we are to assume an equivalence between his voiceless point of view and that of his Native counterparts. Indeed, it would not be entirely misleading to speak here of a hierarchy of absences. For if the film offers a narrative for the Chief, it casts women as the mere instruments of that story. They are his objects, his possessions, his obstacles, and his salvation. Indeed, it is only around the women—as the object of desire and as "sign" (Mulvey 1975; Cowie 1990)—that the presumed heterosexual male viewer can begin to identify, however tentatively, with the Chief. The gratuitous scene in which a young woman gestures with her hand and is said to be throwing a kiss anchors this other narrative of desire, which is then woven into, but not negated by, that of salvation. Such identification is ultimately subverted by the inescapable opposition between Native "Other" and the viewing Euro-Canadian "Self." But it is nonetheless possible to discern several potential subjectivities, each differently positioned, within the filmmaker's utterly opaque realm of alterity. One must therefore ask after the Native *points* of view, and not simply substitute a totalized subject for a complete absence.

Narration and Lack: The Mechanisms of Meaning

The narrative structure of *Saving the Sagas* is organized around the poles of disappearance and salvage. This structure then provides the viewer with a "way of seeing," to borrow John Berger's term—an interpretive context in which the fact of cultural "contact" (a euphemism for colonization) is to be understood.[5] As such, it manifests an otherwise tacit model of cultural history, a paradigmatic narrative, as I have termed Edward Bruner's notion of ethnography (Bruner 1986). However, the full extent of the film's capacity to influence, if not determine, the viewer's subjectivity is to be found in the relationships between the various levels of absence or lack in the film.

It is, I think, widely accepted that narrative derives its impetus and its *telos* from a principle of initial lack. That lack may be conceived in two mutually reinforcing ways. Couched in the language of plot, it implies a drama of resolution whose origin lies in an initial conflict or problem; in terms of the viewer's cognitive experience, the lack is one of knowledge and the film's narrative then becomes a temporal journey toward comprehension. In psychoanalytic terms, that lack is said to operate through the mechanisms of desire, such that the viewer's own lack (of power and knowledge conceived in terms of the phallus, in either its Freudian or Lacanian formulation) is projected and located in the film.[6] But for my purposes here, lack can be generically considered an attribute of the plot and of the viewer's relationship to that plot. It is an emphatically temporal and temporary state. The ultimate compensation for such a lack constitutes the closure of the narrative (Nichols 1981:72, 90), though, of course, not all narratives achieve closure. In ethnographic film, this absence is inflected in a particularly scientistic way, both necessitating and legitimating the exposition. The ideology of the ethnographic film states that the film must fulfill some knowledge function; it must provide information that makes the events depicted intelligible. It is possible for films to provide this contextualization in the beginning by establishing a tableau in the first sequence through voice-over narration (as in *Box of Treasures* or *Potlatch . . . a strict law bids us dance* [1975]) or through visual montage (as in, for example, *The Nuer*). But the construction of an initial synchronic frame in which action can take place is not necessary for narrative (Barthes 1980:81), and is not the case in *Saving the Sagas*. It can also be a product of accumulated shots and sequences that refer to a basic context; the tableau can be constructed intermittently with the diegesis.

In B. E. Norrish's film, the narrative begins *in medias res* with characters already in the field. The tableau is essentially the condition of absence or potential absence, the disappearance of cultural lifeways. And it is from here that the process of salvage begins. However, as Roland Barthes points out in his exquisite analysis of Jules Verne's *The Mysterious Island,* the two terms of any such narrative equation are not strictly correlate (Barthes 1980:82). Absence is an existential state, a condition of stasis, whereas salvage is a temporally extended and ultimately active process. To quote Barthes (1980:82), "[T]his disturbance . . . 'opens' (like a first key) the process of analysis, by revealing two codes: one which is static . . . the other, which is dynamic."

What does all this mean for an analysis of *Saving the Sagas*? The film can be viewed as three separate strands that are woven together through the organization of visual imagery and textual narration. There are three distinct and relevant foci of lack in the film, each generating its own drive toward resolution and conclusion: (1) The two anthropologists are engaged in a process of collection and recording through which they will acquire (previously unknown) ethnographic information; (2) the Native cultures under consideration are defined in terms of loss, and the film narrates their gain of an alternative mode of existence through conversion; and (3) the presumed absence of knowledge on the part of the viewing subject is addressed and, in the course of the film, negated or supplemented. Thus, we have lack as a motivation for ethnography, as a condition of aboriginality, and as a justification for the film itself.

According to Nichols (1981:244), in an "analysis of narrative a lack is inevitable and its resolution is the function of a complex mechanism that enforces closure by masking contradiction." The congruence between these different planes of narrative is not merely coincidental. Nor are their respective mechanisms and processes of masking independent. Rather, they are all informed by a particular conceptualization of "Western culture" that attributes to it a redemptive capacity. It is this vision of a moral unity, underlined by a divinely sanctioned mission to extend itself, that permits the activities of the two scientists and those of the missionaries to be identified in a relationship of analogy and correspondence.

The assumption of loss that bound the different kinds of "lack" was widely expressed by ethnographers of the era (Bruner 1986; Clifford 1986b). Bronislaw Malinowski articulated the same sense of urgency and irony that accompanied ethnography when he wrote: "Ethnography is in the sadly ludicrous, not to say tragic position, that at the very moment when it begins to put its workshop in order, to forge its proper tools, to start ready for work on its proper tasks, the material it studies melts away with hopeless rapidity" (1961:xv). While an understanding of the past as loss may be very old (Williams 1973), the particular sense of historical discontinuity that is embedded in terms such as "traditional" almost certainly has its origins in the rapid industrialization of the nineteenth century (Clifford 1986b; Terdiman 1985). As a product and manifestation of modernity (Buck-Morss 1989), then, it is not surprising that loss is an integral concept organizing the perceptions of, and policies toward, those people identified as premodern or nonmodern. A "structure of feeling" (Williams 1973:12) but also a point of origin for narrative and other representations, the notion of a vanishing Indian calls into being the twin ideas of salvage and assimilation. "Salvage" itself shares with "salvation" the etymological connotation of wholeness, the antithesis of fragmentation and disintegration. No wonder, then, that it could or would become the vehicle for those "totalizing narratives" now so inextricably linked with modernity and modernism (Lyotard 1984).

These are the means for masking the contradiction inherent in the simultaneity of cultural disappearance and physical survival. How can a culture appear to have disappeared while its members continue to exist? How can anthropology preserve cultural diversity and at the same time chronicle the homogenization that attends contact, a contact that is itself prerequisite for anthropology? The paradox is ultimately unresolvable, and the purpose of the film (this film and all salvage ethnographic films) is to mediate the paradox.

Franz Boas and the Ethnography of the Technical

Franz Boas's massive corpus on Northwest Coast cultures begins in 1887 with the publication of "The Coast Tribes of British Columbia." A champion of historicized social science and a fervent opponent of Victorian evolutionism, he contributed immensely to the reconceptualization of the culture concept. Throughout his lifelong attachment to the Northwest Coast, Boas consistently pursued a single set of theoretical problems having to do with the relationship between the general and the particular, the historical and the innate, the objective and the subjective in culture. In *Race, Language and Culture,* he defined the anthropological program in negative terms, as follows:

> In my opinion a system of social anthropology and "laws" of culture development as rigid as those of physics are supposed to be unattainable in the present stage of our knowledge, and more important than this: on account of the uniqueness of cultural phenomena and their complexity nothing will ever be found that deserves the name of a law excepting those psychological, biologically determined characteristics which are common to all cultures and which appear in a multitude of forms according to the particular culture in which they manifest themselves. (1940:311)

Despite not only the vastly problematic distinction between psychology and culture but also the presumption of a nonsocial psyche, Boas's argument defines culture as something that, if not completely irrational, resists rationalization on a cross-cultural level. He was particularly dismissive of any attempt to construct laws that would comprehend culture in terms of a causal relation between "soil and history," referring to such prescriptions as "only vague, empty generalities" (1923:629).

Culture, for Boas, was analogous to language, but not in its denotative sense. Rather, culture and all of its products were construed in the sense of connotation, with meaning being contextually and subjectively determined

(McDonald 1986:24). Within such an analytic system, it becomes logically impossible to theorize and therefore to generalize cross-culturally. Context is all, and the understanding of particular beliefs, social institutions, and practices then requires the mapping of multiple and elaborate relationships between diverse phenomena, a process that is itself contingent upon encyclopedic knowledge of a culture's objective forms and practices. It is precisely this pursuit of the encyclopedic that marked Boas's work, at least insofar as his written ethnography is concerned: so much so that his ethnographies often read like shopping lists of material culture. Several comprehensive studies of Boas's written ethnography have been carried out, the most notable being those of George Stocking (1968, 1974), and I shall not rehearse here what has been said elsewhere. I do, however, wish to examine Boas's film, *The Kwakiutl of British Columbia* (1930), in light of his historicist project and to compare it to other films of the same period. The synopsis below will provide a point of departure for further discussion. First, however, it is necessary to sketch the historical background of the film's making.

Boas filmed the scenes of *The Kwakiutl of British Columbia* in 1930 when he was seventy years of age and on his last trip to the Northwest Coast. Accompanied by the Russian anthropologist Yulia Averkieva, he carried with him both a 16mm camera and a wax cylinder for recording sound. Possibly, Boas hoped to create a synchronous sound film, not knowing that the technology of the time would not yet permit it (because the spring-wound camera was itself rhythmically irregular and because the lengths of recording surface for film and audio were not identical). Alternatively, he may simply have wanted two separate records, one of sound, the other of visible action (Ruby 1983:28). In a letter to Ruth Benedict, dated November 10, 1930, Boas indicated his hopes that the footage amassed in the field would give him "adequate material for a real study" of dance (Ruby 1983:30). Unfortunately, Boas lost or misplaced the footage (he actually believed it had been stolen) and did not complete the analysis. Nor did he edit it into a distributable film. That task was completed in 1973, after the footage had been relocated. With the assistance of several Kwakiutl informants, Bill Holm edited the sequences into a two-reel film for the University of Washington's Burke Museum. For this reason, the actual sequential arrangement and structural organization of the footage is of less importance for my purposes than it might have been if Boas himself had completed the postproduction work. Instead, I want to look to the internal construction of scenes and shots and to the cumulative effect of the imagery taken together.

Synopsis: *The Kwakiutl of British Columbia* (1930)

The first frame of the film is a title reading simply "Fort Rupert." The camera pans along a beach in a long-shot, revealing a row of wooden houses. The next title indicates a "street," and the camera pans along the same length of waterfront lined with houses, which are now visible in greater detail, before continuing on to the water and pausing on Beaver Harbour and the islands of the strait.

In the third sequence we see a woman drinking from a large ladle. Behind her is suspended a cradle, which the woman rocks by pulling on twine fastened to her foot on one end and the cradle on the other, with her hands left free. The title is a single word: "Cradle."

The next seven scenes depict various technological processes. In the first, titled "Woodworking," we see a man kneeling on the beach working a single cedar board (large enough to be a house-board) with an elbow adze, a hand adze, and then a roughly serrated knife. The second shot, "Drilling," features the same man using a hand-drill on a similar board. A closer shot shows him wetting his hands and then twirling the drill between flattened palms. This is followed by another sequence at the same beach location titled "Making Cedar Rope," in which the same elderly man is seen stripping bark from a cedar sapling.

Here the film moves to activities performed by women. We see in a sequence of alternately profile and full-frontal shots, titled "Weaving Baskets," a woman weaving natural fibers while seated on the beach. Following, we see the same woman as she beats cedar bark with a blunt instrument, flattening the fibers that are now separating. Still at the same location, we are introduced to a scene of "Spinning" in which three consecutive shots (profile, frontal, and three quarter) show us a woman spinning a coarse thread or yarn on a spool about two feet long and a disk-shaped whorl.

There follows an extensive sequence of shots and titles devoted to the subject of play. "Ring Game," "Throwing Sticks," "Children's Games: Ball," "Hitting a Ring," "Guessing," "Kicking," "Carrying and Hairpulling," "Pretending to Sleep," and finally "Bone Game" are each identified in titles and imagery. Women are featured only in the more sedate games: "Counting," in which we see a girl marking off a row of twigs that are neatly arranged on the ground in front of her, and "Guessing," in which a woman separates sticks into two groups while a man has turned his back. At this point, the first reel of the film ends.

The second reel of the film is dedicated exclusively to ceremony, dances, ritual, and shamanic practice. The initial two scenes feature chiefs engaged in competition and exchange. In the first, "Chiefs Boasting," we see two men wearing hats and blanket capes, gesticulating at each other. Each picks up a pole, shakes it, and then stabs it at the ground, shakes fingers at the other, throws down his blanket, and stamps his feet. In the "Use of Copper Plates in Speeches," the same two men are featured. In turn, they each hold up a copper, pass it between hands, and place it on the ground. Both of these scenes are filmed outside, with a single wooden house in the background and the two men standing in the path that leads to its door.

The bulk of the film's second reel is composed of dance sequences, with seventeen separate dances identified with titles. They are listed as follows, in order of appearance: (1) "Cannibal Dance," (2) "Woman's Cannibal Dance," (3) "Healing Dance," (4) "Woman's Winter Dance," (5)

"Tooqwid Dance," (6) "Bird Dance," (7) "Dance of the Trees," (8) "Salmon Dance," (9) "Paddle Dance," (10) "Woman Grizzly Bear Dance," (11) "Begging Dance," (12) "Newettee Shaman's Dance," (13) "Shaman's Dance," (14) "Feather Dance," (15) "Mitla Dance," (16) "Nanlum Summer Dance," and (17) "Nootka Dance." In many of the scenes we see not only the men or women performing but also spectators and, on occasion, the outer limits of the outdoor stage or performance circle in which the dancing is taking place. In the extremities of some frames, we can even see the sound-recording apparatus. Dress varies from one dance to the next and includes everyday Western attire (trousers, shirts, and vests for the men, skirts and blouses with sweaters for the women), cedar regalia, capes, carved masks, and feathered head-dresses. Some dances feature vigorous movement, particularly of the upper body and head such that the face of the dancer is transformed into that of the mask and then restored again in rhythmic succession. The mask itself is placed on the crown of the head and when the dancer lowers his or her own head, the human face appears to metamorphose into a raven, an eagle, and so on, depending on what the mask represents. Other dances are relatively restrained, with small steps and little body movement; but in all cases there is the characteristic shaking of cupped hands.

The final scene of the film, however, is not a dance but a healing ceremony titled "Shaman Curing a Patient." Pictured here is a woman clad in a blanket cape with cedar bough head-dress. She is kneeling and passes branches and then her hand alone over a stick, which is upright in the earth. We see her continue this motion with a closed hoop, and the final shot has her shaking a rattle. A title announcing "The End" draws the healing ceremony and the film to a close.

What are we to make of this extraordinary collage? Jay Ruby's estimation of the film (1983) focuses almost exclusively on the dance sequences, an emphasis that receives impetus from Boas's daughter's suggestion that the film was to be used in an experiment with Laban dance notation (Ruby 1983:30). In Ruby's analysis, the concern with dance and expressive forms is central to Boas's refutation of historical materialism and is merely a continuation of a project that generated his 1927 publication, *Primitive Art*. At the same time, however, Ruby claims that it may have been part of another extended project (carried out mainly by Boas's students) whose objective was the refutation of "the alleged racial determination of mental and bodily conduct" (Efron, cited in Ruby 1983:33). Yet, although there is more footage devoted to dances than to any other single subject (the games sequences are a close second), Ruby's exclusive consideration of dance seriously misrepresents the film and, I believe, Boas's intentions. In fact, it cannot account for more than half the original footage. We need instead a more comprehensive framework, something capable of addressing all of the film's content and of realizing the "plural" of its text (Barthes 1980).

The Arresting Visions of Franz Boas

The question of where to begin is paramount. In the final edited version of *The Kwakiutl of British Columbia* we have a mélange of the everyday and of the spectacular. Both the mundane activities of physical survival (in the scenes of weaving, stripping bark, woodworking, etc.) and the elaborate rites of spiritual existence (the dances and shamanic ceremony) are pictured here. Although the titles label the activities, clarifying for the viewer that what might appear to be aggressive hostility is in fact play, and distinguishing among dances that only the tutored Kwakiutl dance enthusiast could recognize, they provide little in the way of contextual information. To be sure, the titles constitute an interpretive gesture, but they are merely the verbal articulation of a particular profilmic analysis and the construction of the profilmic event as a discrete and identifiable object.

When Bill Holm took up the postproduction work for "*The Kwakiutl,*" it was necessary not only that he consult Boas's notes and correspondence about the film but also that he call upon Kwakiutl expertise (Ruby 1983: 26), seeking out the surviving actors from the film and asking them to describe the scenes and the ceremonies of which they were a part. Ruby (1983:29) claims that "the footage makes sense only if one believes that behavioral events removed from their normal social and physical context retain sufficient validity to reveal patterns of culture." The point, however, is not whether the footage makes sense but, rather, what kinds of meaning can be assigned with and without reference to extrafilmic sources. In Colin Browne's (1979:190) annotation of the film, we are told that the actors featured in the film are Mrs. and Mr. George Hunt, Sam Hunt, Frank Walker, Sarah (Hunt) Ohmid, and Charley Wilson, all of whom were key informants for Boas's written ethnography. In addition, Browne states that the ball used in the game is made of skunk-cabbage leaves wrapped with cedar bark and that the yarn being spun by Mrs. Hunt is mountain-goat wool with nettle fibers. This additional "denotative" reading relies on sources other than the film and could not be performed with the film alone, save by the film's actors. The "recognition" factor is simply inadequate. In fact, the film does not necessarily denote anything for a given viewer. Not even Holm could interpret the image-track that Boas left behind.

It may be said that the constituent sequences of *The Kwakiutl of British Columbia* are all concerned with the "how" of existence in this Northwest Coast culture; they are descriptive or, rather, demonstrative. But to a certain extent, its imagery is free-floating and without context, so that we do not know for what reasons a cannibal dance would be performed or what powers the Shaman is invoking when she carries out her curing ceremony. We cannot be sure when adults might have joined the children in the leisurely pursuit of play, nor what provoked the boasting antics of the two Chiefs. The intentionality of these acts is entirely absent. Taken as a whole, the footage provides a powerful demonstration of the degree to which photographic and filmic imagery arrests social process, stripping objects from their systems of meaning in the moment of their inscription. It presents us with what John Berger and Jean Mohr (1982) have described as the "shock of discontinuity," the sense not only that the image is distanced from its supposed referent but also that what it signifies has been loosened from its moorings in the historical world.

In the absence of Native exegesis, a different kind of interpretation becomes both possible and necessary. From the film's fragmented totality, its rough-hewn montage, we might construct a relatively coherent "picture" of the Kwakiutl or, rather, of the Kwakiutl as Boas imagined them. To begin with, we could establish that, to the extent that Fort Rupert is representative of other Kwakiutl villages, the people live in a forested environment; all of the houses appear to be wooden and in many scenes there are large stands of cedar in the background. The village is coastal but protected, as evidenced by the pan out to the water in the early scenes; a vast expanse of water is dotted with islands whose effect would, we can surmise, be to break oceanic storms. Woodworking and basketry appear to be practiced with great dexterity and skill, although with few and seemingly simple implements. For the viewer, these images of simple technology prompt a sense of ingenuity, for we have seen the great length of the cedar plank on which George Hunt labors and are left to marvel at the amount of time and energy that must be expended to reduce a tree of about fifty feet to a single plank using only hand tools. That sense of ingenuity and patience is a hallmark of ethnographic film, a function of its radically othering tendency, but it is at its most extreme in a film like *The Kwakiutl*. As viewers we are to be astounded that these "simple people" with their "simple technology" can manage such great feats of aesthetic and intellectual endeavor.

The cumulative logical effect of the edited sequences featuring games and dances must inevitably be an impression of bounty. Both the number and array of games, and the fact that adults—as well as children—are seen playing, suggest that there is substantial leisure time, and this would necessarily be contingent upon more than adequate food supplies. Similarly, the number of separate dances, some of which are seasonally restricted, and the existence of elaborate masks and regalia suggest a great deal of time devoted to ritual activity; this too, we are to suppose, would require a store of food and surplus produce. The titles "Woman's Winter Dance" and "Nanlum Summer Dance" indicate, if vaguely, a complex and seasonally structured ritual cycle. Thus, in addition to the technological ingenuity and economy, the film evokes a "global signified," to use Barthes's term (1985:195), in the form of bounty or abundance.

What else might the ethnographer extract from *The Kwakiutl of British Columbia?* The information on such abstract anthropological categories as social organization or the division and professionalization of labor appears to be scant on first sight. However, the tacit messages contained here are numerous. The footage and its accompanying narration indicate quite clearly, though perhaps unwittingly, that the society in question is characterized by a notable degree of stratification. This knowledge is provided by the shots of the chiefs, in which two men are seen in an act of verbal and demonstrative competition. We are also led to infer a gender-based allocation of duties. The woodworking, drilling, and rope making are depicted as the province of men, whereas the sequences of weaving, spinning, and shredding bark feature only women. In the one scene of child care ("Cradle"), only a woman is shown. Although a skeptical and critical viewer might claim that what is represented need not be considered exclusive, that difference may reside in the unseen and the unspoken, the "film" provides us only with information suggesting a strict, if complementary, division of labor. Silences, visual and otherwise, speak volumes here, colluding with the assumed viewer's expectations of the domestic sphere and its particular gendered structure.

Earlier, I suggested that the decontextualization of social and technological practices deprived them of the intelligibility that would accrue to them in a Native exegesis. We lose all connotations of the cannibal dance (What did it signify, and why was it performed?) and of the boasting ceremony (Under what circumstances is boasting a mode of political conflict, between what kinds of people, and with reference to what kinds of attributes?). Without an expository narration or additional footage, it becomes impossible to interpret what might be the particular significance of any of these images. Decontextualization in this manner becomes a mode of objectification in the sense that the subjective and objective dimensions of practice are rent apart; the image becomes something akin to the (collectible) material artifact and need no longer be interpreted with reference to any Native meaning system. Instead, it is incorporated into the meaning system of its viewer and possessor: transposed, relativized, and recontextualized in a completely new chain of signifiers.

This process of decontextualization, appropriation and reinsertion is not, of course, a feature of Boasian anthropology in particular. It is an inevitable part of all hermeneutic endeavors, whether they are involved in the traversal of literary-textual or cultural divides. Perhaps Boas's relentless collection of data was part of an effort (albeit a compromised one) to stave off the ultimate necessity and responsibility of interpretation. And yet this seems unlikely given the degree to which he did address such issues as historical change, the social psychology of behavior, and the aesthetics of culture. But even when he acknowledged his own centrality to the interpretive process,

Boas seems to have desired an impossible degree of objectivity. The result of that desire can be seen in the footage that forms the basis of *The Kwakiutl.* When Bill Holm approached the material for editorial purposes, he not only had to compensate for Boas's interpretive reticence but also had to negotiate the history of Northwest Coast ethnography since then. In the end, we have a film that simultaneously honors Boasian method, with its rigorous attention to material objects and its categorical exploration of behavior, and incorporates the knowledge of contemporary Native "performers" and exegetes. *The Kwakiutl of British Columbia* is a profoundly synthetic historical artifact. Holm's editorial style is remarkably loyal to Boasian ethnography, approaching the problem of historical re-vision with scrupulous reserve and utter fidelity to the goals of the discipline's patriarch. And, in the final analysis, the narrative montage of *The Kwakiutl* is not so much an imposition of narrative meaning as it is an effort to imbue each image with a signifying ability not yet realized in the original footage. Toward this end, Holm employs titles, a device that is itself pregnant with historical evocations. It is to this issue of titular reading that I now want to turn.

Boas via Holm: A Titular Reading

At the literal or denotative level of the filmic text, the titles continue to identify things that are foreign to the non-Native viewer (we can remind ourselves here that Boas intended the film only for academic audiences, and these did not include Native anthropologists). As Barthes describes it, the "caption . . . helps [one] choose the *correct level of perception,* permits me to focus not simply my gaze by also my understanding" (1985:197; original emphasis). This "repressive" ·function of the caption is part of the film's ideological tool-kit, binding us and blinding us to the cumulative effect of the imagery. The footage appears to us as *pure denotation.* At the same time, it connotes for us—because the imagery is now to be understood in *our,* which is implicitly to say non-Native, terms—such abstract and essential qualities as ingenuity, economy, bounty, excess, and even barbarity (how else does the bourgeois Western viewer understand cannibalism?). Clearly, the same values would not be signified for the Kwakiutl observer, of any status. The potlatch, for example, a symbol of excess for early missionaries and legislators, may have represented honor, tradition, social obligation, and the power of the ancestors for high-status Native participants. It may also have meant other things, including onerous labor, inequity, or a joyous opportunity to partake of others' wealth, for lower-status Kwakiutl. But the point is the same: The participants' perception is excluded from the interpretive frame provided for the viewer by Boas's own camera work and Holm's subsequent editing. "As for the signified of connotation," writes Barthes, "its character is at once general, global and diffuse; it is, if you like, a fragment of ideology" (1980:91).

To be sure, Boas was well intentioned and sympathetic to what he perceived as the Native cause, combining his academic enterprise with a practical commitment to racial equality and justice. But he was also a product of his time, and, though highly cognizant of the forces that dominated thought in this period, he was nonetheless also constrained—as we all must be—in his ability to transcend the era's ideology. Boas himself recognized this fundamental epistemological and political problem when he wrote,

> It cannot be said too frequently that our reasoning is not an absolutely logical one, but that it is influenced by the reasoning of our predecessors and by our historical environment; therefore our conclusions and theories, particularly when referring to our own mind, which itself is affected by the same influences to which our reasoning is subject, cannot but be fallacious. (cited in Stocking 1968:160)

Boas's hopes for liberation from previous intellectual traditions notwithstanding, his own comments support the procedure followed here—namely, the analysis of Boas's own thought and representations in terms of his own social milieu.

And so, we return to *The Kwakiutl of British Columbia* and its global significations: ingenuity and economy of technique, bounty of resources, diversity of ceremonial forms and rites, and, finally, the ultimate barbarism of cannibalism. These qualities or essences, which Boas and Holm manage to diffuse almost imperceptibly amid the mere cataloguing of culture, are not neutral, of course, but form the conceptual latticework of a normative ethical system. Included within that system is a vision of the Native as Adamic, as originary. This is the image of the savage as custodian of the paradisiacal garden, where labor is neither onerous nor constant, and where leisure can be pursued energetically. And how well this image of savagery meshed with the economy of abundance assumed to have been the basis of pre-contact cultures on the Northwest Coast (Suttles 1987; Drucker 1955; Boas 1966).

Yet, when Boas made *The Kwakiutl of British Columbia,* the residents of Fort Rupert were living in anything but luxurious conditions. The population reduced through disease, the ceremonial life virtually strangled by federal (Canadian) legislation banning the potlatch, limited access to the resources that had been the staple of Kwakiutl life, and widespread poverty and cultural dislocation were the dominant qualities of Kwakiutl life in 1930. Boas was not simply recording the processes of the present, but reconstructing a culture—an imaginary culture—still pristine and innocent of Euro-Canadian ways. This falsification of the present is carried on throughout the footage in the presentation of old technologies whereas those of the

(then) present are conspicuous in their absence; demonstrations of traditional political forms (boasting) and healing practices are retained whereas.
references to contemporary Band structures or bio-medicine are excluded.
All narrative, Hayden White (1980:10) reminds us, "is constructed on the
basis of a set of events which *might have been included but which were left
out*" (original emphasis). To ask what might have been represented, what
other possibilities exist in the silent spaces that can be discerned only by
reading "against the grain," is to understand the full implications of anthropological narrativity. What version of reality is being represented, what ideal
is being conveyed in *The Kwakiutl of British Columbia?* Reconstruction, as a
methodological tool, effaces the supposed impurities of cultural change, and
thereby elides the reality of cultural contact, colonization, and historical
process. The impetus to reconstruct is a quintessentially nostalgic impetus,
born in the assumption of loss. Recognizing this, one detects a more heroic
ambition. Salvage would become resurrection, and the salvage ethnographer
would become more than the collector of *aides de mémoire;* he or she would
become the facilitator of continuity, even if that continuity were to entail the
isolation of the museum's glass chambers.

   As facilitator or *réalisateur,* the ethnographic filmmaker becomes a director and people become the instruments of her or his vision. There is no
doubt that Boas had the scenes of *The Kwakiutl of British Columbia* staged.
The dances and ritual exchange of boasts would normally have occurred inside during a potlatch or feast, but Boas would not have been able to film
the events with natural light and so constructed a stage outside. He seems to
have been without diffusers or any other technical apparatus that would provide light in sheltered areas. As for the performers, they carry out their ritual
activities before and for the camera. They occupy what Richard Schechner
(1985:92) has called the "subjunctive frame," where they are simultaneously re-creating the rites of a ceremony no longer in practice, an event of
the past, and enacting them in the present—for cameras, recording equipment, and the curious ethnographer. Even the use of the hand adzes had
partially given way to other technology appropriated from the encroaching
Euro-Canadian culture. It would perhaps be extreme to describe different
scenes in *The Kwakiutl* in the (rather heavy-handed) terms that Schechner
uses to describe Shaker dances, as a "way of physically re/membering
(= putting back together what time has dis/membered) an extinct behavior"
(1985:48), but there is a sense in which Boas's film constitutes a kind of
"restoration." The use of the term "extinction," when applied to a ritual
event that had been performed less than a decade before and was still fresh
in people's memories, seems extreme. Nevertheless, in Boas's footage we see
clearly the props of reconstruction: the makeshift stage, the self-conscious
performance, even the recording equipment in one corner of the frame.

   It is possible that Boas wanted to include in the film the visible signs of this acting frame or stage as a gesture of reflexivity and self-awareness. But this seems unlikely given the poor quality of the prints, the shakiness of the camera, and other technical flaws that suggest a more haphazard film style. Perhaps Boas would even have edited out this aspect of the footage, had he not lost track of the material himself. But such considerations are peripheral to the main issue: of cultural reconstruction or restoration, and the attempt to resurrect an endangered authenticity. This resurrection did not, however, aspire to reinstate practices into a contemporary social milieu, merely to preserve them for academic scrutiny. In a sense, this kind of filmmaking attempts to "reverse the acculturative process and salvage elements of traditional behavior for posterity" (Balikci 1975:191). It has been argued that such filmmaking strategies hold the possibility for comparison and contrast between a reconstructed past and an experiential present (Balikci 1975: 199). For myself, such comparisons merely point to the differences between present constructions of the past and present constructions of the present. But we may postulate that Boas would share Balikci's aspirations. His concern with the problem of culture change and assimilation (the latter term was first used in its current sense by Goldenweiser in 1912 [Leaf 1979: 170]) was mirrored in his physical anthropological work on "hybridization" (Stocking 1968:49). It was also expressed in his work on modern life (Boas 1923), in the introductory remarks to James Teit's (1898) volume on the Thompson River Indians (echoed in the title of this book), and in numerous other contexts.

This returns us to the problem of narrative and the nostalgic longing for purity embodied in the image of disappearance. But in methodological terms, that return is somewhat problematic. On the one hand there is the claim that *The Kwakiutl of British Columbia* is informed by the narrative of disappearance and, on the other, the apparent lack of narrativity in the film's composition; how does one reconcile the two? To begin with, the absence of narrativity as a framework for the selection of imagery should not be mistaken for the absence of a paradigmatic or metanarrative framing the perception of the profilmic event and its representation in film. Although the different levels of narrative are parallel, as in *Saving the Sagas*, where the two converge on each other in mimetic identity, this is not always the case. In *The Kwakiutl of British Columbia*, the lack of continuity between shots and the seeming concurrence of events seem to rob the film of its narrative potential. The narrative frame, the ideological construct of the vanishing Indian, is inserted into and signified in the film through the mechanisms of montage and repetition and emerges surreptitiously through the saturation of the viewer's visual consciousness with a highly specific kind of imagery.

Technically, Boas's footage leaves much to be desired. *The Kwakiutl* is raw and unaccomplished, a fact quite independent of postproduction editing. The camera is shaky, the image often unfocused and without a continuous center. Boas did not make much use of the range of camera shots available to him, opting almost exclusively for a single medium-range shot, which produced a flattened perspective and indiscriminate vision. It is as though he did not understand the exigencies of film's own ideological apparatus, the need to create a subject position for the viewer (Baudry 1974–1975; Chapter 2). However, the apparent lack of specifically cinematic literacy probably entailed more than mere technical incapacity. Boas seems to have thought such a film style was the means to observational neutrality. He did, after all, want the material gathered on this last voyage to be the basis of a final, *"real* study." Despite his own technical naiveté, however, he did imagine film as the basis for an expanded anthropology. Perhaps that conviction emerged from his association with Harlan Smith, the relatively unknown archaeologist who shared his obsession for the Northwest and his hopes for a visual ethnography.

Harlan Smith and
the Art of the Ethnographic Film

In 1911 Edward Sapir, who for just one year had been chief anthropologist in the Division of Anthropology at the National Museum of Man (under the auspices of the Geological Survey of Canada), hired Harlan Smith; and during the next twenty-six years, Smith produced one of the most comprehensive collections of ethnographic films on a single culture area by a single filmmaker, anywhere in the world. In terms of quantity, his only real competition comes from Jean Rouch, whose massive corpus of more than one hundred films is surely unrivaled anywhere. Smith's films were shown mainly to museum audiences as part of a Saturday morning lecture series, but some were also lent out to schools (Zimmerly 1974:5). Since then, they have been only infrequently used; indeed, many anthropologists are unaware of their existence, which is unfortunate because Smith's most accomplished films exhibit a literacy and complexity achieved by few documentary filmmakers of the time. Not only is the quality of the image good but the films are tightly organized, coherent, and exquisitely consistent, indicating his aesthetic and technical maturity as well as the degree to which Smith valued the editing and postproduction part of filmmaking.

Synopsis: *The Tsimshian Indians of the*
Skeena River of British Columbia (1925–1927)

The film opens with a title reading "The Canadian National Railway speeds through the mountain walled valleys of British Columbia toward the land of the Tsimshian, where totem poles and costumed Indians recall the glories of a vanished past." The title is followed by a series of shots showing the geographical environment: the river, its treed shores, and the mountains. A man in Tsimshian dress, with fringed blanket cape, is shown inside a house, illuminated by a single shaft of sunlight from above, and the film then cuts to a map of British Columbia on which the Tsimshian territory is clearly indicated with a pencil.

Another title describes the Skeena River as the link between the Tsimshian and their coastal neighbors; the accompanying imagery depicts the river from various angles, and in long-shot we see the canyon with a village perched on its banks.

Shots of a young black bear and a river teeming with salmon follow an introductory title that describes the environment as "abundant." Following are two sequences featuring various villages that, as the intervening title informs us, have been built on the river's edge.

"Fishermen and hunters, they have lived here for untold generations." The image-track shows us an elderly man in medium range, his "costume" fully visible and with the ovoid designs of his blanket cape prominent; then it cuts to a close-up of his face. Next we see an elderly woman who is seated, as well as shots of children playing. This is followed by a shot of a young woman carrying an infant in an "Indian baby carriage," a wooden box strapped across the shoulders and carried behind.

In the following five sequences, the film provides informational imagery of food, particularly salmon, and depicts the fishing technology and preparation processes. We see, in turn, young men gaffing fish from protected enclaves along the river-bank, women carrying fish, smoking them, and then storing them in a house built especially for the purpose. Berries (soap-, blue-, salmon-) are described as supplements to the diet, and we see scenes of berry picking, whipping, tasting, cooking, and drying. Finally, wild cow-parsnips are added to the menu, and we are shown someone searching for and then eating the vegetable.

A subsequent series of shots and titles deals with transportation. The narration describes trails in the place of roads and primitive transportation, whereas the imagery shows paths snaking through a forested area and a woman laden with pack and suitcase. She is accompanied by a dog that is similarly burdened with a smaller pack tied to its back. "The River itself was the main highway" and, according to the title, was traveled in cottonwood canoes. These and the enormous trees from which they were carved are shown in sequence along with images of men paddling and poling their way along the river.

"From Cottonwood to Cedar": The following title describes cedar as the material for homes, furniture, and storage boxes. In its wake are images of a man using an elbow adze to carve a totem pole—first in medium range, then in close-up—and finally continuing his wood-work with a knife. Soon we see another man working on a wooden bowl.

The woodworking is followed by sequences of women weaving baskets, which are displayed for the camera, and spinning mountain goat wool. The "beautiful blankets" of the title are modeled by men who wear them as capes while posing next to the house entrance or near totem poles on the river bank.

The poles themselves are featured in the next sequence, where they are described as "statues" carved professionally to "honor" the men. A montage of totem images follows here—poles seen from the bottom with the camera panning upward, poles that lean or are broken, and then detailed close-ups of the carved figures emerging from the wood.

A series of shots in which individuals and groups of people are shown dancing, most often with a drummer visible, is introduced by a title reading: "Strange dances are held near these totem poles. Masked actors impersonate the characters in well-known tales." There are several shots of the dancing, which occurs in a crowd of onlookers who occasionally obscure the camera's object. In the final shot of this series, an automobile is visible in the background of the frame.

The next title describes death as having "knocked at the door," while a single shot of a dark cloth suspended over a doorway is shown.

The final four sequences transport the viewer into "this new age" where "tombstones and grave-houses replace the older totem poles." The footage focuses on tombstones and grave-houses in an unkempt field, where long grasses obscure the markers. We are introduced to the tourists who, we are told, "come from far and near to view the totem poles." They are pictured looking at the poles, pointing upward to the tops of the columns, and taking photographs. Two shots of totem poles being raised are prefaced by a title attributing responsibility for their resurrection to the Dominion government. Finally we see a large and broken pole lying on the ground. But according to the title that precedes the image, this "fallen pole" has been "re-erected with others and reproduced on the ten cent post stamp." The film's last shot is of the upright poles, towering above the village.

From this verbal rendering of the film, it should be possible to glimpse the extraordinary linearity of its narrative; each sequence of cinematic images and text anticipates the next and stages it as almost inevitable. The opening title of the film transports us to the scene of the action with the trope of the frontier journey. The train, of course, is an image of familiarity but, more than that, a gesture toward the heart of a Canadian national consciousness forged both in the imagination and in the construction of a transcontinental line. Not merely an image of transit, it moves the viewer (we can momentarily imagine ourselves in the place of those early audiences) between cultural spaces, from that of the dominant Anglo-Canadian milieu to that of the Tsimshian, both literally and metaphorically. Other Smith films make use of the same trope. In *The Bella Coola Indians of British Columbia* (1923–1924), for example, the opening title reads: "In 1873 Sir Alexander MacKenzie the first white man to reach the Pacific overland through Canada discovered Bella Coola." In that film, the epic journey is explicitly defined in terms of exploration and discovery, and an identification between the explorer and the viewer is generated much in the same manner that identities are created between ethnologists and viewers in Norrish's *Saving the Sagas*. The journey opens up the narrative, serving as the film's "once upon a time," and, in doing so, materializes its rhetorical function and the ethnographic act of intellectual voyage between the foreign and the familiar.

That movement is never once abandoned in *The Tsimshian,* whose cyclical structure returns the viewer from the end to the beginning in its affirmation of the viewer's presumed Euro-Canadian or perhaps American identity. In its beginning we arrive with the trains in the territory of the Tsimshian, like explorers in uncharted terrain. We are permitted, indeed encouraged, to fantasize ourselves as adventurers, and the problem that confronts us in our newly intrepid status is the comprehension of the foreign circumstances in which we find ourselves. In this manner, the film constructs its scientific objective, the fulfillment of a knowledge function, and the familiarization of something otherwise alien and opaque to our investigative eye. At the same time, it positions the viewer as a passenger on this intellectual voyage. We become tourists, voyeurs, subjects of a narration that exists solely *for* us. That position as armchair traveler/observer is reaffirmed in the closing sequences, which feature camera-toting tourists. But it is also inverted there as the viewer becomes not merely the subject (agent) of narration but also its object. The tourists, donning what appear to be Shriners' hats, are like the images of the train: metaphors for culture contact.

To this extent, Smith's films demonstrate a formal continuity with the travelogues that were so popular at the turn of the century. Of course, this correspondence between popular and institutionally professionalized accounts of otherness is not unique to film; it is part of the anthropological tradition in general. And although the separation of different forms of representation has been thorough to the point of militancy in more recent years, the "discursive practices [of the discipline] were often inherited from these other genres" (Pratt 1986:27). It is not merely coincidental that Smith constructs the ethnographic film as a journey. His trope of travel is at one with those accounts of exploration and discovery that so entertained the previous generation. And, as in those earlier literary productions, it works to draw the viewer into the narrative frame.

The point may be obvious but nonetheless important for all that; the "topos of travel," as Johannes Fabian calls it, is a crucial rhetorical device for distancing an "Other." It emerges in the context of a secularization and spatialization of time that finds its apotheosis in Victorian evolutionism but persists well into the present century (Fabian 1983:2–21). In the nineteenth century, there arose a conception of time and space in which, "relationships between part of the world (in the widest sense of both natural and sociocultural entities) can be understood as temporal relations. Dispersal in space reflects directly, which is not to say simply or in obvious ways, sequence in Time" (Fabian 1983:12). From our point of view, at a time when Concorde jets and space shuttles have rendered travel banal, eighteenth- and nineteenth-century accounts of voyages have all the magic and unbelievability of an H. G. Wells or Jules Verne novel. Unfortunately, such accounts did not always receive such elegant articulation. But regardless of their aesthetic appeal, the romanticism of travelers' tales had largely been dismissed by the self-defined scientific discourses of the late nineteenth and early twentieth centuries—especially by an anthropology that was at pains to distinguish between the tourism of colonial elites and the fieldwork experience of social scientists.

But the motif of travel, and the understanding of travel as a passage in time, did not disappear. Instead, it was subsumed "under the reigning paradigm of natural history" (Fabian 1983:8), where the signs and products of evolution were mapped onto a global landscape whose rough terrain was temporally marked by the sites of origin. It is not incidental that Harlan Smith was initially employed at the Museum of Natural History in New York and that he first began developing his skills as a photographer and cinematographer there. Nor, I think, is it incidental that his post in Ottawa was officially under the auspices of the Geological Survey of Canada and the Department of Mines. The historical linkages between geology and history, not to mention archaeology, are profound. It was, after all, the revolution in geology spurred by Lyell's *Principles of Geology* (1830) that led to the initial fluorescence of natural history and to the development of a fully secular anthropology in which travel could become not so much an exercise in spiritual salvation as an act of scientific discovery and recovery. And it was in geology that time acquired its particular depth, its extension, and its spatial dimensions—as the sedimentary layers of an earth that served as time's iconic ground. It seems to me that the history of anthropology in Canada and elsewhere must be understood in terms of its relationship to geology. Such an institutional affiliation must surely have had a determining impact on the kinds of research carried out and on the definition of the discipline as a whole: its cognitive orientation, its ideological project. The precise nature of that intersection remains vague (Fabian's interventions aside), at least until further research is done, but it was this complex and ambiguous tradition that Smith brought to the making of *The Tsimshian*. And it is only in such an institutional and ideological context that one can fully appreciate the degree to which time and temporality were axes of meaning in the film's and its era's representation of other cultures.

The first sequence of *The Tsimshian* situates the viewer and the object of her or his gaze in time. The Tsimshian, we are told, "recall the glories of a vanished past." We are delivered up upon the banks of the Skeena River where the past is made present again through the workings of memory.

How odd, how utterly magical, that we can see this past in the present—as though we were privy to the Tsimshian mind's eye. The film performs for us what the ideology of cinema claims for itself: providing us, that is, with the very residue of time, its presence arrested in a past to which we are now fantastically permitted entry. That possibility is, of course, the possibility of preservation and re-creation, carried out by the dominant culture in the pursuit of pristine origins. The tensions between past and present that lie at the heart of modernity's nostalgia for a vanishing authenticity also lie at the heart of cinema. And not surprisingly, for cinema was, as Annette Michelson (1984) so cogently reminds us, modernity's "philosophical toy." Perhaps for this very reason, because of their shared historical roots and ideological orientations, film appeared to offer salvage ethnography its ultimate vehicle. Understood as the presence of the world in time, it seemed to hold out the possibility of realizing H. G. Wells's fabulous dream of time-travel.

However, to understand how these different but related dreams of time-travel come together in the films of salvage ethnography, we must return once again to those questions of temporality that philosophy posed with respect to film and photography. I do so not, as I said earlier, because I find such ontologically oriented debates of much use in understanding how film works, but because it was in the effort to oppose film and photography that so much film theory and, by extension, film practice was developed. Roland Barthes—whom Maureen Turin (1985:8) sees as "one of the most recent and articulate perpetrators" of the realist assumption that film operates on an indexical and denotative level—gives contemporary and eloquent voice to those early but still powerful notions about film and photography. His sense that the two modes of representation are distinct in their temporalities is evocative of an entire representational ideology:

> The type of consciousness that photography involves is indeed truly unprecedented, since it establishes not a consciousness of the *being-there* of the thing (which any copy could provoke) but an awareness of its *having-been-there*. . . . Film can no longer be seen as animated photographs; the *having-been-there* gives way before a *being-there* of the thing. (Barthes 1985:200–201)

What strikes me as being of particular interest about this statement is the very specificity of its position. And what takes it out of the purely or merely relative is Barthes's own consciousness of that specificity. Barthes writes: "Film can *no longer* be seen as animated photographs" (my emphasis). But there was a time when film was conceived in precisely those terms. Hence the word "movie." One might imagine that such a literalist concept of the motion picture could have been borne only when film itself was a brainchild. But the idea had extraordinary staying power and continued to influence philosophical debates for decades, briefly forgotten and then reborn again with the technology of slow motion, freeze frames, and video playback.

The point is that all of the filmmakers discussed here—Norrish, Boas, and Smith—were producing films during the period when film was being reconceived as something other than just moving pictures. Let me go further and suggest that that moment marked a transitional phase in the history of cinema (at least ethnographic cinema) when, in Barthes's language, the *being-there* of the film eclipsed the *having-been-there* of animated photographs. By this I mean not that a new cinematic technology was invented but, rather, that cinema was reconstructed in a new image. Boas's cinematic naiveté then appears to us in a new light, as a kind of representational anachronism; his work seems to realize that earlier idea and *The Kwakiutl* appears merely as a series of moving pictures.

To say that the *being-there* of film eclipsed that of the *having-been-there* of photographs is not, however, to say that one replaced the other. Ethnographic film has never fully surrendered the latter; it continues to derive its authority from a claim to indexicality and to deny its own aesthetic and narrative conventions. But the debate about the relative importance of aesthetic and documentary value in ethnographic film largely postdates Smith's films, which are themselves quite ambivalent about the nature and the function of the image-track. The tendency to conceive of narrativity as external to the imagery, as something that must be inserted via the title (subtitle, intertitle), implies the concept of the moving picture. In Smith's films the image-track and the narration are not yet fully integrated, and continuity derives less from the logic of the images and their arrangement than from the omniscient narration that binds them.

This ambiguity of tense and temporality is reflected and repeated in the grammar of the titles themselves. Consider, for example, the descriptive titles that are applied to the Tsimshian. The Tsimshian, we are told, "built their houses on the banks of the river," where they "have dwelled" for an unspecified but decidedly lengthy period of time. Subsequently, the narration informs us that salmon "is their staff of life," that "they dry it in summer for winter use." From the simple past to the past indefinite to the present indicative, the titles move in rapid succession. Some activities, such as the storage of personal effects in wooden boxes and the carving of totem poles, are narrated in the past tense. Others, including the dances and placement of tombstones, are articulated in the present. Nor can this discrepancy be resolved by separating out practices into categories of the existent and the disappeared. The accompanying footage depicts these activities (weaving, spinning, carving, etc.) as present, and to this extent the film is qualitatively different from mere photographic montage, which would signify only the past existence of an object (Berger and Mohr 1982).

The filmic construction of history, the situation of the imagery in the past, is accomplished by the narration, which, in many cases, actually seems to repress what might otherwise be implied—namely, the continuation, persistence, and survival of cultural ways and forms. I do not mean to suggest that the image-track in some way embodies an unmediated reality that is then, and only then, denied or obfuscated by narration; rather, my point is that ethnographic film demands to be viewed on the assumption of indexicality: the *having-been-there* of the filmmaker-cum-anthropologist. Moreover, the indexicality of the ethnographic image is understood as an indication that what we see is what would have existed regardless of our presence and, indeed, in our absence (Nichols 1981:241). In *The Tsimshian,* then, an awkward juxtaposition of titles in the past and present tenses comes together to destabilize the overt message of the film, which, on the diegetic plane, narrates the disappearance and commemoration of aboriginal culture in a single, linear continuum.

In the first title of the film, the Tsimshian past (by which the film means the Tsimshian essence) is identified as "vanished." Later in the film, old ways of marking burials are being replaced by new and culturally foreign ways, and the totem poles, symbols of the Northwest Coast cultures since first contact, are being raised anew "for posterity" and commemorated with a postage stamp. Almost certainly fortuitous, this image of the postage stamp nonetheless manages to condense the logic of the modern commodity culture, where authenticity is reduced, reified, fetishized, and circulated as a "sign" of the nation-state now longing for its (authenticity's) return. As the counterpart to the *having-been-there* of the film, posterity connotes the *present-becoming-past;* to do something for posterity is to do something *ad memorium,* as a token for that which must cease to be. Like the Chief's recognition of his own mortality in *Saving the Sagas,* the gesture toward posterity is a prophecy of destruction. Ironically, then, the postage stamp, currency of the new Dominion, becomes a mnemonic device, evoking the cultures whose existence had been suppressed by that self-same state. Almost all of Smith's films feature this ambivalent nostalgia. In *The Bella Coola,* it is expressed explicitly in titles that describe enormous houses of which "only shadows" remain and totem poles that have disappeared except for a few stubborn but inferior survivors. In *The Nootka,* the film's "graphic voice" (Nichols 1983) tells us that "today the big whale hunting canoes of hollowed cedar have rotted and of the mighty cedar themselves only stumps remain."

In the end, what redeems Smith's films, but what also marks them as typically romantic, is his profound respect and admiration for Northwest Coast cultures. He marvels at and praises the skill of Native craftspeople, referring to them in effusive and superlative terms. His attention to detail, the pause and fixing of his camera's gaze on crafted objects such as masks and baskets, underscores his own sense of and quite sincere regard for all the cultures on the Coast. Ultimately, though, such respect could not mitigate the sense of imminent demise; it only imbued that presentiment with lamentation.

There is, however, one additional and important respect in which Smith's films are worthy of praise. More than any other filmmaker of his generation, Smith was prepared to acknowledge and to represent the heterogeneity of change and contact. Although he assumed the previous existence of a pristine and atemporal state, undifferentiated except through colonization, he also evoked the experiential reality of the time. His films are not reconstructive in the sense that Boas's were, and there does not appear to have been any effort on his part to efface the signs of contact. In the end, the internal contradictions generated by his simultaneous commitments to the narrative of disappearance, and to the lived reality of the present, threaten to explode the narrative and to rob it of all credibility. But the instabilities of the film need not all be interpreted as signs of incapacity; and it seems to me that Harlan Smith's inability to maintain this separation of tenses is at least partially a function of both his discomfort with the strictures of the category "nonfiction/ethnographic film" and his sensitivity to the plenitude of experience being elided by the dominant narrative. In this respect, Smith is a particularly important figure for the history of ethnographic film. And this despite his utter neglect by film historians more devoted to realism than was Smith himself.

Following his production of *Cheenama the Trailmaker* in 1935, the Canadian Museum of Man abandoned its film program, which included distribution as well as production, and as it did so, Smith's potential contributions to the discipline were abruptly and severely restricted. Although it is impossible to gauge what might have been the direction of ethnographic filmmaking on the Northwest Coast had his work remained in circulation, it is clear that the tradition that did finally emerge was influenced by other forces. As shall become apparent, the films produced in subsequent decades were equally concerned with the problems of history and salvage. However, they express quite different assumptions about the function and the object of salvage, a disparity that can be understood primarily in terms of their answer to the documentary question "What to do with people?" (Nichols 1981) and its correlate, "What to do with time?"

Replay: Norrish, Boas, and Smith

Let me review briefly. Looking at, though not really *looking* at *Saving the Sagas,* I argued that the film exemplified the era's dominant motif, namely that of redemption. Boas's never-completed film *The Kwakiutl of British Columbia* seemed to defy such an analysis in its truncated montage and its utter inhabitation of the "moving pictures" concept. But for that reason, it permitted the reading of a meta- or paradigmatic narrative, whose ideological values were signified in the film's aspiration toward a neutral vision and a reconstructed past. The methodological and stylistic problems related to the construction of narration and the presumed relationship between events and their representations were raised in reference to Boas's film but made central in the consideration of *The Tsimshian*. For in Smith's film, the contemporaneous histories of film and ethnography were themselves implicated in the film's attempt to mediate past and present through the trope of travel.

If the aesthetic value of the films is passed over in such a process, the political dimension of cultural production is gained. However, the point is not to efface one in the act of foregrounding another but to reveal them as being implicated in and by each other. That is to say, aesthetic strategies have ethical and political implications (Pryluck 1988). And in this sense the duality of the term "representation" is more than etymologically fortuitous. Narratives ensconced in the legal and political apparatus of a dominant group are not merely related; they are lived. The narrative of disappearance made Canada's Indian Act of 1874 and the policies of wardship both possible and legitimate, made the banning of the potlatch almost inevitable, and made the ethnographic enterprise an ethically credible exercise in salvage. It is for this reason that we can, with Hayden White (1980), pose two questions simultaneously: "What is being narrated?" and "What is being moralized?" By "moralized" I do not mean that Norrish or Smith or Boas were personally and intentionally accountable for the policy of assimilation, and certainly Boas was adamantly opposed to it. But as people in a particular time, as historically situated individuals, they could not but articulate the assumption that power and authority were vested in a Euro-Canadian and/or Euro-American cultural center. At best, they could speak the alternatives of their era. But because authority was naturalized in an ideology of historical progression, assimilation could not be contested, only regretted. Hence the bitter and desperately nostalgic lineage that is salvage ethnography.

This is modern allegory as Walter Benjamin described it, the story of a world fragmented and in decay, whose crumbling pieces are the fetishes of the past's devout connoisseurs (Benjamin 1977; Buck-Morss 1989). Not new, this groping after lost authenticity: It is as intrinsic to the *Book of Genesis* as to Milton's Satan, as to the pages of the British Romantic poets and the German painters of the same era. But each era has its own construction of the rupture between past and present. What is particular about the loss addressed by the century's early ethnographers is that the vanishing Other, which was ultimately its vanishing Self, was contemporary. In the early decades, it was a *vanishing* and not yet *vanished* authenticity. Thus, not only was time spatialized, as Johannes Fabian (1983) claims, but spatial distance was temporalized through the creation of carceral spaces more euphemistically termed "reservations." In their carefully circumscribed "islands of history" (cf. Sahlins 1985), Native North Americans could be conceived as somehow ancestral, as original, as primitive. Almost inevitably, they were thought to be dying, those not yet dead chanting their own funerary rites over future graves. In a complex process of distanciation, these people could be simultaneously absent and present through the representational endeavors of the ethnographer. As James Clifford remarks, "The other is lost, in disintegrating time and space, but saved in the text" (1986b:112). The films of Norrish, Boas, and Smith seek precisely this kind of redemptive role. They make present what is on the verge of dissipation and, in so doing, save it for observation.

This much at least is shared by both the films and the written ethnography of the period. What is not shared is the functionalism (and later structural-functionalism) by which the totality of a culture's practices are seen as interdependent and logically necessary. Smith's films come closest to the monograph form associated with functionalism and its later variants. However, the equilibrium model of culture requires an elaborate analysis of causality, and all of the films produced in this period are deficient in that regard. None of them exhibits a sense that culture exists as an ideological and sociostructural abstraction, and thus systematic relations are not addressed or represented. Part of the failure to pursue that kind of ethnographic abstraction can be explained by the way in which film was conceptualized. The utter opposition of narration and imagery, the tacit postulate that the film text is always doubled, always divided between voice and image, where image itself is understood as mere picture, made such a film style inevitable (cf. Mitchell 1986). Film's presumed indexicality could never be reconciled with language's arbitrariness, and so ethnographic documentaries remained mired (as many do today) in a fetishism of material culture and specularized practice. This is why Boas imagined using his footage for an extrafilmic study, and why Smith, despite attempts to fuse verbal narration and pictorial narrative imagery, was ultimately unable to create a fully filmic ethnography. Such an endeavor would ultimately have to be carried out on the assumption that film, far from being vision's extension, is the quintessential "mixed media." However, that possibility seems to have been banished from visual anthropology's imagination; although later films would take different positions on the narrative of disappearance, they remained enthralled by its claim to capture the world on a celluloid strip whose frames provided—they thought—the only limits to a museological gaze.

Notes

1. This service was intended to promote morally acceptable films, and to insist upon the educational value of movie-going. In effect, its role was to police the local movie industry.

2. The other is a film titled *Nass River Indians* (1927), directed by J. S. Watson and filmed by Watson and C. M. Barbeau. The film bears a striking resemblance to two other films, *Fish and Medicine Men* and *Saving the Sagas*, and may be a reedited version of the same footage. However, the fact that Barbeau is given cinematographic credits for *Nass River Indians* suggests that his involvement in *Saving the Sagas* may also have entailed more than his appearance in the film.

3. Of the scores of so-called Native films listed in Colin Browne's (1979) filmography, *Motion Picture Production in British Columbia: 1898–1940,* only twenty-seven can fairly be called ethnographic films. Not included in this category are those films in which Native persons are featured only in passing, as part of travelogues or newsreels about royal visits; rather, in keeping with the notion of genre, ethnographic films are exclusive to those productions whose primary objective is the documentation and explicitation of cultures.

4. For this discovery I am indebted to Pierre Stevens, archivist and filmmaker at the National Archives in Ottawa.

5. The phrase "way of seeing" occurs in Berger and Mohr (1982).

6. Most feminist film theory attends to the gendered embodiment of that lack and the degree to which the desire of a positionally (heterosexual) male viewer is mobilized around the body of a woman (Mulvey 1975; Cowie 1990; de Lauretis 1984; Heath 1987). Homi Bhabha (1983) has shown how these principles of desire work in the construction of racial stereotypes by generating a tension between attraction and repugnance, thereby paving the way for an analysis of the ways in which gender and race converge in certain constructions of otherness. This is far too brief a sketch to even hint at the richness and complexity of a debate that has now been at the heart of film studies (though not ethnographic film studies) for more than a decade and a half. I refer to that debate here in order to indicate my own (qualified) sympathies with the kind of analysis that is being developed in the interstices of psychoanalysis, film theory, literary criticism, and history. However, though such an analysis may be congruent with my purposes here, it is not immediately or transparently applicable to the current subject. Indeed, it remains to be seen whether the interpolation of subjects is the same for audiences of Hollywood and ethnographic film. Mulvey's germinal article "Visual Pleasure and Narrative Cinema" (1975) was, after all, almost exclusively addressed to mainstream Hollywood cinema, and most of the criticism it has since generated is focused there. Nor can I fully accept the phallocentric and culturally relative lineage of most psychoanalytic film theory. The development of psychoanalytic ethnographic film criticism will require a thorough exploration of that cultural bias. My ambitions here, tempered by a sense that further work needs to be done, remain more modest. I offer no universalizing theories of need or desire (indeed, I resist the tendency to universalize desire altogether) as the ground for understanding filmic narrative.

4

Totems and the Potlatch People: Absence, Presence, and the Denial of History

In a world that is well on its way to becoming one vast quarry, the collector becomes someone engaged in a pious work of salvage. . . . The past itself, as historical change continues to accelerate, has become the most surreal of objects—making possible, as [Walter] Benjamin said, to see a new beauty in what is vanishing.

—Susan Sontag

To experience a thing as beautiful means: to experience it necessarily wrongly.

—Friedrich Nietzsche

Where Have All the Natives Gone?
New Modes of Salvage

WHAT HAPPENED TO THE VISION of the vanishing Indian that so character-ized the films of the early years? The National Museum of Man's (1935) withdrawal from filmmaking activities created an enormous vacuum in Canadian visual anthropology (Zimmerly 1974). Without an institutional locus, filmmaking withered and the situation was only worsened by World War II, during which time strategic considerations and supply shortages made movement and production on the coast difficult. In a negative sense, then, the War marks a transition point in the development of a Northwest Coast visual anthropology. At its end, a new generation of anthropologists and filmmakers were waiting to make use of a matured film technology, and, once again, the cameras were turned to the coast.

Catastrophic events usually provide the demarcating lines for the eras of grand histories. Accordingly, Edward Bruner (1986) sees this moment as the transition point in the history of ethnographic narratives: as the moment in which the narrative of disappearance gives way to one of renewal. Perhaps Bruner's analysis is useful in reference to conventional, nonfilmic ethnography of the continental United States (I am not in a position to judge that), but it does not speak to the tensions and contradictions within visual anthropology. Nor does it attend to the persistence of the collection ethos that oriented most Northwest Coast ethnographic filmmaking during the 1950s and 1960s. The films of the immediate postwar decades (from the mid-1940s to the mid-1960s) are ahistorical in the extreme, and essentialist in their foundations. Often at odds with the written ethnography of the time, their assiduous cultivation of the vanishing-Indian trope requires additional consideration. To understand such tensions and ambiguities requires, as stated previously, that narratives be considered contextually and that they be understood in their relationship to a whole discursive field.

I think of this period as a kind of pause that, from the vantage point of the present, constitutes a protracted moment of transformation and exploration. To entertain such a notion is to admit that history is always written from the present and that the positing of a linear development is, on some levels, an act of retroactive teleology. But we write necessarily from the present, and writing the past of the present is, by definition, selective (de Certeau 1988). Perhaps what is most intriguing and promising about an analysis of this postwar era is the degree to which it is a period of hesitation and one in which alternative representational strategies are tried out. Thus, it is possible here to imagine other histories and to partially unsettle the sense of inevitability that comes with the moralizing narrations of the present (White 1980).

There are two major representational possibilities raised during this era. In the first of these, Native authenticity is construed as something completely absent, vanished, or irretrievably past. Here, salvage ethnography becomes a kind of abstract social archaeology, and preservation is displaced by the process of recuperation. In the second, historical rupture is denied altogether, and acculturation is refused or delegated to the superficial level of form and appearance. This latter scheme rests upon a deeply essentialist commitment by which the pure and invisible Being of cultures is impermeable to external influence. In this latter case, the representation of individual Native cultures becomes the most extreme act of aestheticization. Total absence or pure presence: In either case the historicity of Native cultures is denied.

It is possible to imagine here a third alternative in which authenticity would be reconceptualized as something historically contingent, but such a move would require the unsentimental abandonment of bipartite categories: primitive/modern, simple/complex, cold/hot, ahistorical/historical, and so on. In the 1950s and early 1960s, North American anthropology was still not prepared for such a relativist position, and it was not until much later that the theoretical denunciation of binarism began to make itself felt in representational strategies, filmic or otherwise. However, the first two modes, what I shall term here the archaeological salvage and presentist modes of ethnographic inscription, were fully developed in the two decades following the end of World War II. They are considered here in turn, beginning with a set of films focused on a salvage expedition to the Haida village known as Nintstints (encompassing examples of the social archaeological motif) and concluding with Robert Gardner's voluptuous film about the Kwakiutl, *Blunden Harbour*. First, however, I want to trace some of the more general developments in anthropology and to look again at the context in which most filmmaking of this period took place. Doing so, we will want to ask how or why the visual and the written ethnography of the time could have become so rent apart in its substantive concerns and ostensible objectives as to seem irreconcilable. For the legacy of that separation—by which filmic ethnography is confined to the picturing of material culture—is, along with ethnographic film today, haunting its theory and encumbering its activities.

Personality, Function, Ecology: The Potlatch as Topos

Perhaps what strikes the viewer most about the century's earliest ethnographic films is the degree to which they aspire to universality. True, their titles identify them as being about the Kwakiutl, the Nootka, the Tsimshian, or the Haida, and so on, but the exposition tends toward generalization and if there is a predominant "global signified," to use Barthes's term, it is Nativeness or primitiveness writ large. Recall here the narrator of Norrish's film exclaiming, "We know *Indians*." Or the introductory arrival into the heart of forested darkness in Smith's piece, where "costumed *Indians* recall the glories of a vanished past." The peoples imaged in these films are instances of a grand type, relatively undifferentiated except at the boundaries between "White" and "Indian" (though these terms are themselves incommensurate). The Northwest Coast exists here as geographic space, not yet as culture area. Although A. L. Kroeber had conducted his statistical analysis of culture traits as early as 1917, it was not until Boas's students achieved dominance in the field, during the 1940s, that the culture area concept became widely disseminated and, indeed, taken for granted.

By this point (the 1940s), one can see three separate but interrelated approaches to culture on the Northwest Coast: (1) the culture and personality analysis exemplified by Ruth Benedict (1959), (2) structural-functionalism, and (3) cultural ecology. All of these analytic frames had the potlatch at their center and assumed that, as a ritual moment of condensed symbolic value, it held the key to understanding coastal social, political, and economic life. Without exception, the potlatch was treated as a window onto a cultural universe, the entrée to its particular logic. Structuralism, which offered the only serious (though still problematic) alternative to this monologic but spectacle-centered analysis, made its way across the Atlantic only slowly and had little impact on the Canadian field until the 1970s. Ironically, poststructuralism would later return to the potlatch or, rather, to the puritanical representations of potlatch produced during this period, in its attempt to find the moments of excess where rationalist (modernist) logic fails. Because of its centrality in debates about the postmodern, and because of its importance to the history of ethnography, we need to go back to those early representations and to consider them anew, asking both when they were employed and to what ends, and why the films of the era were so uniformly silent about potlatching. For, in doing so, we begin to see how the cultural politics of representation play themselves out, how certain groups and peoples are privileged and allowed to stand for others, and how typification comes into play.

In her narration of *Box of Treasures,* Gloria Cranmer-Webster remarks that the Kwakiutl have been the most anthropologized people in the world. Though an extraordinary and ultimately dubious claim,[1] Cranmer-Webster's assertion points to a palpable tendency in anthropology and to an ongoing fascination with the Kwakiutl. Helen Codere (1961:431) referred to the Southern Kwakiutl as "the famous Kwakiutl of the North Pacific Coast," and for anthropologists the latter seem to require little other introduction.

As Codere noted more than forty years ago, most of the work on the Kwakiutl has relied upon the enormous body of material amassed by Boas during his fifty-year association with the area (1950:78). W. Holm and G. Quimby (1980:31) have added to Codere's recognition the insight that Boas's work, like Curtis's, was almost entirely dependent upon the cooperation and collaboration of a single man, George Hunt, an informant who had been employed by the Indian Reserve Commission as a translator in the 1870s (Cannizzo 1983:45). Despite his own reluctance to generalize about coastal cultures, Boas clearly contributed to Ruth Benedict's psychologizing classification of Northwest Coast peoples. His own concern with psychology is evident in almost all of his writings. It was on the basis of Boas's Kwakiutl texts (Cannizzo 1983:47) that Ruth Benedict (1959) elaborated her notion of the Dionysian and identified the Kwakiutl as such. For Benedict, schooled in the classics and enamored of tragic drama, the Dionysian connoted paranoia, megalomania, the overgrown, and the obsessive. In fact, it appears as a pathology in the Freudian sense, and indeed, in her cultural auto-critique, it is to the Dionysian elements of American society that Benedict attributes the moral and political crises of the time. But the movement between Northwest Coast and Euro-American cultures in Benedict's work is awkward and tenuous at best, both too broad and too vague to be ethnographically convincing. The chapter on the Northwest Coast in *Patterns of Culture* is unabashed in its identification of the Kwakiutl with an entire area (1950 [1934]:175). Except for rare asides in which the Kwakiutl are contrasted with their neighbors, such as in Benedict's claim that the Salish were comparatively less concerned with hereditary privilege (Benedict 1950: 226), *Patterns of Culture* constructs a monolithic cultural personality that extends from the Puget Sound to Alaska. For all its poetic insights and its sympathetic, if compromised, pursuit of the expressive in non-Western cultures, Benedict's book virtually reduces the Kwakiutl and the entire Northwest Coast to rivalry, "its chief motive" (Benedict 1950:246). The potlatch, which ethnographers and legislators alike had understood as the competitive institution *par excellence,* was posited as the very embodiment of the area's collective personality.

This conception of Northwest Coast culture (note the singular), based on the conflation of a single linguistic group with an entire area, had enormous influence on Northwest Coast studies, even among its detractors. In the vast literature of the Northwest Coast, even studies of non-Kwakiutl potlatching are constructed in reference to the model of the potlatch that had been elaborated for the Kwakiutl. The latter is the necessary reference point, the comparative and the ultimate instance. Considering this monolithic representation, it is worth noting that Boas, who had termed the potlatch a kind of life insurance (1898:54–55), seems to have used the term in ways that his informant, George Hunt, did not intend. Goldman, for example, claims that Hunt rarely used the word "potlatch" in his notes and translations (1975:131; see also Cannizzo 1983:55). And others, including the early ethnographers J. R. Swanton and K. Oberg, took pains to distinguish the potlatch from the feast, Swanton (1909:155) noting differences in the degree of ritualization and Oberg (1934:98) attending to the social context and function of both. Although early writers provide little reason for privileging the potlatch over other institutions, it was the potlatch and not the feast that became symbolic of the Northwest Coast. And it was the potlatch that came to connote all those things that were the necessary counterpoints to the representing culture and its interlocutors. The potlatch became absolutely central to the anthropology of the time: a veritable "topos" of the ethnographic imagination (Fabian 1983:111).

In the period under consideration, the potlatch was the subject of many ethnohistorical studies that were themselves part of an attempt to reconstrue though not reconstruct Northwest Coast cultures. Helen Codere, in a ground-breaking reevaluation (1950), argued that the potlatch was a substitute for warfare and, in doing so, allied herself (perhaps unwittingly) with Benedict's claim that the institution was premised upon rivalry. Others, such as Stuart Piddocke (1965), emphasized its economic functions, as Boas

(1966 [1895]) himself had done. The vast majority of anthropological analyses focused on the sociopolitical functions of the potlatch. McLellan (1954:96), for example, argued that the potlatch served to "strengthen and affirm basic social groupings," whereas Garfield (1939) emphasized the validation of titles and the importance of status, and Allen (1981) saw in the potlatch a vehicle for maintaining social equilibrium. On a number of issues, these theorists converged. And this despite the often vitriolic debate that filled the pages of anthropological journals. Piddocke's claim that the potlatch served to redistribute uneven resources is, on some level, compatible with Allen's argument for cultural homeostasis, and McLellan's analysis of potlatching politics runs parallel to Garfield's concern with status. Even where differences of opinion are most pointed—regarding the relative scarcity or abundance of resources, for example—there is no question among any of these writers as to the importance of the potlatch *per se*.

A spectacle, the potlatch drew attention. But more important, and as Benedict herself recognized, the potlatch was a rite of consumption that provided a familiar reference point for Western viewers and analysts. It seemed to be the most extreme moment of consumer culture, but in a displaced and exotic form. As a cultural projection, it was out there and hence available for scrutiny. This, then, is the other side and even the underside of Boon's (1982:6) suggestion that every anthropology produces what it requires as other. The North American ethnography of the Northwest Coast did not simply incarnate its own opposite in the representation of coastal cultures. Rather, it projected itself outward and embraced the potlatch because the potlatch itself (in its latest manifestations) seemed a reflection, albeit a distorted one, of that consumerist excess which seemed at times to drive and at others to threaten capitalist relations in Western economies.[2]

It is both relevant and necessary to ask how a single institution could become emblematic of an entire culture. Such synecdochic representations are, of course, common in anthropology—think, for example, of cock-fighting in Bali or Trobriand *kula,* to name only two. Yet, this kind of representation, which fetishizes the fragment in a doctrine of the invisible and abstract whole, also has a history. Malinowski's *Argonauts of the Western Pacific* (1961 [1922]) is perhaps the first and certainly the major instance of that strategy and treats Trobriand *kula* as both the object form and the condensed enactment of Trobriand culture. At the same time that it reveals a cultural logic, the *kula* provides Malinowski's monograph with its structure, its narrative frame. Doubling over, one upon the other, both form and content of the monograph reinforce functionalism's twin assumptions: that all practices are motivated and that cultures are wholes whose every component is enmeshed in relations of dependency with every other component. The first reacts against the doctrine of survivals, the second responds to the perceived *ad hoc* comparisons of James Frazer. Together, these two assumptions made it possible to see in a single institution the refracted totality of a social universe.

It is, of course, unnecessary to assume that because one institution is related to all others, it can act as a microcosm for the ensemble of institutions that together constitute a society. To the contrary, such a move requires a great act of intellectual maneuvering—a veritable leap of (il)logical faith. Nonetheless, the leap was made, and from an argument that posited the potlatch as central to Northwest Coast cultures, the ethnography of the area quickly moved to an analysis of culture via the potlatch and, finally, to a tacit equation of the potlatch ethos with a principle of Northwest Coast culture in general. Twenty years after *Argonauts* first appeared, Malinowski's methodological intervention had been completely entrenched in the discipline as a whole, and Northwest Coast studies were no exception.

Filmic Ethnography and the Reign of the Museum

If, as I have argued, the potlatch had become the predominant symbol of the Northwest Coast and the point around which all written ethnography revolved, one would expect it to have been equally prevalent in the films of the period. After all, film lends itself to spectacle as does no other medium, save theater. And the potlatch was spectacular in every sense of the word, being both an occasion of special and heightened social activity and a literal spectator event in which witnesses were invited to publicly validate the claims and prerogatives of those in whose honor the potlatch was being held. Yet our expectations are not met. The films of this period, from the mid-1940s through the mid-1960s, are not only *not* centered on the potlatch; they hardly even make reference to it. Why? Why were films so radically different in their subject matter and iconography? Is there something about film which precluded the holism of literary functionalism and structural-functionalism, which ensured that ethnographic film would never achieve the status of filmic ethnography in the monograph tradition? Certainly, that conviction drove a great deal of filmmaking and its criticism. I have already indicated my own skepticism in this regard. But there were other factors, and the primacy of the museum as a context for production was central among them.

The sheer volume of films produced in this period is daunting for any historian. But, of the scores of reels made, a large percentage were produced directly under the supervision or with the input of a mere handful of anthropologists working out of the University of British Columbia. Wilson Duff alone was responsible for nineteen films. Most of these run less than five minutes and are exclusively concerned with natural resources and technology. Films like *Fishing* (1950) and *Cedar Bark* (1952–1953) exemplify this cataloging of techniques and are often the simple composites of a few extended shots, using only one camera angle and a single focal depth. A few of Duff's films, *Mythology* (1952) being the most notable instance, address the abstract dimensions of cultural and/or symbolic production, but these are a distinct minority. Mostly, his films attempt what the museum exhibits and their coffee-table publications achieve: the showcasing of material culture as an artistic creation. All of Duff's films were produced under the auspices of the British Columbia Provincial Museum (BCPM), as were those of G. Clifford Carl, whose small corpus included the alliteratively titled *Mungo Martin Makes a Mask* (1953) and *Nature's Candles—Eulachons* (1947–1948). Carl's work shares with Duff's a strikingly uniform narrative and is singular in its attention to the production of material artifacts.

It would, I think, be almost impossible to overestimate the significance of the museum in determining the nature of ethnographic film during this period. As the sponsors of production and often as the sites of filmmaking, the museums demanded that films provide a documentary service that could augment their own documentation, which in turn took the form of collection and display. The demonstrative imperative is unequivocally clear in all of these films, where laborious footage reveals to the viewer the hidden techniques of aesthetic creation. Ultimately, this obsession with material production meshed with a similar obsession with the object, and indeed these films serve as exercises in the visual objectification of culture in general. Knowledge becomes technique and technique transforms the given into the cultural. The trajectory moving from nature to culture is perfectly realized in A. L. Kroeber and S. A. Barrett's film (of the self-explanatory title), *Wooden Box Made by Steaming and Bending* (1962), as well as in their accomplished subsequent production, *The Totem Pole* (1963).

The Totem Pole is but one of fifteen films, produced mainly for the BCPM,[3] that deal exclusively or primarily with totem poles as material artifacts. Indeed, totem poles are the cinematic fetishes of the period, rivaling the potlatch as the synecdochic symbol for Northwest Coast culture in the visual media. And like the written ethnography of the time, a disproportionate amount of filmmaking energies were devoted to the Kwakiutl. George Hunt, who had been so utterly central to Boas's ethnography, was also a key player in the films of the early salvage ethnography. In an ongoing tradition, the films of the neo-salvage era relied on a select group of actors and informants: Mungo Martin, David Martin, Henry Hunt, and Tony Hunt. All of these men were affiliated with the BCPM, as cultural performers and interlocutors, and that affiliation was unquestionably the major factor in determining their status as "ethnographic movie stars." Even Kroeber and Barrett, of the University of California at Berkeley, worked out of Victoria and featured Mungo Martin and Tony Hunt in *The Totem Pole*. No wonder, then, that when screening these films one is constantly struck with a sense of *déjà vu*. The recognition of faces and scenes, of storylines and props, frequently inspires an intimation (and an occasional dread) of an "eternal return." But it is important to recognize that, despite the parallels of structure and the continuity of characters, that intuition is not simply a product of the films' overt imagery. It also emerges from the experience of a completely coherent and internally consistent representational ideology, variously played and replayed in all of these films.

Produced by a mere handful of actors and cinematographers, filmmaking on the Northwest Coast remained an essentially museological activity— perhaps even more so than had been the case with early salvage ethnography. In the place of the glass cage and the softly lit halls of cultural preservation, the film provided both a literal and a metaphorical framing device by which material culture could be isolated. Combined with documentary's literalist realism—its assumption that the only truth available to film exists in visible surfaces—the museological bent of ethnographic filmmaking prompted an exclusively object-oriented documentary style. The obsession with material culture that defines the filmmaking of this era, and the absence of attention to ritual practice, particularly the potlatch, seem to have been the direct result of filmmakers' confining assumption that film could not provide the medium for abstraction. That obsession also reveals the collecting impulse that lay behind anthropological museums in the first place. In ethnographic filmmaking of this kind, the collection of images comes to substitute for the collection of objects.

At this point, however, the visual image with currency in anthropology's political economy is limited to the material artifact. The potlatch, an abstract social and ritual institution, could answer the ethnographic desire for collection only when it was mediated or embodied as artifact. Indeed, from the museological perspective of the time, the potlatch was a social, political, and ritual *context* for display and was evoked only as part of the explanatory exposition in which objects were embedded. In and of itself, it did not possess the materiality prerequisite for appearance in the glass catacombs that curators dedicated to a vanished past.

George Stocking rightly correlates this "object orientation" with the predominance of the museum in early anthropology: "[A]nthropology had a strong internal intellectual push toward the collection and study of material objects permanently embodying moments of past cultural or racial development. Within the evolutionist framework, human physical remains, archaeological finds, and contemporary material culture were the most ready means of graphically illustrating the development of mankind" (Stocking 1985: 114). In his analysis of funding for American anthropology, Stocking further points out that "material objects served as both commodity and medium of exchange within the restricted political economy of anthropological research" (Stocking 1985:113). Although such a political economy was opposed from some quarters within anthropology, particularly by Franz Boas, Stocking notes that this orientation did not give way until well after World War II, despite the demise of evolutionism (which provided the ideological justification for the museum) and only when alternative funding from philanthropic organizations became available. Only then, when institutions such as the Rockefeller and the Ford Foundations could sustain anthropological research outside of the museum, did the discipline begin to loosen itself from its naively materialist orientation.

In Canada, the situation was somewhat different. Lacking the vast capital resources of a northern Rockefeller or Ford, anthropology remained wed to the museum until and even after the discipline was thoroughly ensconced in the university system (McFeat 1976). These economic circumstances were further reinforced by a centrist policy and a general Canadian reticence to allow academic disciplines to become dependent on corporate financing. At the center of Northwest Coast Studies at the University of British Columbia (UBC), the separation between anthropology and the museum was never finally achieved. Instead, the Department of Anthropology was itself tied to the University's Museum of Anthropology, from which it derived much of its public credibility. Prior to the establishment of the University's own Museum of Anthropology,[4] however, anthropologists worked closely with the British Columbia Provincial Museum. And nowhere is that association more apparent than in the ethnographic film it produced. In the productions of UBC anthropologists, it is as though ethnographic film itself is the ultimate museum, but better than the cultural mausoleum because it is mobile and infinitely reproducible.

Objects and Contexts:
Museology and Structural-Functionalism

Perhaps ironically, the objectifying tendencies of museum-based anthropology were buttressed by the emerging theoretical paradigms of functionalism and structural-functionalism. Functionalism, as Marilyn Strathern (1987) has noted, was essentially a doctrine of contextualism. It necessitated a new taxonomic orientation toward the museum display, calling for contextual information as the supplement and explanation for the object (making comparison of the Frazerian type utterly untenable). A parallel movement has been traced by Susan Stewart in her analysis of the history of collection and representation in *On Longing* (1984). Stewart claims that the institutions of collection, especially the modern museum, work by creating an identity between contextualization and representation. By removing objects from the social and historical locus of their production and then according these objects a symbolic status (i.e., by making them "stand for" a culture),

Stewart claims that museums replace social relations with "the illusion of a relation between things" (1984:165). A fetishism of the object thus becomes the literal objectification and, more important, the reification of culture.

But the functional context is a kind of ideal space, the abstracted representation of all that might or should exist. Temporality is expunged from this paradigm, which ultimately assumes that the goal of collection is the arresting of time's corrosive capacity. The understanding of structure as a fundamentally immutable abstraction made such a synchronic bias inevitable. And it meshed perfectly with the particular commodity fetishism described by Stewart, whereby social and historical relations are reconstrued as relations between coexistent objects. In this light, the supremacy of the totem pole, as image and artifact in museums and filmmaking, assumes new significance. In an important regard, it is the doubled sign of ethnographic process; the pole itself becomes the totem that ethnographers assign to Northwest Coast culture in general. And in the soft incandescence of museum halls, where Tsimshian and Kwakiutl, Haida, and Salish poles stand, the history of coastal cultures is surreptitiously reduced to these towering sculptures and the relations between them, spatialized relations of contemporaneity and proximity. Often the only differences remarked in the museum display of totem poles were formal ones, having to do with particularities of "ovoid" form (an elongated but slightly squared oval considered definitive of the Northwest Coast style), the use of certain mythic icons, or the like. And it is only recently (see Chapter 5) that museology has begun to reconceive ethnographic objects in terms of their historical and performative contexts.

But during the postwar decades, functionalist and, later, structural-functionalist assumptions ensured that the era's anthropology and its filmmaking would treat the disappearance of a single institution as the disappearance of authentic culture. Change rendered totems as the ciphers of a lost authenticity. And thus ethnographic filmmaking, still motivated by a desire to gather the material residue of evolutionary process (Stocking 1985), became a kind of abstract social archaeology, whereby salvage was not merely an endeavor to save the contents of a house on fire, but an act of recovery and of discovery in which the past, irrevocably separated from the present, could be contained and collected.

What does this mean, concretely, for a specific analysis of individual films? Not all coastal films exhibit the same attributes in the same measure. The boundary between eras is inevitably a tenuous one. Thus, many of Wilson Duff's films continue the tradition of Boas and were conceived as the filmic counterpart to field-notes—as the yet unadulterated data for further research and analysis (Hockings 1988; Marazzi 1988). Duff's work focuses on technological process and is dominated by sequences in which a single object is produced from raw materials. His films echo those of the earlier period and share in the "burning house" ethos; they are the last-ditch attempt to record old ways, through staged performance and/or reconstruction. Others, such as the "totem films" to be discussed below, inhabit the abstract social-archaeological film tradition with less ambiguity. Some earlier films, such as Norrish's *Saving the Sagas,* even feature dual narratives in which the disappearance of authenticity is matched by its recovery through anthropological salvage. In the same tradition, there is Robert Gardner's quite exceptional film *Blunden Harbour,* which, despite significant innovations, remains mired in the same island of no history through its aestheticizing insistence on the ethnographic present.

In the discussion that follows, I provide a synopsis of *Totem,* a film about the 1957 salvage mission to Anthony Island. When the analysis can be augmented, I include reference to another film about the same trip, *The Silent Ones,* although no synopsis is provided. My purpose here is not so much to compare these two films as to draw out both the continuities and discontinuities with filmmaking of the prewar decades. The technical advances made possible by synchronous sound recording are evident in both films, where voice-over narration has replaced the brief intertitles of Norrish's, Boas's, and Smith's silent (but not speechless) documentaries.

Synopsis: *Totem* (1959)

The first few sequences of *Totem* introduce Anthony Island. There are shots of the shoreline from the water and the sound of waves smacking against the boat's hull. The voice of Bill Reid speaks to the viewer, describing the island as small, about one and a half miles long, protected on the eastern shore where the Haida villages of Nintstints and Squonquai (Red Cod Village) are located.

A point-of-view shot permits us to look over the bow of the boat as it approaches the shore. As narrator, Reid notes: "We came as visitors too . . . taking what remains of their world and preserve [*sic*] it and show the outside world something of the wonder of the old ways." The camera closes in on booted feet as they move across the beach and cuts to the totem figures that stand along the shore. The camera pans across the island. "We were late," Reid tells us, adding that it has been seventy years since the village was abandoned. Again the camera zooms in on the totem poles.

Reid describes the anthropologists' first few hours on the island, remarking, "And to think also of what had been lost: not only the poles and other material things that had been destroyed, or been allowed to decay through neglect, but all the rich pattern of legend and ceremonial that lay behind these massive expressions of a rich and powerful way of life." The visual imagery here is of the poles, with close-ups of the faces and characters that adorn them. The narrator goes on to describe the poles as representations of a family's origins, the achievements of a family head, and then comments on the society that produced them as one in which "paint-ing, sculpture, song, dance, and legend were the major part of a pattern of life."

The camera follows a pole upward from its ground, and the voice notes the wealth of detail still visible on some of the poles: "We weren't too late." We are told that the forest that had "almost reclaimed" the poles also pro-tected them. A mother bear figure is identified on one of the poles, followed by a sequence featuring mortuary poles. The frame of a house is shown and the narrator remarks that it is small by Western standards.

Here the narrator introduces the salvage team as consisting of four an-thropologists, an amateur expert on Haida housing, several camera men, and a Native crew. Reid himself is described as a descendant of the Haida and a representative of the Canadian Broadcasting Corporation. Ironic comments about camp life follow (the city dwellers grow beards, the Na-tives use electric shavers), along with a sequence of shots featuring the sawing and segmenting of totem poles. The largest pole falls with the aid of ropes, and as it does so, we hear thunder. Cut to the sky, which is laden with heavy storm clouds, and there follows a series of shots showing rain-fall with accompanying narration describing a storm and the discomfort it produces for the anthropologists.

On a fortuitous walk, the anthropologists discover shell heaps that they say indicate the existence of another village; in particular, they provide the first evidence of cave dwelling among the Haida. The narration highlights the lack of knowledge about early Haida culture, noting that the first Whites arrived in the area less than two hundred years ago. We are told that our knowledge of the Haida at that time has been colored by the inventions of "prejudiced missionaries, ignorant traders, and half-informed scholars" and that only now is the confused image being slightly "unscrambled." The ac-companying images include a black and white etching of Indians on the coast and an Edward Curtis portrait from the Vanishing Indian collection. Reid tells us the Haida were handsome, ingenious, and able to "fashion a great material culture with relatively primitive tools." At this point a second Curtis photograph is shown.

There follows a description of Northwest Coast canoes and construction processes, with photographs of Indians on the beach. "But it was when the practical skills and sure sense of design borne of necessity were applied to the lavish heraldry of ceremonial life that the full splendor of Haida art was born. And though the White Man brought disruption and eventual destruc-tion of these people, he also brought a flood of new wealth and new tools to augment the stone hammers and adzes and the few iron knives they had had before. And so for a little while during the first two thirds of the last century, creativity on the West Coast flourished as it never had before—and perhaps never will again."

A sequence of photographs follows and the camera zooms in on them, panning along the shoreline pictured in the old photographs. More Curtis portraits follow. The arrival of new currencies is discussed, as is the con-tinuing importance of California abalone (a major trade item on the coast), and we see in close-up the earrings and bracelets that adorn the figure in the Curtis image. The scene shifts and we see another photograph of a group of Native men in Western turn-of-the-century clothes.

The camera zooms in on the group photograph, moving from face to face. The narration begins: "This story of Nintstints was typical of nearly all the villages on the coast. A forgotten history, hundreds perhaps thousands of years long, when the culture slowly developed, the stimulation of early contact with the Europeans with peaceful trading giving impetus to old art, and then distrust, suspicion, disease, liquor, violence. . . . And then 1862— when a traveler to Victoria unwittingly brought the seeds of sudden disaster." The narrator continues, telling of the spread of smallpox on the coast and of the total collapse of Nintstints, while the camera fixes on the canoe at the bottom of the group photograph.

We are returned to the scene of the salvage mission with a shot of rippling water and of men pushing the open crates to the ocean's edge. Toward the film's end, the narrator reads from Wilson Duff's report of the expedition, repeating Duff's assessment that the end of the village was the end of a society and not only the death of a few hundred people. The final sequences include shots of the poles being towed across the inlet in their crates and close-ups of their cracked visages.

The New Salvage Ethnography and the Problem of Authenticity

On the diegetic plane, *Totem* tells the story of the Anthony Island expedition and its mission to rescue the relics of a village abandoned sometime before the turn of the century. Its principal members—Harry Hawthorne, Wayne Suttles, Wilson Duff, Michael Kew, and John Smiley—were or would later be among the most prominent scholars of the Northwest Coast; Bill Reid became the central figure and the driving force in the revival of Haida art. The nature of the mission inevitably lent itself to a narrative of disappearance. Indeed, the narration seems to ask, rhetorically, what else can be spoken but a eulogy for this magnificent but vanished community? When Nintstints, now a UNESCO-designated "World Heritage Site," was abandoned by the survivors of smallpox, it became a kind of ghost-town. Hence the ceaseless references to endings and tragic ruination that emerge so readily from a consideration of the expedition's circumstances. But that tale of final endings is too simple, and one must, I think, resist any easy acceptance of the film's overly transparent account of total denouement.

Totem and, to an even greater extent, *The Silent Ones* express a profound concern with absolute cultural destruction on a level that far exceeds the local concerns of Nintstints and Anthony Island. That desire for a transcendent narrative becomes clear both at the end of *Totem* and in the report that Duff wrote after the expedition; in the latter, a narrative structure moving from origins to death becomes apparent. Both texts transparently embody the object orientation that motivated not only the expedition—which retrieved the poles for display at the British Columbia Provincial Museum and the Museum of Anthropology at the University of British Columbia—but all the filmmaking of the era.

Like the films of B. E. Norrish and Harlan Smith, *Totem* and *The Silent Ones* are organized around the trope of travel and discovery. Each begins with images of boats and then uses point-of-view shots to situate the viewer on a vessel as it approaches the island. The island itself bears great poetic value, being a symbol of both temporal and spatial isolation. And it is an image favored among anthropologists. One can hardly count the number of introductory "passages" by which the ethnographer introduces his or her reader to the subject of the text: endless arrivals upon the seemingly deserted shores of tropical islands and then the move inward, to another world, in the fashion of Conrad—or Malinowski. In the previous chapter we saw how such iconography establishes a narrative frame in which anthropology is itself an object for observation; I shall not reiterate that argument here. What interests me in this chapter is the way in which *Totem* and *The Silent Ones* construct and evoke authenticity through the use of old photographs, especially those of the Curtis collection, and how these then function in an identification of Nintstints with Haida culture *per se*.

The anthropological interest in Nintstints is not in itself surprising. As the site of some of the most refined Haida pole carving anywhere, it would have been expected to draw considerable attention—if only because such aesthetic excellence is the collector's greatest desire. But *Totem* and *The Silent Ones* are not unique in their almost exclusive focus on poles; films about totem poles[5] are so numerous during this period that they practically constitute their own genre. This obsession enacts the discipline's ideological orientation and its economy of collection. Incorporated into the heroic tales of rescue that *Totem* and *The Silent Ones* tell, the poles become the buried chest, the trove of gold and jewels, in anthropology's version of *Treasure Island*. Less photogenic topics, such as the negotiation of land claims or Native language–education programs, remain invisible to the camera eye, and we find virtually no films devoted to them at this time.

It is not, however, merely the aesthetic appeal of the poles that made the trip to Anthony Island so ripe for cinematographic coverage. The tale of Nintstints has great—indeed, epic—tragic value. A community not merely deteriorated but utterly destroyed made it possible to imagine, if not to image, the Haida village in its purely authentic and originary state. Moreover, the narrative reconstruction of Nintstints required complete discontinuity— an event clearly demarcating "before" and "after," on either side of which is Haida cultural presence and absolute absence. "Culture contact," in Bill Reid's narration, is, at least in its initial stages, a source not of destruction (although physical/biological contact *was* destructive) but of artistic fluorescence. In fact, contact is depicted as fuel for Haida culture, an external force generating the realization of cultural (largely aesthetic) potential. The Euro-Canadian presence is, in some ways, encompassed and incorporated by the Haida and made internal to it. Accordingly, authentic Haida culture is not temporally restricted to the pre-contact period; and in this respect *Totem* embodies a much broader vision of aboriginal authenticity than did many earlier films in which contact and assimilation were the sources of corruption and death. But the full ambiguity of continued engagement is not yet palatable film material, and thus the narrative still requires a moment of transformation, an ending that displaces and defers the questions of contemporary Haida existence. That moment is provided—can *only* be provided—by some kind of monumental catastrophe.

The problem for the filmmakers therefore became one of depicting the previous period. And inevitably they stumbled upon the problem of how one constructs and presents authenticity in a period defined as complete decay. The poles themselves are cracked and rotting; no original images remain for comparison. Nor is there any visual record of Nintstints before the devastating arrival of smallpox. An artist's rendition on the basis of socio-archaeological speculation might have been possible, but such explicitly and transparently artificial images would not have had the indexical value that documentary film required. And it is clear that the filmmakers did not want simply to represent authenticity; they wanted to present it. Thus, *Totem* uses Edward Curtis's photographs from the turn of the century, taken not long after the disastrous spread of disease claimed Nintstints, in order to erect its edifice of authenticity.

The Curtis photographs show us, or claim to show us, what the Haida of the area looked like in the period before devastation. The first Curtis portrait is juxtaposed with narration contrasting the prejudiced understandings of early missionaries, traders, and scholars with that of the present generation of anthropologists. The image is surreptitiously attributed the scientific authority that Duff, Suttles, Hawthorne, Kew, and Smiley embody. The narration goes on to tell us that "*we know*" the Haida to have been handsome, ingenious, and so on, and again a Curtis portrait is shown, validating the claim to knowledge with its sentimentally posed beauty. At the same time, the omniscient voice assures the viewer that the exquisiteness of the photograph is not simply the imputation of an artist's gaze, and so the picture itself is corroborated as a true and unmediated presentation or reality. But this is too easy an alignment, and we now know that the Curtis photographs were carefully staged to fulfill the photographer's own vision of purity. Lyman (1982) has deconstructed the supposed authenticity of Curtis's photographs and pointed out how frequently Curtis removed the evidence of contact by retouching his prints to efface the material traces of change.

Specifically, he often "burnt out" watches or foreign technological trappings from his portraits, which were themselves posed and shot in "traditional" clothing supplied by the photographer.

The authenticity to which Curtis aspired could not accommodate any contact, and his reconstructive vision was far narrower than that of *Totem*. For Curtis, any foreign accretion was a sign of decay, but, as we have seen, *Totem* construes the initial engagement with traders as the external source of a Haida apotheosis. Yet, in using the Curtis photographs, the filmmakers effect an ironic kind of transformation. They restore a secondary image of traditional Native appearance such that it can become a part of the presumed historical reality. If I understand Richard Schechner correctly, it is to this that he refers when he claims that restored events can feed back into history: "Restorations need not be exploitations. Sometimes they are arranged with such care that after a while the restored behavior heals back into its presumptive past and its present cultural context like well-grafted skin. In these cases a 'tradition' is rapidly established and judgements about authenticity are hard to make" (Schechner 1985:65). As in Schechner's (1985: 55–65) analysis of Stall and Gardner's film *Altar of Fire,* the problem of authenticity in *Totem* is extremely vexing. But not because one doesn't know which practice or which artifact was reinserted. Rather, the problem arises because there are two radically different notions of authenticity in operation, each entailing its own assumptions about the level at which cultures exist. Were the filmmakers aware of Curtis's penchant for theatrical stagings and retouchings? Perhaps. And perhaps not. Yet, regardless of that knowledge or its lack, the photographs guaranteed the film its own claim to authenticity because, as photographs, they themselves proclaimed indexicality. Accordingly, the filmmakers could and did employ photographs in an otherwise filmic composition, invoking the *"having-been-there"* of the former as a means of asserting the *"being-there"* of the salvage mission. In this manner, buttressing the validity of the film with the assumed infallibility of the photograph, *Totem* constitutes itself as documentary.

At the same time that they underline the film's veracity, the photographs ensure the beautification of Haida culture. The sepia-tone magnificence of Curtis's Natives is, by now, familiar to historians of visual anthropology. Leafing through the gorgeous pages of his coffee-table collections, one senses a Keatsian romanticism dedicated to a "Beauty that must die." In a combination of paternalistic pessimism and prophetic hope, Curtis himself remarked: "I feel that the life of these children of nature is like the dying day drawing to its end; only off in the West is the glorious light of the setting sun telling us, perhaps, of light after darkness" (cited in McLuhan 1972:viii). When the photographs, with their soft shadows and luminous, almost angelic visages, are juxtaposed against an exposition on the physical beauty of the subjects, the Natives themselves become the currency of a photographic exchange that runs exactly parallel to the museum's traffic in masks and poles. There has been considerable attention paid to the reevaluation of exotic artifacts as art—from the primitivist valorization of expressive African sculpture onward (Clifford 1988b; Torgovnick 1990; Williams 1985)—but comparatively little has been said about the constructions of Native persons as human artifacts. Gerald Vizenor (1987) has addressed the issue with bitter cogency in his discussion of Ishi and the Curtis portraits, but his is a specific analysis of one man's museum life, and Northwest Coast studies have generally been slow to recognize the relationship between aestheticizing representations and the reifying or fetishizing objectifications of culture. To understand how complex is that process and how multidimensional its operations, one has to read the references to personal beauty in the context of the film's rather highbrow concern with the culture of *art*.

In *Totem*, the narrator's comment about Haida handsomeness acquires additional significance when we recall his repeated references to the artistic virtuosity of the Haida and his claim that "painting, sculpture, song, dance, and legend were the major part of the pattern of life." The allusion to Ruth Benedict's *Patterns of Culture* in the last phrase, whether self-conscious or not, reveals a shared essentialism whose vision of Haida culture identifies the final moment as the truest. Where art is defined as the center of culture (as in the romantic concept of High Culture), the effluorescence of art comes to signify the realization of cultural potential, the manifestation of ideal Being. Benedict's own schooling in the classical (Greco-Roman) arts should not be overlooked, and in the correspondence between her interests and those of the filmmaker one glimpses that powerful tendency by which essentialism and cultural aestheticization are so invariably linked.

More than that, there are shades of evolutionism in *Totem*. The film privileges the most recent phenomena and treats anything resembling Western high culture, with its artistic specialization and professionalization, as an indication of advancement. This is perhaps not surprising when one considers the biography of the film's narrator and script-writer, Bill Reid, whose status as a sculptor is nothing short of monumental. But, and this is an important "but," *The Silent Ones*, which was made without Reid's input, is equally concerned with Haida art. In this film, the voice-over narration tells us that the harsh environment demanded craftsmanship but that the Haida sculptor (always a singular male in the narration) went beyond this into the sublime realm of the creator-hero, and "achieved pure artistry." The film describes the anthropologists when they first landed on Anthony Island as struck by awe: "Even in this day and age they had to marvel at the craftsmanship achieved." And in Duff's and Carl's many reels devoted to the carving of masks and poles, a similar testimony is made. A familiar pattern emerges, though it is a pattern of representation rather than of culture: The beauty of Haida art is extended and becomes the beauty of Haida culture. Totem poles and Curtis portraits are of the same functional and symbolic order in this rendering of culture as aesthetic and collectible object.

There is an obvious sense in which Stocking's analysis of anthropology's political economy applies here. In ethnographic filmmaking, the pursuit of material artifacts and the cultivation of a refined code in which to evaluate those objects (both monetarily and aesthetically) are wed to the process of cultural salvage. A slippage occurs and, as the trade in material culture provides the economic logic of a museum system, ethnographic filmmaking establishes its own morally credible economy by rendering cultures as artifacts for which film itself is the medium of display. But it would be unfair to argue for a simple causal relationship between the museological orientation of anthropology and the filmmakers' concern with art forms on the Northwest Coast. After all, ethnology was similarly determined by the museum and was less concerned with poles and carving than with ritual systems, and with the potlatch in particular.

The deceptively obvious solution to this problem of discrepancy is that poles are material objects; they have duration, they retain their visibility, and, hence, they can be photographed. Potlatches, being transitory rituals, vanish as the last guest departs the big house. Having ceased, however temporarily, the potlatch recedes into invisibility, into memory and potential, and beyond the camera's gaze. Yet we have already seen that *Totem* used old photographs, and that its verbal narration wove together reconstructive and archival images. There is no reason for film to have avoided the potlatch on the grounds of its pastness or its ephemerality. Photographs of potlatching and potlatch paraphernalia existed in archives, and there were many who remembered the forms well enough to reenact them. Yet neither *Totem* nor *The Silent Ones* makes extensive reference to potlatching. In the implicit discussion of pole-raising ceremonies in *Totem*, the matter is described as a "family affair" in which "each was rewarded according to rank" and "the right to use crests was established." In *The Silent Ones*, however, an unnamed and unknown Native is invoked: "If he were a chief he saved for years. Then he gave it away at great potlatches to win admiration and affirm the greatness of the clan." Both films perfectly manifest the filmmaker's tendency to reduce culture to the objects which it produces. Thus, *Totem* discusses potlatching only via the potlatch pole, focusing on the technological aspects of construction and design in a listing of pole types. The potlatch itself is described as "an occasion of feasting and distributing wealth," a phrase that might as easily have been attributed to the less formalized feast described earlier.

Yet, though it evades the representation of temporally unstable events, *Totem* does note that there were phases of intensive carving and pole raising along the coast, with different cultures (Haida, Kwakiutl, Tsimshian) enjoying periods of increased productivity at different times. According to the film, the intensification of artistic activity had a wave-like quality, with pole carving reaching its height among the Haida in the middle of the nineteenth century, among the Kwakiutl after 1880, and among the Tsimshian between 1900 and 1940, depending on the level of integration with the Euro-Canadian economy. The history narrated in *Totem* leads the viewer to infer that the end of pole carving among the Haida corresponded to the fall of Nintstints and, further, that Nintstints was a microcosm of Haida culture, whose death it symbolically embodied.

And here we begin to see how the synecdochic representation of Nintstints could be tied to the use of the totem pole as the symbol of Native culture on the Northwest Coast: not in opposition to the discourse on potlatching but in tandem with it, and in a complementary division of representational labor by which film attended to material culture, and written texts focused on the abstract institutions of social life. On the Northwest Coast, the raising of a pole always entailed a potlatch, because the use of crests had to be validated publicly. But potlatching had been banned in 1876 by federal legislation in Canada. In many ways, that legislation embodied the same assumptions about excess and decadence that Ruth Benedict had summarized under the rubric of the Dionysian. But the extremity of potlatching on which Benedict (like so many contemporary postmodernists) based her model was historically particular, as Helen Codere (1961) observes in her important analysis of culture contact and its impact on the Kwakiutl. Codere describes a pattern that has since been generalized to most of the cultures of the coast, although in different time frames (see also Allen 1981), and it is strikingly akin to the waves of artistic activity that Bill Reid describes in *Totem*. Codere divides the history of the Kwakiutl into three periods, which she designates as the pre-potlatch (1772–1849), potlatch (1849–1921), and post-potlatch (1921–1955):

> The century and a half of Kwakiutl culture history shows a single outstanding development, the rise and fall of the potlatch. The earliest period of Kwakiutl history is one in which the potlatch is present as an institution but in competition with other institutions on a fairly equal basis. The middle period is the one in which the potlatch came to be the central and all-encompassing institution. This is also the period for which we have rich ethnographic materials and which we are tempted to think of as "classic" and most characteristic of Kwakiutl culture. In the final period the potlatch as an institution died, a fate that has been met by many other highly specialized institutions. (Codere 1961:434)

Codere goes on to examine the features of Kwakiutl culture that persisted, along with those that vanished, in the face of contact with Anglo-Canadian culture. From a list of twenty-two distinct forms of material culture, social institutions, and interests, Codere can find only one that lasted through the post-potlatch period and that was "social status and its maximization" (Codere 1961:509). Though "maximization" was almost identical to the competitive principle that Benedict had identified as the core value of Kwakiutl culture, Codere refers to the "quick and relatively painless loss of an old culture followed by an equally painless and quick and seemingly competent taking on of a new one." She is able to dismiss suffering and to gloss over the unevenness of history because she believes Kwakiutl and Anglo-Canadian culture to have been fundamentally convergent, both resting upon similar moral and economic assumptions (Codere 1961:513). The operative term in Codere's analysis is not change but replacement or displacement. However, though she carefully refuses to accord any one of the three periods greater validity or representativeness, Codere clearly believes there to have been a fundamental rupture in Kwakiutl history, a rupture that can be located in the thirty years following Dan Cranmer's illegal potlatch in 1921. Nor is she alone in this assumption. Rosemary Allen (1981) echoes Codere in her cross-cultural survey of the potlatch literature; and although she notes a residual "concept of potlatching" among the Tlingit, her final conclusion is that the potlatch had died by the mid-1950s.

In explicitly functionalist terms, but arguing against the theories of cultural megalomania, Allen remarks that the potlatch was a "mechanism for the maintenance of social equilibrium," and that it "played its part in the retention of a fairly well integrated tribal culture" (1981:52). Like Codere's analysis of integrative functions, Allen's treatment leads to the conclusion that the termination of potlatching constitutes the rupture of history, because no culture can continue in the absence of its nucleus, its functional center. Codere's neo-Platonic insistence that outward forms can be deceiving, that belief systems are frequently lacking in material indicators, or that some values can persist after conversion while others are eroded does little to mitigate this conclusion and its tacit "all or nothing" paradigm. For all her labors against the lingering evolutionism of Northwest Coast ethnography, Codere's placement of the potlatch in the center of a linear continuum, whose antipodes were the pre- and post-potlatch eras, encouraged those who would argue that the potlatch was both the last and the ultimate realization of Kwakiutl or other Northwest Coast cultural Being. In this manner, evolutionism continued to enjoy an ideological dominance in Northwest Coast studies and its visual anthropology long after it had been ejected from other areas of anthropology, and despite Boas's relentless efforts to secure its banishment. The potlatch, being in some regards last, became first among attributes in the image of Northwest Coast cultures.

Back to the Future: The Potlatch of Signs

In this context, we may do well to consider the continuing importance of the potlatch as a concept in contemporary theoretical endeavors. The naturalization of recent history that so marked the ethnography of this period finds itself reproduced and extended in poststructuralist theories aimed at the deconstruction of rationalist economics and their ideologies. Here, for example, is Bataille (1967:274, cited in Pefanis 1990:19), writing against discourse, writing about "an endless and baseless substitution whose only rule is the sovereign affirmation of the play outside meaning. Not a reserve or withdrawal, the infinite murmur of a blank speech erasing the traces of classical discourse, but a kind of *potlatch of signs* that burns, consumes and wastes words in a gay affirmation of death: a sacrifice and a challenge." Without wanting to delve into the many complex attempts to theorize gift economies (see Pefanis 1991 for an excellent summary and analysis), I think it sufficient here to note the thematic continuity between disparate schools and to observe among these schools the centrality of the potlatch as an image of the nonrational (in the sense of not rationalized) economy. A sign of excess, the potlatch familiarized by early anthropology was created, we must recall, in the image of those final Kwakiutl potlatches where commodity-saturated economies were playing themselves out. This is the distorted vision naturalized in Baudrillard's (1975) concern with the death-drive and in Clastres's (1980) reading of primitive exchange as the aversion of war. The French theorists of the potlatch and, more generally, of the gift-economy were, of course, approaching the potlatch through Marcel Mauss (1954) and not through their contemporary North American ethnologists. But the data on the potlatch generally came from the same sources and referred to the same period—namely, the two decades on either side of the *fin de siècle*. If this vision of economic excess seems opposed to Codere's claim for an incipient Protestant ethic, it must be remembered that Codere herself notes a spiral effect at the end of the potlatch period, potlatching being both magnified and distorted as a result of an increased circulation of both capital and foreign commodities. Naturalizing that moment of spiraling consumption, both North American ethnology and French postmodern theory reiterate—in very different ways—Benedict's vision of Dionysian extremity. In doing so, they ironically corroborate the sentiments of those early legislators who also perceived the potlatch as a threat to Protestant capitalism.

But I have digressed in an effort to point out the continued relevance of these debates to contemporary theoretical and political matters. Let me return, then, via Mauss to the potlatch as totality. For it was Mauss who first conceived of the potlatch (which he construed as but one variety of the gift) as a total social fact. The theory of ritual totality underpinned an apocalyptic essentialism that saw the end of the potlatch as the end of Northwest Coast cultures. And this is where the connection between literary ethnography and ethnographic film emerges most obviously. The end of potlatch made ethnography itself an exercise in the recovery of those material forms which embodied the potlatch cultures. In the films just discussed, *Totem* and *The Silent Ones*, we no longer find the "vanishing Indians" of a racial twilight; instead, the potlatch people are already gone and totem poles are all that remain as memorials to now-dead ways. In *The Silent Ones,* poles are likened to skeletons, and, to give force to the simile, one of the anthropologists is shown discovering some human bones amid the brush and grasses. In *Totem,* the poles are described as remains. Even *The Totem Pole* emphasizes the collapse of artistic traditions when it refers to the carvers employed by the British Columbia Provincial Museum as simply reproducing the older poles that had been badly weathered and were now threatened with complete decomposition.

The Center Will Not Hold:
New Visions in Visual Anthropology

Northwest Coast ethnography has always been inseparable from collecting, and, as will be discussed in Chapter 5, the collection of artifacts is inextricable from a will-to-power through possession. The ceaseless gathering of objects along the Northwest Coast, sometimes through purchase, sometimes through legal confiscation, not only generated support for salvage ethnography but later became the basis for the symbolic reclamation of Native cultures. But before turning to the later era, I want to reconsider the aesthetic implications of salvage ethnography.

The representational manifestation of the object orientation that Stocking attributes to anthropology's museum economy is to be found in the privileging of visual metaphors that drives both written and filmic ethnography (Fabian 1983:105ff.). The complementarity of literary and filmic representations in this period can, I think, be best understood in these terms. It emerges at the confluence of two related epistemological and ideological lines: a general empiricism that emphasizes the sensorially perceptible surfaces of things; and the different dimensions of the image that empiricism locates in the text and the "image-track" (cf. Mitchell 1986). Thus, dividing the representational fields of text and film as those of abstraction and immediate presentation respectively (see Chapter 2), salvage ethnography constitutes a Northwest Coast Other as collectible object. As Fabian (1983) sees it, the linkage between visualization and objectification is mediated by a third factor, namely aestheticization. In order for a political economy of collection to operate, the consumable object—Native cultures and/or their artifacts—must also be a desirable object. This is why films of the period pay such assiduous attention to the artistic virtuosity of Haida carvers, to the delicacies of silver and abalone bracelets, to the "noble brows and supple bodies" of particularly beautiful individuals. Not that these forms were immediately appealing to a broad audience. The transposition of the "primitive" in this century from the rude to the sublime has been a long, complex, and frequently ambivalent process. On the Northwest Coast, as elsewhere, that transposition has largely been a redefinition of value involving a (still incomplete) movement from value based in scarcity to that located in supposedly inherent aesthetic qualities.

Though never completely separated, the tension between these two modes of value is abundantly clear in this era. A period of transition, it is characterized by a growing diffuseness of representational strategies. As the decades passed, a number of alternative narratives began to appear, such that, by the 1970s, representational heterogeneity had virtually exploded the reigning paradigm; salvage ethnographic film gave way to revivalist accounts. But in the 1950s and 1960s, the salvage ethos was virtually hegemonic. Virtually, but not absolutely; there were other visions as well. In the films thus far considered, we have seen the concern with scarcity value as a primary motivator of the salvage project, even when that concern has prompted tributes to artistic achievement and cultural sophistication. In this context, it will be instructive to examine a film that was neither produced in the museum context nor oriented around the assumption of disappearance. Robert Gardner's *Blunden Harbour,* released in 1951, seems to defy all the conventions of the period. Unlike *Totem* or *The Silent Ones,* it shuns the notion of cultural death and asserts instead the persistence of an essential Kwakiutl character. *Blunden Harbour* is the very apogee of cultural aestheticization, an exquisite rendition of what the museum ethnographers could achieve only in awkward and too-obvious ways. Yet, for all that, it draws on many of the ideological assumptions that also underlay the salvage films. In the following pages, I examine the film in its many aspects, attending to both the continuities and the departures from salvage ethnographic films.

Synopsis: *Blunden Harbour* (1951)

The film begins with shots of a coastline, taken from a boat offshore. The camera pans along the shoreline as the boat moves parallel to it. A line of wooden houses is visible just above the beach.

The initial narration, spoken in the first person, introduces Halestes (a killer whale) as the "Chief at the beginning of the world" who roamed the earth until finding a sandy beach that he liked. When Halestes explains himself to one of his visitors, he says, "I am Halestes and I go spouting around the world but I wish to become a real man in this place. So, I built my house in Blunden Harbour." As the narration proceeds, we see the village in closer range and then the camera zooms in on a group of women seated on a wooden boardwalk.

As the women sort fibers and place them in baskets, the narrator continues, but now in the third person: "A forest and a sea kept apart by a thin line of houses and people. Here is a friendly arrangement where nature toils for the reasonable human. No struggle for survival, no encroaching jungle, no men against the sea. These ones have an ancient formula for success, ancient and simple."

The visual imagery continues to focus on the women, all of whom are clad in modern Western dress. "From the water, life," states the narrator. Here the film cuts to shots of women and children walking along the beach where the tide is out. They continue past the camera. Several shots of women gathering and digging on the beach follow as the narrator speaks: "Each day a little different from the next: gathering, saving, cooking, eating, sleeping. . . . There is a time and place for everyone, the old, the young, the dead, the quick."

Scenes of women digging for clams and then preparing them for eating are accompanied by occasional remarks and singing voices in the background (though we see no one singing). "There is as much to look back upon as there is ahead. . . . Old methods with new tools, old tools with new methods." We see in close-up a two-pronged digging stick, and the narrator says, "This sliver of humanity has done well by the judgment of a whale."

As the scene shifts from the women on the beach to men carving, the narrator states simply, "From the wood, a way of life." Following are a series of unaccompanied shots—of children playing inside a house, of a man's hands carving, of a woman holding her child, of a toy boat tied to a stick, of men in a boat and of the nets that they draw in. There are shots of a meal in a house where framed photographs sit above a painting of the mythic serpentine character, Sisiutl, and where the table has tinned milk as well as processed, packaged food on it. Further images from the interior, of a viola and a boy sleeping, and the wooden eyes of a carved face, are supplemented by soft, singing voices in the background.

The narrator interjects, "A way of life and a way of death," while the film shows a pile of mortuary boxes and poles. The scene then shifts to show children playing inside on a swing, followed by the faces of various men and women. There are shots of men fishing and several of men carving with hand adzes and knives. We see many close-ups of the masks, and again the narrator speaks: "A way of life, a way of death, a way of dreams, a way to remember."

In the final sequences, there is a linear montage of shots: of masked dancing, detailed close-ups of buttoned blankets and of hands shaking rhythmically, of coppers[6] and the faces of dancers that periodically disappear behind masks. There are also shots of the audiences who watch the dance performance. These are intercut with images of woman and children, including a swing sequence, which appeared earlier in the film. In its finale, we see women looking toward the water, where boats can be seen on the horizon. The film closes on a shot of a barrel in which water is stored and a ladle dipped. Here, "The End" is graphically announced.

Visible Culture and the Cult of the Visual

Critics of film and the plastic arts are quick to remind their readers how difficult it is to convey in words the effect of an aesthetic creation that is not exclusively or primarily literate. Such apologies often assume the primacy of the pictorial regardless of the artwork's implicit valuation of visual and aural signs. Yet in a film like *Blunden Harbour*, the movement between genres is especially difficult—not so much because the film uses the visual to express nonverbal sentiment as because the film attempts to evoke the invisible and the ineffable. *Blunden Harbour* eschews the verbal dimension in favor of the visual as it seeks the pure presence of culture. Whereas Harlan Smith's films lacked extended narration by virtue of technical necessity, *Blunden Harbour* is relatively "silent" for aesthetic reasons. And whereas the intertitles of *The Tsimshian* served to identify or denote and, hence, to specify the imagery, the voice-over narration of *Blunden Harbour* does precisely the opposite; it opens up the film and generalizes it, taking it onto a plane of universality. Nowhere does Robert Gardner's narration define the object of viewing or the locale. Nor does it name the people filmed. In Bill Nichols's terms, the narration is poetic rather than expository. The brief aphoristic remarks, so oddly reminiscent of *Ecclesiastes*, serve the essentialist project perfectly, evoking a truth that must remain unspeakable if it is not to be distorted.

The distinction between the poetic and the expository is extremely important in Bill Nichols's typology of narrative principles. For Nichols, the poetic mode of discourse is a "predominantly metaphoric mode that deflates the metonymic and syntagmatic aspects. Stress falls upon the present moment" (1981:80).[7] For the most part, Nichols sees the poetic as the primary mode of representation underlying experimental film, but not as a significant principle in documentary or ethnographic film (Nichols 1981:73). He does, however, note that narration in ethnographic films often uses poetic forms and that filmmakers such as Frederick Wiseman may elevate it to an organizational principle through the construction of documentary mosaics (Nichols 1981:211). But the poetic mode lacks temporal movement, and it aspires to a synchronic vision something like the viewer's experience of a single visual image or tableau. As a result, it is often the representational strategy most likely to emphasize the dimensions of coherence, mutuality, and unity in culture.

Blunden Harbour, like *The Nuer*, which Nichols labors to recuperate, is a collage of sensuous imagery whose overall effect is a sense of calm, control, and solidity. The film renders the life of Blunden Harbour utterly familiar; there is nothing chaotic about it, nothing unpredictable. There is no violence, no tension, no conflict of values in the scenes of an eminently communal life. Everything about the narration and the visual imagery strives to evoke the everyday and then naturalizes it as normal. Unlike almost all of its predecessors, drama and conflict are banished from the film. Thus, when the voice of Richard Selig, Gardner's narrator, tells us that there is "no struggle for survival" and that Blunden Harbour does not pit "men against the sea," we are being told something both about the predicament of these villagers and about the tradition in which the film was made.

Almost all of the classic ethnographic films prior to 1951 (and many since) were organized around a monumental struggle between humanity (usually men) and the elements. Robert Flaherty's *Nanook of the North* and his later works, *Moana* and *Man of Aran,* are perhaps most exemplary in this tradition of epic ethnography, and their shadows haunt the statements about encroaching jungles (*Moana*) and struggles against the sea (*Man of Aran*). Although Flaherty was roundly criticized for projecting bourgeois individualism and Western nature/culture dichotomies onto non-Western peoples, the tradition continued in such films as John Marshall's *The Hunters* and Jean Rouch's *The Lion Hunters. Blunden Harbour* stands out for its refusal to partake of this vision, this fantasy about a masculine humanity being forged in eternal conflict with an implicitly feminine nature.

However, the rejection of a conflict motif does not liberate Gardner's film from the gendering of a nature/culture dichotomy. The opposition between male and female is, in *Blunden Harbour,* defined as categorical complementarity. Consider once more the image-track and its narration. Scenes of women gathering at the water's edge are accompanied by the comment "From the water, life," whereas those of men carving are narrated "From wood, a way of life." Women become the vehicles of biological life, sustenance, continuity, and birth. Maternal by nature (in Gardner's vision), they provide nourishment. But the provision of food is removed from the cultural realm with the distinction between "life" and a "way of life." In contrast, the men are the crafters of culture, fashioning both objects and a cultural style, a whole "way of life."

Yet, in significant ways, *Blunden Harbour* did depart from the standards of postwar ethnographic film. Its refusal of conflict as a locus of narrativity is a significant development and places Gardner's work at odds with dominant film practice. However, there are ironies in this departure: Gardner's refusal of conflict is as much a product of his own radically aestheticizing tendencies as it is a critique of salvage ethnography's latent frontier mentality and its swashbuckling tales of recovered Native treasure. Not that the films of Flaherty, Norrish, Smith, or Boas are in any way "unaesthetic," but the principles at work in a film like *Blunden Harbour* are dramatically different from those of *Totem* or *The Silent Ones.*

It is now rather common practice to assume that the ethnography of the everyday is inherently democratic, that it restores the common person to a place of rightful value and centrality, and that it somehow rectifies the errors committed by bourgeois individualism in the name of heroic drama. As far as it goes, this seems a reasonable approach, and attention to the "people without history," to use Eric Wolf's (1982) term, is, I think, a politically necessary act. But as a revolutionary tactic, compensatory accounts do not go so far. If, in its rejection of conflict and the high drama of the potlatch, and in its delicate attention to everyday details, *Blunden Harbour* escapes the melodrama of salvage ethnography, it nonetheless achieves its own reifications in the vision of organic completeness.

The narrative closure that marks *Totem* or *The Silent Ones* is a moment of finality and resolution to which the story inexorably leads. It is one (extremely significant) moment in a temporalized process. However, completeness in Gardner's film is a dimension of the initial tableau. Indeed, it is an existential state: a synchronic state, of satiety and functional perfection. It is a vision most eloquently articulated in Selig's remark, "this sliver of humanity has done well by the judgment of a whale." The reference to the "judgment of a whale" recalls that other archetypical judgment of Western culture, the pronouncement of the seventh day when the world is found to be good and complete.[8] Completion and totality are what we see in *Blunden Harbour*, where the many aspects of daily life are presented as facets and emanations of a single whole whose *telos* is reproduction and continuity. The narration moves the viewer from one pole of existence to another, from life to death, from youth to age, and from dreaming to memory. All are presented as part of an organic unity that, in its all-encompassing scope, also assumes the aura of finality. That which is final, satisfied, or otherwise whole is also stopped short in history and cut off from its future. At least this is the implication in the context of that linear and progressive temporality which Gardner, like all the filmmakers considered here, inhabited.

As discussed earlier, allochronic discourse, the denial of an other's temporality (or other temporalities), is inherently reifying. And we have seen how important visual processes can be in the constitution of an otherness that is spatially and temporally removed (Fabian 1983). In *Blunden Harbour*, the scarcity of narration gives the visual imagery a primacy and an autonomy that it is rarely accorded in ethnographic films. If one thinks of *The Axe Fight* (see Chapter 2) or Mary Lee Stearn's Northwest Coast film *Those Born at Masset* (1977), the "silence" of Gardner's becomes abundantly apparent. There are no diagrams, no ponderous ethnographic explanations of kinship alliances and obligations, nor functionalist analyses of ritual activities. Instead, *Blunden Harbour* is constructed on the assumption that meaning is visible. What Bill Nichols (1981:252) says of *The Nuer* is equally applicable here. In *Blunden Harbour*, "poetic imagery gains only minimal specificity from verbal commentary or synchronous location sound (. . . sound appears to derive from the general location, tribal songs, for example, but not necessarily from the scene depicted)."

This is not to say, as Jay Ruby (1983) claims for Boas's *Kwakiutl of British Columbia*, that the film assumes the constituent parts of a culture to be independently meaningful and that, as a result, they can be decontextualized without losing that meaning; rather, Nichols's statement implies that culture and meaning are objective in the visual domain, although still relational and therefore dependent upon holistic analysis. In *Blunden Harbour*,

Gardner is at pains to present all aspects of the culture and to relate these to each other in the brief but laconic remarks of the voice-over narration. For Gardner, culture can be objectified because it is objective; it can be filmed because it is material and therefore visible.

The result of Gardner's particular materialist commitment is that the scene loses specificity. Without any narration to locate the visual image, the "pictured" floats free of its historical context. *Blunden Harbour* remains a series of organized shots and sequences featuring particular and perhaps identifiable individuals; but ethnographically, the film lacks a location. This is an almost unbelievable irony when one considers the importance assigned to location shots in the construction of realist (Hollywood) veracity. In *Blunden Harbour* we are not even told that Blunden Harbour (now Clayoquot) is a Kwakiutl community, never mind that the dances and coppers are part of a potlatching tradition, or that the myth at the film's beginning probably belongs to a particular clan identified with the whale and that this story of origin may not have been shared by all members of the village. Like *The Nuer, Blunden Harbour* "attempts to restore a sense of the poetic to the everyday world of another culture" (Nichols 1981:252). Yet, although this strategy may indeed be a healthy antidote to the tradition of exalting the spectacular, it nonetheless entails its own risks. A "poetic strategy" almost always "pries the film away from any claim to representing historically specifiable situations or events" (Nichols 1981:252). Here, the supposed timelessness of aesthetic experience and the ahistoricism of poetic representation in ethnographic film converge.

However, the gaze entailed by ethnographic film is, in many ways, more complicated than any transcendentalist aesthetics can suggest. The missing element is the pyschological one: the desire that aestheticizing representations elicit. *Blunden Harbour* does not merely objectify nor even reify the Kwakiutl community that Gardner filmed. It makes this community both desirable and consumable. We do not simply observe daily life here, we look at it; and our look is implicated in all those structures of commodification and marketing by which the Native artifact can be rendered as art object and as museum display. In fact, the film accomplishes what André Malraux (1953) has attributed to photography—namely, the creation of a "museum without walls." Seemingly paradoxical, but mutually dependent, the processes of distanciation and consumption lie at the heart of salvage museology and its particular film form.

However, it must be remembered that the consumption of ethnographic film (of all film) is only, and always, the promise of consumption: endlessly deferred in the space between the viewer and the filmed object. Susan Sontag (1977:42) speaks cogently to this fact when she describes the photographer as "supertourist, an extension of the anthropologist, visiting Natives and bringing back news of their exotic doings and strange gear. The photographer is always trying to colonize new experiences or find new ways to look at familiar subjects—to fight against boredom. For boredom is just the reverse side of fascination: both depend upon being outside rather than inside a situation." Sontag's insight, that the photographic impulse is dependent upon a relationship of distance and externality to the event or object of photography, has obvious applicability to ethnographic film. And it provides a cautionary note against any easy equation of possession and consumption.[9] In the end, it is perhaps only a dressed-up version of the maxim "You can't have your cake and eat it too"; but the distinction between possession and consumption is imperative if one is to understand the construction of value, especially in the museum context. For the glass wall invariably separates the viewer from the artifact, and museum pieces are those that have been removed from circulation in the more mundane market of tourist arts—for reasons of scarcity and/or aesthetic merit. Thus, if both possession and consumption assume the prior objectification, and hence distanciation, of the ethnographic object/other, they are not wholly reducible to it.

Native History in Absentia

There are unexpected convergences between *Totem* and *Blunden Harbour*, despite the profound differences of camera style and narrative structure. In both films, one finds oneself transported to a realm of suspended time, in which history is absent because stopped or external to the lived time of the everyday. In *Blunden Harbour*, the pure presence of the visual domain runs parallel to the denial of continuity that characterizes the motif of cultural death. Although the narrator of the film claims that "there is as much to look back upon as there is ahead," the film's only concession to considerations of time past is its introductory myth. And myth, as Levi-Strauss (1975) points out in his identification of mythic and poetic language, is notoriously ahistorical. By definition, myth-time lacks chronological specificity; it takes events out of historical time and relocates them in a realm of immutable perpetuity.

And yet I do not want to reduce all of these films to a single ideological project—the denial of historicity—even though all of them share in this. Rather, my point is that their strategies are different but related, deriving, as they do, from a single cultural-historical perspective. James Clifford (1988b:230) offers a poignant summary of this (anthropological) orientation when he remarks that "'cultures' are ethnographic collections," of a Western "art-culture system." It is difficult to conceive of a film more clearly a part of the Western "art-culture system" than *Totem*, with its quest for museum artifacts. But *Blunden Harbour* shares a similar impulse, even—or especially—when its aestheticization of culture is working through people rather than through material objects.

In many ways, *Totem* is a film about the end of history in a Haida community, and about the end of Haida history more generally. Indeed, it takes place in the afterward of Native history. While explaining the cataclysm that befell Nintstints in a sugar-coated rendition of contact (Anglo-Canadian culture is the source of Haida self-realization, and disease comes via a Native man), *Totem* magically covers over the historical circumstances of the salvage mission. We know its intrepid anthropologists only as members of an expedition. Salvage anthropology, Canadian cultural policy, and the museum drive for acquisitions remain blind spots in the film's narrative. In analyzing *Totem,* one can speak of a stilled history, of a history relegated to, and equated with, the past. More than this, history comes to the Haida from without. It is not of their making, certainly not of their choosing. They are its instruments and, quite emphatically, not its agents.

It is in this very familiar isolation (one wants to say "islandification") of Native cultures that *Totem,* with its brash heroism and epic aspirations, approaches the serene tableaux of Gardner's *Blunden Harbour.* Gardner's film gestures toward time (never completely assimilable to history) with the reference to technological change: "Old methods with new tools, old tools with new methods." But the film signifies repetition, continuity in the form of reproduction, and a ceaseless but unchanging existence. Its rhythms are those of the rocking chair: familiar, regular, and sedate. The narration renders each image universal, and any hint of an external context is expunged. Thus, Blunden Harbour becomes an island, surrounded, one presumes, by a sea of historical happening, but removed from it. The film tells us nothing about relations with non-Kwakiutl communities or about changes since contact with Europeans, about political forms or state interference with ritual practice, about missionization or the Provincial school system. The viewer is merely enthralled by the mundane beauty of it all. Thus enraptured, she or he is seduced away from history and into Dufrenne's realm of aesthetic communion.

Between Page and Screen

Earlier, I suggested that there was a link, albeit a complex and implicit one, between the written ethnography and the ethnographic film of this period. I want to reiterate that conclusion here while at the same time acknowledging the increasing divergence of representational strategies. It is, I think, clear that *Totem* (and other films of its style, including *The Silent Ones* and *The Totem Pole*) responded to, and expressed, a notion of vanished authenticity that was equally integral to the literature on potlatching. In tracing the relationships between such patently archaeological films as *Totem* and the various histories of potlatching, one sees how the assumptions of functional necessity and structural totality worked in perfect complementarity with the vision of loss. One sees also how this paradigm logically transposed change into rupture.

In this context, *Blunden Harbour* seems oddly placed, for it denies historical rupture altogether. Like *Totem,* it constructs Native culture as something unchanging and leaves its viewers with yet another version of the dichotomy between historical and ahistorical societies. But whereas *Totem* locates authenticity at the level of visible, material culture, *Blunden Harbour* posits authenticity on a plane of essential being and thereby renders it immune to change, rather than subject to complete extinction, as is the case in most of the later salvage films.

In the following chapter, we shall see the emergence of films that are similarly intent upon resisting the conclusion of early salvage ethnographers: that Native culture was dead after having been poisoned and corrupted by external influence. However, in these later productions, the problem of history is central. *Blunden Harbour* sometimes hints at this possibility and is, in many ways, a significant step toward a recognition of cultural survival—even though that suggestion of survival is achieved by effacing the sources of possible transformation. But if it escapes the facile oppositions of salvage ethnography, it is also waylaid by its own aestheticizing aspiration toward universality. I want to offer Gardner a generous reading, for there is much in *Blunden Harbour* to commend it above the self-glorifying narratives of salvage ethnography. Indeed, at the time of the film's making, an endeavor to find universality in places more commonly imagined as completely foreign probably seemed to hold out great promise for a politically sensitized ethnography. That the film would end up presenting some of the most tenaciously reifying visions of Native culture could not, perhaps, have been fully anticipated. As has so often been the case, the obsession with objects was replaced not with an egalitarian vision but with a romance of ethnographic subjects, and that romanticism performed its own objectifications in the name of tribute.

At several points in this chapter I have suggested that, in their different denials of history—the denials of absence and of pure presence—the filmic narratives discussed here were made inevitable by the fetishism of the potlatch that characterized the contemporaneous written ethnography. But I have also tried to show how this elevation of the potlatch—particularly the Kwakiutl potlatch of the early twentieth century—was itself ideologically compromised. What we see in the relationship between film and written ethnography, therefore, is a bifurcation of representations along the lines of media and/or genres. Under the influence of museum-based ethnography and the growing market in Native artifacts, this period sees both a blossoming of filmmaking and the entrenchment of a radical opposition between film and written ethnography. The former is burdened by a visual bias that leads to a concern with material culture, whereas the latter is freed to pursue questions of social function in the analysis of ritual. Thus separated into complementary but relatively valued modes of ethnographic representation, the particular concerns and distortions of either genre feed each other.

We therefore find ourselves, at the end of this period, and at the end of this chapter, on the threshold of a new era. As the heady days of ethnic consciousness and Native revival opened in the 1960s, ethnographic films of the salvage variety began to be displaced by narratives of renewal and of survival. Even before that decade of transformation commenced, there emerged a sense of instability. New film forms were tried out, new narratives explored. Many were deeply ambivalent about questions of cultural identity, authenticity, and history. And many were conflicted in their deployment of images and narrative strategies. More than anything, though, the period saw the beginnings of a representational pluralism, and although structuralism will yet reign as the last great paradigm of totality, there were cracks visible in the edifice of anthropology's particular hegemony. Native peoples began to "talk back" and to insist on a space in which to do so. Ethnographic film provided one such space and became a potent tool in the political battles to be waged over the reclamation of all those objects, rights, and places that had been confiscated or destroyed as salvage ethnography told the tale of endings.

Notes

1. One has only to think here of the Balinese or the !Kung to realize how exaggerated is Cranmer-Webster's claim.

2. J. Baudrillard argues that it is consumption rather than production that drives postindustrial capitalism (1975 [1973]). I do not want to take on his argument here, or to make any claims for the relative importance of consumption or production in the maintenance of an economic logic. The point has to do with appearances, and consumption is the dominant focus of reference in both self-perception and ethnographic representations of the Northwest Coast.

3. Other films were made for the Canadian National Film Board, the Canadian Broadcasting Corporation, and the British Columbia Department of Recreation and Conservation.

4. The UBC's Museum of Anthropology is now housed in Arthur Erikson's architectural fusion of Northwest Coast house styles and cubist forms.

5. Distinctions among totem poles, funerary poles, house poles, and so on, are rarely made in any of these early representations.

6. "Coppers" are hereditary ritual objects resembling masks and used in public displays of power and personal history.

7. Nichols refers here to the structuralist semiotics of Christian Metz, whose psychoanalytic text is titled *The Imaginary Signifier* (1982).

8. The implicit evocation is: "And God saw everything that he had made, and, behold, it was very good.... Thus the Heavens and the earth were finished" (Genesis 1:31, 2:1).

9. I am grateful to Margaret Rodman for her insightful discussions on this matter.

5

Remembering:
The Narratives of Renewal

But we never forgot.
—Gloria Cranmer-Webster

Second Takes

IN THE LAST CHAPTER, I examined the later developments of the narrative of disappearance and attempted to trace the intertextual relationships between anthropology's visual and written representations. I argued that the images and analyses of Northwest Coast cultures elaborated in either genre were significantly influenced by the institutional structures in which they were produced. And it became apparent that the ethnographic museum and its particular ideology of collection was absolutely fundamental as a determinant of representational strategies. My own narrative sought to explain an apparent discrepancy between written and filmic representations and ended by observing that while film and written ethnography differed in their overt imagery and explicit problems, they were united by a common ideological project and a common, indeed mutually sustaining, assumption of loss and radical ahistoricity.

Yet, having followed the narrative of disappearance to its own inevitable horizon, we (and ethnographic film) saw the emergence of several alternative visions. The profusion of films during the postwar years continued through the 1960s and 1970s, and with that quantitative growth there came also a diffusion of styles and of stories. Robert Gardner's poetic presentism was the most unprecedented and dramatic departure from the reigning conventions, but others were quick to follow. The results were often ambiguous. Sometimes, aesthetic experimentation produced films that were philosophically and/or politically at one with the productions of early documentary realism. Sometimes, formally conservative films made the most daring interventions into the political scene. Native-produced films, which entered the field for the first time, had to negotiate the vast and difficult terrain that was—and is—the history of representing cultures. And anthro-pologists had to respond to new voices. What we see in the period begin-ning in the late 1960s is a tense and often tendentious endeavor to reconsti-tute the object of representation *as* subject, but through the mechanisms of objectification. The paradoxes and difficulties of such a project should be immediately obvious. The ontological necessity of objectification in all rep-resentation and the political necessity of asserting the subjectivity of those represented often seem at odds with each other. The solutions explored in ethnographic films of this era are inescapably partial but nonetheless impor-tant for all that. As we shall see, they focus on the problems of time and voice, two of the main axes of meaning in Western notions of the subject.

Following the neat paradigmatic accounts of the previous chapters, this one may appear comparatively lacking and with few definitive conclusions. This is, I think, a reflection of the complexity of the topic, which burgeons and involutes in the decades of Native activism and consciousness-raising. But, in addition, this lack of resolution is a function of the historiographic problem, of writing in the present about the present. Looking at the films of the post-1960s period, we find ourselves in a field almost too vast and varie-gated to permit an integrated vision. Nonetheless, there are tendencies vis-ible: iconographic strategies and narrative continuities that seem to present themselves as such. And if one hesitates (and I do) to pronounce confident summaries of processes that are still dynamic and pliable, it is yet possible to analyze them for their shared and opposed meanings, their deeper assump-tions and their positioning within the field of both aesthetic and political representation.

Contexts for Change:
New Pictures and Public Policy

Revisions came slowly, more slowly in visual anthropology and Northwest Coast studies than in many other spheres of mainstream anthropology. In part, the transformation of narratives within the academy was a function of more general sociopolitical conditions in North America. In the United States, John Collier, who was commissioner of Indian Affairs between 1933 and 1945, supervised and implemented changes in both the policies and the practices instituted by previous administrations. Collier's "Indian New Deal" urged the protection of Native religious practices and encouraged what was then labeled "tribalism" but what might today be designated ethnicity (in the United States) or multiculturalism (in Canada) (Jonaitis 1981:5; Philp 1977). Collier's "tribalist" position ran the risk of repeating a "divide and rule" ideology, and it ran directly counter to the pan-Nativist movements that later emerged around Wounded Knee. But it also seemed to unsettle the totalizing and racially oriented visions that had previously grounded the State's undifferentiated and undifferentiating reservation policies.

Collier's efforts, considerable though they were, had limited effect and were severely attenuated versions of the demands that Native peoples themselves were making: demands for the return of sacred objects, land, and land-use rights. Nonetheless, Collier personifies a broader reorientation of bourgeois attitudes. What appeared first as an expanded primitivism became, over the decades, a more ambitious (though not always unambiguous) commitment to the right of self-determination for non-Whites. In the "culture industries" we see this development in the movement from the first Native art shows in San Francisco (1939) and New York (1941) to the growing publication and consumption of Native autobiographies (early 1960s onward) (Krupat 1985) and, gradually, the demise of anthropological accounts prophesying doom. In Canada, a parallel development occurred, though somewhat later, whereby the arts of Woodland, Inuit, and Northwest Coast cultures acquired increased prestige as museum artifacts and as marketable artworks. At the same time, local activities aimed at self-expression and self-articulation increased, particularly in the area of broadcast communications. However, if the first inklings of revival were immanent in the primitivist shows of the early 1940s, they did not make themselves evident in Northwest Coast visual anthropology until the 1960s. Despite occasional works, such as the 1956 CBC production *People of the Potlatch,* it was another ten years before ethnographic film began to directly confront and contradict the narratives that had previously animated it: narratives of death and destruction.

This chapter considers more recent filmmaking efforts in their relationship to earlier films and filmmaking strategies and focuses on those productions that explicitly seek to enact a narrative of revival. Choosing such a focal point is inevitably a political act. If there is representational diversity in the immediate postwar years, a veritable explosion of film styles characterizes the 1960s and 1970s. In general, the revivalist project is dominant (though not exclusive) during the latter period, and my analysis mirrors a broad historical tendency within the genre. However, my treatment here does not claim the status of pure and neutral reflection. It actively privileges an ethnography that self-consciously attempts to articulate local perspectives, and that makes a space for Native voices. Admittedly, this problem of voicing and of subjectivity is a difficult one to negotiate, and the attempt to do so requires an analytic scrupulousness that often seems impossible to achieve. For if the language of the engagée comes easily, it often conceals more profound philosophical conundrums. Insofar as my own position is concerned, I try to avoid substituting the essentialism of the ethnographer with an essentialism of the "Other" self, particularly when (as in the case of anthropology and its subjects) that self is so frequently constructed in terms that the ethnographer her- or himself has mediated. The problem is one of recognizing the internal contradictions, tensions, and ambivalences of a "community" ("collectivity" is perhaps a more accurate word) while allowing that strategic unity that permits opposition when such a community is suffering oppression. This problem—of representational politics—afflicts all social analysts who write in the present moment, and who write with a commitment to political emancipation. In this chapter I respond by analyzing the films produced by and/or for Native communities as I have analyzed others, retaining the same skepticism toward the assumed transparency of film and realist aesthetics with *Box of Treasures* as I did with *Saving the Sagas*.

In the many films to be considered here, there is a shared iconography that is dominated by three motifs: the potlatch, salmon fishing, and land. All of these motifs are related through the trope of repatriation, which defines them in terms of ancestral rights and the conflict with local and federal governments. The vast majority of films are concerned with the efforts of various Bands to repossess territory or repatriate objects that were confiscated or deceivingly purchased during the nineteenth and early twentieth centuries. They are, in short, depictions of Native resistance to state hegemony, and their primary narrative objective is to make a case for the continued viability of coastal cultures. In this regard, they are diametrically opposed to the earlier representations discussed in previous chapters. Yet they frequently employ the same tropes and rhetorical strategies, structure their narratives around similar assumptions about the nature of social organization, and operate within the same paradigm that elevated ritual and art to the level of cultural patterns. Nor is disappearance absent from these productions. It is displaced into futurity but remains as the possibility against which Native Bands must ceaselessly struggle.

The existence of formal and iconographic similarities between films of such radically different narrative paradigms immediately raises questions about the degree to which contemporary filmmaking about the Northwest Coast (whether Native produced or not) has truly escaped the ideology of salvage ethnography. It also raises questions about the mechanics of resistance in general: about the relationships between individual signs and hegemonic structures of meaning, and about the possibility of an alterior consciousness operating in and through signs that simultaneously constitute the representations of the totalizing state. We can and must ask of recent films whether and to what extent they make use of old concepts and symbols to tell different stories, and to what extent such filmic intertextuality supports or undermines an attempt to undo the narratives of an earlier era. These are urgent questions, for those earlier narratives were both determined by and complicit with the institutional policies aimed at the elimination of aboriginal cultures.

The genocidal dimensions of that policy should not be underestimated. Theodore Roosevelt, who wrote an introduction to Edward Curtis's *The Vanishing Indian,* described the U.S. General Allotment Act of 1887 as a "mighty pulverizing engine to break up the tribal mass" (Berkhofer 1978: 175). And somewhat less dramatically, John A. MacDonald, while still minister of Indian Affairs in Canada, had defined Canadian national policy on Native matters as one in which the government would "wean them slowly by degrees, from their nomadic habits . . . and by slow degrees to absorb them on the land" (Ponting 1986:26). In Canada, the seemingly endless amendment of the Indian Act produced virtually no substantive change until the 1960s—and even then, many proposals, including those of the famous "White Paper," were retrogressive. Of course, American and Canadian policies were significantly different on many counts, Canadian policy being by far the more liberal. But, as in many other domains, Canadian attitudes were deeply influenced by American ones, the latter entering into the national consciousness via the innumerable channels that bind Canada to its southern neighbor in relations of social and political dependency. In any case, the ideological basis for assimilationist policy, whether understood as a bulldozing or a more benevolent (but no less dubious) paternalism, also provided the ground for the films of salvage ethnography, and it is for this reason that one wants to be so careful about employing old strategies in new narrations. The ideological baggage of these iconographic traditions is heavy indeed.

Cultural Revival and the Reconstitution of Museology

In considering the history of Canadian (and early American) anthropology, we have observed the degree to which the discipline was associated with the museum. We have also seen how much visual anthropology remained rooted in museology, with which it shared a definitive object orientation and a particular economy of collection. In Canada, the major institutional development was the movement away from the National Museum of Man in Ottawa to the British Columbia Provincial Museum in Victoria. Although this shift undoubtedly had many implications (not the least of which derived from the loss of Edward Sapir's extraordinary direction), visual anthropology remained fundamentally museological in character. However, this orientation began to change as the National Film Board began to assume increasing power and control over documentary production in Canada.

Equally important was the growing involvement of Native people in film production.

Ethnographic filmmaking under the auspices of the National Film Board (NFB), previously known as the Canadian Government Motion Picture Bureau, grew slowly after World War II but retained the stamp of its founder, John Grierson, in its orientation toward the politically committed exposé. In the late 1960s, the NFB instituted a program that, among other things, aimed to encourage Native persons to develop filmmaking skills. Although none of the features produced under this program, titled "Challenge for Change," dealt directly with Northwest Coast cultures, many were relevant to the predicament of Northwest Coast Natives in their battles with federal and provincial governments; almost all touched upon the issue of territorial jurisdiction. Ultimately, "Challenge for Change" may have had more rhetorical significance than importance for Native skills acquisition, but it remains a significant point in the development of Native control over communications resources, and of the slow movement toward self-representation.

Native filmmaking developed well beyond the context of the NFB and the "Challenge for Change" program, both in Canada generally and on the Northwest Coast in particular. With Band funds and federal assistance, filmmakers and Native advisers have taken on the task of representing coastal cultures anew. Among the more active of these have been the Kwakiutl (Kwakwaka'wakw) of Alert Bay, the Nishga, and the Git'ksan and Wet'suewet'en Tribal Councils. The Kwakiutl of Alert Bay—under the leadership of Gloria Cranmer-Webster, who is curator of the Band's museum (the U'mista Cultural Center)—have produced two related films, *Potlatch . . . a strict law bids us dance* and *Box of Treasures*. The Nishga have been the subjects of four films—*This Land* (1968), *This Was the Time* (1970), *The Nishga: Guardians of a Sacred Valley* (1977), and *The Nishgas: A Struggle for Survival* (1977)—all of which deal with land-claim disputes. The Git'ksan have more recently released their own production, *On Native Land* (1986), and have been the subject of several others. Though cast in ethnographically specific terms, all of these films have a common political and thematic project: the narration of Band struggles with provincial and federal legislative and judiciary systems. All of them provide a justificatory account by which the particular legal claims being made are grounded in an invocation of tradition and origins. And the origins invoked in the films then become the moral basis for both a rejection of externally imposed historical change and a demand for restitution.

In general, these films appear to be directed at educated audiences, at those in the upper strata of Canadian (and, to a lesser extent, American) society, at those with a university education and some access to political power. Spoken in the language of a broadly defined functionalist anthropology and frequently making reference to specific provincial and federal legislation, the narration of these films assumes their audience to have some familiarity with the history of Native-State relations and with the academic discourses about them. The National Film Board productions are circulated through NFB offices throughout Canada. Films of the various Band councils are generally available through university and public film libraries, and are frequently part of undergraduate curricula in both Canada and the United States.

Although it is difficult to estimate how often these films are used on reserves, at Native community centers, and in Native museums, or which segments of the Band populations indeed make use of them, it would seem that their educational utility is greatest for members outside of the cultures featured. The Band-produced films are cautious exercises in self-presentation that inevitably feed into the local discourses and experiences of self, but whose primary value lies in the mediated communications with others. The film narratives tend toward metatheorization and are laden with the heavy vocabularies of social science. Films produced on behalf of or in sympathy with Native Bands share this didactic tone and reiterate what must, for most Native viewers, be all too obvious. When Gloria Cranmer-Webster says, "Contact with outsiders . . . severely limited our lives" in *Box of Treasures,* it becomes apparent that the film wants to address precisely those outsiders whose arrival so reoriented Kwakiutl culture. A promotional advertisement for *On Native Land,* with glossy color stills and fast-paced copy, is particularly revealing in this regard. It describes Git'ksan life as something foreign to the viewer—with whom the reviewer surreptitiously identifies. We are told that the film shows "*their* deep-rooted connection to the land," and narrates "*their* memories . . . *their* perspective . . . *their* truth" (my emphasis). One can, I think, fairly well assume that the Native productions are part of larger lobbying processes, of attempts to effect changes in the conceptions of Native cultures that predominate in the ideology of national power elites. They are unabashed attempts to promulgate a different version of aboriginal cultures and histories, a version that might then form the basis for redefined State policy.

One might expect that this kind of committed filmmaking would require independence from the museums, the institutional guardians of Euro–North American possessive culture. In Canada, where provincial and national museums are, by definition, funded by government, a conflict of interest over representational strategies would seem inevitable. This expectation is heightened in proportion to the degree that recent films include in their narration a demand for the repatriation of those objects that are the mainstay of the museum. Yet, although the present era is one of increasing diversity, with a growing number of private production companies entering the documentary "industry," these expectations are not realized. Filmmaking, Native or otherwise, has not been removed from the museum context and, at least in Canada, government funding still supports a substantial proportion of all production. An understanding of the complex and often ambiguous relations between film narratives and their economic bases necessitates a more cautious understanding of ideological process. More especially, we are called upon to reconsider the nature of museology, as well as the possibilities for appropriation and resistance within the confines of an institution that often appears to be the very instanciation of that possessive drive by which Native cultures were reified and encompassed in the first place.

Much of the recent ethnographic filmmaking on the Northwest Coast has been undertaken in conjunction with Native museums such as the U'mista Cultural Center at Alert Bay. Indeed, *Box of Treasures* chronicles the establishment (in the late 1970s) of the Kwakiutl Museum, which was mandated by the federal government as part of the agreement to return artifacts from the National Museum in Ottawa. As we shall see, Native museums (there are several in British Columbia) are premised upon a taxonomic system rather different from that of traditional anthropological museums. And, in general, contemporary museology assumes a less observational notion of the institution, attempting instead to integrate collections with performance such that artifacts are available to be used in ceremonies but are still given special care when not in use (Ames 1986; Clifford 1988b). It would be inaccurate to attribute changes in the representational strategies of contemporary ethnographic film to the demise of the museum, despite recent claims that anthropology has largely extricated itself from its former locus (Miller 1987:111; Stocking 1985). Rather, museology itself has been transformed, and thus we see in recent films the instanciation of vast institutional and epistemological changes that have a far broader reach in anthropology and beyond.

As Eugenio Donato (1979) argues, the anthropological museum was born along with the library in an effort to represent reality through principles of metonymy. It eschewed the *ad hoc* and used the series as its basic organizational principle, assuming that "the spatial juxtaposition of fragments [could] produce a representational understanding of the world" (Donato 1979:223). However, Donato's claim that the museum is intrinsically impossible because it is oriented toward the spectator rather than the object (Donato 1979:225) needs to be reconsidered in light of recent developments. In at least some Native museums, the synchronicity of metonymic display has been replaced by an order in which space is precisely temporal—not because it assumes an evolutionary continuum but because the paradigm of the museum becomes the temporalized performance itself. More specifically, it takes the form of the potlatch performance and, accordingly, objects are encountered in the temporal order in which they would appear in a potlatch; one moves through these museums as through a ritual. These new museums then provide the ideological frame for a reoriented filmmaking, and, as one might expect in these circumstances, the films are far more concerned with Native exegesis and with questions of history than were their predecessors.

However, such an institutional explanation goes only partway toward an adequate accounting of the changes in ethnographic film. Technological factors also need consideration. The development of light-weight cameras, high-speed film, and high-fidelity recording equipment, all at reduced prices, has been extremely important. Moreover, the documentary film industry benefited from the injection of new capital from sources as diverse as local governments and multinational corporations. If, during the 1950s, film seemed to be losing the battle for audiences with television, the late 1960s saw the reestablishment of cinema as a commercially distinct and viable industry. Not only did television not eclipse film but television became a major source of funding for film production. Programs such as the British Broadcasting Corporation's *Disappearing World* and *Tribal Eye* (for which *Crooked Beak of Heaven* [1975] was produced) and Japan's *Subarashii Sekai Ryoko* (Our Wonderful World) are examples of this trend, as are the films of *National Geographic*. And they provided capital on an unprecedented scale. The sheer increase in documentary activity made experimentation in genre forms possible, thus possibly helping to liberate ethnographic film from its reliance on representational strategies such as the authoritarian voice-over. Not that documentary became a site of radical experiment. It did not; and, in any case, television put its own constraints upon ethnographic film, among which the most pressing were audience expectations of the fantastic and the exotic. Nonetheless, the development of different voicing strategies grew in proportion to the amount of film made, and ethnographic film was redefined accordingly—slowly and ambiguously, but also irreversibly.

Most contemporary ethnographic film differs from its predecessors in two fundamental ways: at the levels of both the paradigmatic narrative and the narrative strategies of individual films. Thus the narrative of revival, which extols heterogeneity and refuses the totalizing gaze so intrinsic to salvage ethnography, calls into being a formal diversity at the level of voice. Whereas early films relied heavily or exclusively on voice-over narration, correctly likened by Bill Nichols (1983) to the titles of silent films, recent films make use of a combination of narrative strategies. Voice-over is either omitted or used in combination with overt Native exegesis; a Native point of view may be elicited through staged interviews or scripting, and translations may be provided by either voice-over or graphic titles. However, it should not be assumed that the inclusion of a Native voice is any guarantee of representational equality. All voices are staged and authorized in the editorial construction of film, and the status of Native voices is often ambiguous in ethnographic documentary, particularly when a major vehicle for Native narration is the elaboration of mythologies.

As early as the making of *Blunden Harbour*, Robert Gardner had endeavored to provide a Kwakiutl perspective through the inclusion of a local creation story at the film's beginning. However, this strategy, though an important departure from the empiricism of salvage ethnography, remains problematic in that Native exegesis is relegated to the realm of myth—understood in its commonsensical dimensions as a kind of unreality. Other films explore the possibilities of mythic narrative in different ways and attempt to acknowledge myth as a legitimate mode of collective knowing in nonliterate contexts. In addition to those films that simply enact myths, explicitly Nativist productions often incorporate mythologizing as part of a broader and more comprehensive exegesis that addresses immediate social and political issues in terms of ancestral ideals. Even then, however, myth tends to be relegated to a realm of pastness, often acting as a universal signifier for disrupted tradition and authenticity.

Obviously, not all Native discourse is confined to the realm of myth. As often as not in these films, Native people are seen and heard speaking among themselves about a particular problem. Sometimes the prompter is made visible; at other times he or she is absent to the viewer. But in either case, the overheard conversation becomes part of an objectivist strategy that positions its viewer as the innocent observer. In such cases, we are led to believe that we are privy to intimate sentiments and that we have special access to the internal workings of a community. This effacement of the viewer occurs even in films, such as those of the U'mista Cultural Center, where questions about a given issue are being posed by Natives in meetings that are clearly staged for the camera's eye. Yet it would be a mistake, I think, to equate the objectivism of the prompted dialogue with that of the salvage ethnographer's omniscient exposition. Although many contemporary films allow viewers the happy fiction of voyeurism, the concealed staging permits Native exegetes an opportunity to articulate a clearly thought-out political position, and thus to achieve a kind of self-representation denied by the unsolicited disrobings of the voyeur's candid camera. Here the tables are turned on earlier filmmaking and on the viewer her- or himself. Representation still occurs for the spectator in the sense that it anticipates, even needs an audience, but the locus of power has shifted, if only partially, away from the viewer and toward the speaker.

In general, most contemporary films employ several narrative strategies in alternation, moving from the voice-over to the staged town meeting, from translated interviews to direct address. The results are potentially as diverse as the strategies employed. The incorporation of several narrative modes into a single film may produce a polyphony that solidifies the narration; if the voices speak in concert, their stories serve to corroborate one another and to give additional coherence to the paradigmatic narrative in which the individual film operates. However, where conventional expository narrative is retained, the movement between a first-person and third-person narration may create tension and ambiguity as much as anything else. This is the case in *Box of Treasures*, where the narrator (Cranmer-Webster) speaks of

Kwakiutl history from both an objective and a subjective point of view, shifting uncomfortably between "they" and "we." But this ironic vacillation of voice and the contradictions it implies make *Box of Treasures* an especially important film for the present analysis. For the film embodies and confronts the innumerable difficulties that inevitably encumber a resistant practice that must be carried out on the terrain and in the language of a dominant and dominating group. In the end, the assertion of Native subjectivity in film can be achieved only through an act of self-objectification—that is, of self-representation. And the stakes are high indeed.

While none of these strategies ever realizes the objective for documentary that Bill Nichols describes as capturing what would have occurred had the filmmaker not been there (1981:241), at least some of them directly confront the problem of construction and reconstruction. Direct address, though discomfiting for many viewers brought up on Hollywood realism, is particularly powerful as a means of disrupting the fiction of found or unmediated material. It also refuses the snug invisibility and supposed innocence of the spectator, who is situated not as observer but as participant and respondent in a simulated and often confrontational dialogue.

Perhaps most important of all, these films attempt to undermine the reification of lifeways that the voice-over produced. No longer limited to a condescending thought attribution, the films permit "Other" voices to speak, breaking down the borders of mutual unintelligibility and collapsing the neat oppositions of subject and object that anthropologists and ethnographic filmmakers have so relentlessly enacted. However, there remains a sense in which Native voices remain Other in these films. The spectator's assumed identity is still, by and large, non-Native and so the Native subject often speaks in the full knowledge that she or he will be a radically foreign object for the listener. Here, then, the objectification of a cultural self occurs as part of the speaker's own project but in terms not completely his or her own. The degree to which ethnographic films privilege the speaker's or the listener's position then becomes a matter of profound significance for the elaboration of its representational politics. Although the relationships are neither simple nor direct, the possibilities for situating voices are inextricably bound up with control over production and editing. Hence one of the most important factors in the development of an alternative ethnographic cinema has been the trend toward Native-directed, -produced, and -controlled films.

The U'mista Cultural Center Productions

Having traced some of the problems and developments in narrative film strategy, I want to turn now to particular texts and consider them in closer detail. It is perhaps already apparent that the films of the contemporary era are infinitely more complex than their precursors. Critical analysis becomes correspondingly more difficult, with the subtleties and sophistications of camera style and content drawing the reader in different and often opposing directions. The synopses that follow are long but I have tried to keep them as stringent as the earlier accounts, balancing the need for information with a recognition that not everything contained in any of these films can be adequately conveyed on the written page.

In the following pages, I discuss what I believe to be one of the most important ethnographic films ever to have been produced on the Northwest Coast: *Box of Treasures.* Before we turn to the film itself, however, it is necessary to consider the history of the U'mista Cultural Center at Alert Bay, which provided the subject matter, impetus, and direction for the film's making. The establishment of a museum at Alert Bay was a condition for the return of artifacts previously held in the Canadian Museum of Civilization in Ottawa. Those artifacts, including masks, coppers, and ceremonial regalia, had been confiscated following the arrest of Kwakiutl potlatchers in 1921, when Dan Cranmer had hosted a potlatch on Village Island. The accused had been given the option of surrendering their valuables or being imprisoned, although some suffered both punishments.

The word "u'mista" means the return of something special, and the cultural center bearing that name was created in the process, and as the prerequisite, of repatriation. As noted earlier, the collection and display of objects in museum contexts entails an entire epistemological position and assumes particular notions of property and possession. Thus the creation of a Kwakiutl museum necessarily risked being a mere replica of a culturally foreign institution—a matter of simply relocating the place of a possessive self peculiar to post-Enlightenment culture (Clifford 1988b:218). A Native museum housing Native artifacts could, in fact, entail that very assimilation against which Native revival movements have been fighting, transforming the Kwakiutl or the Haida (there are two Haida museums) into the arbiters of their own reification and exoticization.

Yet such an apocalyptic scenario is not inevitable. Collection and objectification are inherently relative procedures, dependent upon culturally specific constructions of the artifact, the logic of display, and the relationships between time and space. Indeed, *Box of Treasures* attests to the possibilities of alternative taxonomies and an alternative imagination of the time-space relationship upon which all ethnographic museology must ultimately rest. Indeed, it would not be unfair to say that the Northwest Coast Bands have led the way in the redefinition of anthropological museology (Ames 1986; Clifford 1988b). At the U'mista Cultural Center, potlatching objects are organized spatially according to the temporal order of their appearance in the potlatch. This order itself expresses the relations of social priority, such that temporal distance (movement from the beginning) is correlate with increasing supremacy in the social universe. Thus, the museum constantly reenacts the potlatch by placing the spectator in the place of witness. No longer a simply or straightforwardly consuming eye, the observer is on some level encompassed by the logic of the potlatch; she or he can no longer appropriate the object without also becoming a vehicle in that ritual system of status relations whereby the act of witnessing is itself a mode of legitimation. Moreover, this spatially contained but essentially passive performance mirrors the other functions of the U'mista Cultural Center, acting as a locus and a resource (of materials and expertise) for active ritual performance. The objects housed there can be withdrawn for use on ceremonial occasions or for educational purposes, and the Center encourages both of these activities as part of its project to promote an enacted form of cultural knowledge.

The extension of the museum's contextualizing function into the domain of performance has important implications for any analysis of the museum and/or collection in the too-modern, postmodern world. Other museums, including both the BCPM and UBC's Museum of Anthropology, have begun to reconstrue their own projects in this manner, with objects being loaned for special occasions and performances being staged in the museums themselves. In this context, it seems necessary to reconsider Dean MacCannell's (1989) description of the museum as the symbol of modernity's victory over the nonmodern world. And, equally, to reject Eugenio Donato's (1979) suggestion that the museum itself is rendered obsolete by the new science of thermodynamics and its *telos* of infinite dissipation. Neither the extremity of MacCannell's modernist nightmare—the completely homogenized world—nor Donato's sense that history's end is not a rationalized unity, but chaos—the most radical heterogeneity—adequately addresses the complexity of museum practice today. For Donato, the museum cannot be separated from collection, from the desire for an impossibly complete knowledge of a totalized reality. Hence its incompatibility with the consciousness of thermodynamics. For MacCannell, the museum is precisely an attempt to stave off the sense of loss—of lost heterogeneity—that totalization engenders. But the U'mista Cultural Center seems to want to refuse these very oppositions. The museum mocks the facile dichotomy between the modern and the nonmodern, and denounces the narrative of disappearance that such binarism assumes. In its place, it institutes an architectural but potentially animated space as the locus for objects that are understood not as the congealed signs of a reduced selfhood but as the instruments of collective and performative self-construction (see Munn 1983 and Miller 1987 for a discussion of the object as instrument of subjectification). Whether the Center has succeeded in achieving these vastly difficult objectives is a matter for debate, but its very attempt demands a reexamination of recent social theory and its accounts of museology. For our purposes here, the question of ultimate success is less important than effectivity, and I want now to consider the relationship between new museology and ethnographic film.

Let me thus return to the phenomenon of repatriation and ask what role, if any, the films have played and what status they have in the revival of Native Northwest Coast cultures. In the case of the Kwakiutl, the repatriation of artifacts and the films about that process are at least partly a repayment of the debt of family affection and obligation. Gloria Cranmer-Webster is the granddaughter of Dan Cranmer, whose 1921 potlatch was so thoroughly punished by State authorities. And although Cranmer-Webster is undoubtedly an extraordinary individual (in terms of both the force of her personality and the status she enjoys in the community at Alert Bay), which may explain her success in repatriation efforts, other Bands have sought similar agreements with provincial and federal museums. That their efforts to obtain goods taken by force or by sale are also personally motivated in no way diminishes the sociological significance of these acts. Repatriation is a mode of recollecting what was collected by others for the purposes of domination through possession. Such recollection politicizes the deeply felt commitments to families and communities, and the polysemy of the word itself conveys this doubledness of practice—whereby the gathering up of scattered objects and the remembrance of the past are but two dimensions of the same process. Before considering further the relationships between contemporary filmmaking and the problem of collective remembrance, however, I want to examine one of the U'mista Cultural Center's productions in detail.

There is one additional point to be made before proceeding. Throughout this chapter I speak about films produced by or for Native peoples. Often these films are actually directed by non-Native persons, and production in this sense is a far broader concept than is usually the case in discussions of film. However, the purpose of a discursive analysis is to reveal the myth of the *auteur;* accordingly, the individual biographies of directors and technicians are not as important to the present analysis, whose purpose is an understanding of films that were commissioned by, or undertaken on behalf of, coastal Bands. For this reason, I occasionally use the term "Nativist" in place of "Native produced" to refer to revival films.

Synopsis: *Box of Treasures* (1983)

The film opens with a running title, black on white: "From the Beginning, the people of the Northwest Coast lived off the sea; our cultures, rich in tradition, flourished. Central to our lives was the potlatch, a ceremony of dance and gift giving that provided the key to each family's identity, status, and our link with the past.

"In the 19th century, contact with outsiders—settlers, missionaries, the government—severely limited our lives: where we lived, what we did ... finally, in many cases, what we believed in.

"Attempts to impose change on us came to be focused upon the pot-latch, thought by many to be a symbol of waste and heathenism. In 1884, the Canadian government enacted legislation prohibiting the potlatch.

"In some of our own villages, those of the Kwakwaka'wakw, the cere-mony continued in secret. In 1921, Chief Dan Cranmer held a large pot-latch on Village Island. Participants were sent to jail. Those convicted were given the option of surrendering their masks, ceremonial regalia, and cop-pers to avoid imprisonment. Of the confiscated treasures, some were sold and given away; the rest were consigned to the National Museum of Man in Ottawa.

"There, for many years, they stayed. But we never forgot."

Backing this introductory set of titles are the sounds of chanting voices and drums. There follows a series of close-range shots of masks, each flood-lit in an otherwise dark setting. The scene shifts to the coastline, then to decaying buildings and prostrate poles. The narrator tells us that Village Island is now abandoned. The camera moves from face to carved face on the poles: "On the faces of the totem poles, one senses a change, a way of life succumbing to the effects of intervention."

Alert Bay is described as a community on an island shared by Whites and Native villagers. But, "While in many ways, Alert Bay is similar to other fishing communities, it has also become the center from which we have begun the task of reclaiming all that was almost lost." There are shots of the village from the water, and the camera pans along the shoreline.

Cut to Gloria Cranmer-Webster, identified as the curator of the U'mista Cultural Center: "A lot of people have heard about the Kwakiutl. We're probably the most highly anthropologized group of Native people in the world. But a lot of those people ... think that we are all dead, that we've disappeared because we were the vanishing races those early White peo-ple said we were. And where you look at museum exhibits in a lot of places, it's as if we were gone. There's no reference to us still being alive. And we are."

The scene shifts to an interior. There is a fire in the foreground and a painted wall in the background where people dressed in button blankets are standing. Chanting and drumming can be heard. A shot of a masked dancer is framed with flames. A sequence of low-angle shots of the same dancer follows. The narrator comments, "For years, there were few potlatches. Many people forgot the dances and their meaning. But some remembered."

Cranmer-Webster comments on how the elders continued dancing and potlatching. The scene changes and an elderly woman is shown seated. She recalls, in shaky voice, the potlatch of her youth and describes it as a way of expressing joy.

Again the scene changes. This time a beach is shown. We hear the sounds of chopping wood and the camera pans right to show a man cutting bark from a tree. Cut to a table where the bark is being shredded with a mallet. Subsequently, in a number of shots, men are shown carving or painting masks. The narrator remarks, "Once again artists create tradi-tional masks and poles following designs that are centuries old."

A close-up shot of an unfinished mask follows and the carver tells us that knowledge of the designs permits the artists to produce both masks and poles. He stresses the continuity of design forms, "doing it exactly as the old people did it."

A man is shown mending a net. He says, "You could call us more like the Salmon People. In this area this is all we ever lived on . . . and we still depend on the fishery and the sea." A sequence of shots of the boats and the nets being let out follows his remarks.

The fisherman, shown in close-up, continues. "Our people have always fished when, where, and how they wanted. We can no longer do that. There's a moratorium on black cod, halibut. . . . Next thing you know it will be clams and everything like this." We see boats and nets full of fish. "The ocean is our life. . . . To cut off the life line like the salmon, the fishing, is like taking the dirt away from the farmers. We no longer would exist."

The scene changes to a room in which several men are seated around a table, speaking. We pick up their discussion: "We're now looking at hours of fishing where we used to look at days. I think we've got to tell them, 'This is it. We're not going to be pushed any more.' We can't be pushed any more because we're right at the bottom now."

The narrator speaks over the men, her voice superseding theirs: "Many political battles are being fought in Alert Bay. Of all the things taken away from us, none symbolize our loss more than the masks taken after Dan Cranmer's potlatch." Cranmer-Webster then describes the negotiations to return the masks from the National Museum of Man.

A series of filmed stills showing the construction of the U'mista Cultural Center are accompanied by explicative narration that tells of its unique open structure modeled on the traditional big-houses. An elderly woman is shown and heard speaking in Kwakwala, with subtitles: "This place built on the beach that you call the museum, it is like a storage box, like a body of treasures the old people used to have." At this point, Cranmer-Webster describes the open arrangement of objects as a kind of liberation, explaining that they have been locked up for too long.

The narrator then comments on the other exhibits, including the displays of objects taken from attics and basements, gifts given for the occasion of the Center's opening, and a series of photographs of old village sites, each with its own creation story noted at the side. "The Center was to be more than a museum; it was in fact our box of treasures and a focus for all our efforts to strengthen the culture, language, and history that were almost lost." The word "u'mista" is explained as a term used in reference to slaves ransomed or returned through retaliatory raids, meaning something special that has been returned.

Following are several shots of the opening ceremonies, of dancing in front of the ceremony and on boats in the harbor, of speeches dedicated to the "struggle and suffering." Cranmer-Webster speaks of both the happiness and the sadness of the opening, and how the dedication to deceased elders makes them present again.

The camera pans from the museum to a sunset on still water, and

Cranmer-Webster speaks: "We came very close to losing our culture, our language." She describes the commitment of some of the elders to reinculcate the wisdom of an earlier era. The film cuts to the museum interior where an elderly woman is seated in front of a video camera. The scene is explained as follows: "The old people are our links to our history. So that the past does not die with them, their memories are being recorded at the Center."

There are extended sequences here in which young children are shown learning their language in school and their stories in the Center. The U'mista educational program is described as an "ironic reversal of the situation at the turn of the century," when the indigenous languages were forbidden at school. A linguistic anthropologist, Jay Powell, is shown and heard working with a woman in a kitchen on basic syntax and phrases in Kwakwala. And a teacher describes for us her approach to language education as one that incorporates personal history as well.

Cranmer-Webster speaks about the uncertainty of the educational program as we see children learning dances in an open field. She notes the competition between Native and "modern" sources of entertainment and acknowledges that some children will leave the island for mainland (White) society.

Shots of a class of adolescents being shown masks from "The Potlatch Collection" at the Center are accompanied by an encapsulating narration: "You can sum it all up by saying that it's important that you know your past if you're going to be fighting for your future."

We return to the fishing meeting shown earlier. A new speaker is analyzing the situation in terms of "aboriginal rights," which he defines as inclusive of fishing, the maintenance of culture and language, government, education, local government, and environmental control.

Over shots of children dancing in the field, Cranmer-Webster speaks of battles still to be won, particularly those related to fishing and environmental destruction. Shots of the museum potlatch follow, and she continues, "Most of all, we celebrate the fact we're still alive, still here. . . . We are always going to be here."

Potlatch Reconsidered:
Representation and Repetition

There is much in *Box of Treasures* to recall the written ethnography of the later salvage period. Both this film and the Center's earlier production, *Potlatch . . . a strict law bids us dance,* are focused upon the institution of the potlatch, which is presented as the symbolic and functional locus of cultural survival. *Box of Treasures* begins by asserting as much, and the narrative circles around the ritual opening of the U'mista Cultural Center, constantly returning to images of potlatching in overt exposition and imagery, and through the metaphoric ramifications of the Center itself. Indeed, the

U'mista Cultural Center, with "The Potlatch Collection" as its centerpiece, derives much of its own significance from the fact that it provides the spatial and informational context in which such activity can take place. In order to fully comprehend the transformations in filmic narratives, or to appreciate the limits for such change set by anthropology's discursive traditions, we must return again to the ethnography of the potlatch. In the last chapter, it was argued that the potlatch was a key signifier in the dehistoricizing discourses of salvage ethnography; what remains for a critical analysis of contemporary Northwest Coast ethnographic film is a careful scrutinizing of how the potlatch—as a sign—has been deployed in other narratives. To what extent does the image of the potlatch carry within itself the history of other representations, and to what extent can it be reaccented and reauthorized to generate new representations, and new meanings?

Accentuation and authorization: These are the terms of Bakhtinian linguistics (Bakhtin 1981; Morson and Emerson 1990), originally employed in the analysis of the ethical act and, subsequently, in that of the modern novel. Bakhtin's concern with the novel was primarily a concern with the limits of authorship, and with the possibility that multiple voices might continue to exist in a singly authored text. Limited space prevents me from fully evoking the delicacy and sophistication of his analysis, but Bakhtin's concern with the materiality of signs and the degree to which dialects bear the traces of other, previous voicings is suggestive here. Bakhtin's writings lead us to confront the ambiguity of a sign—the potlatch—that necessarily entails the convergence of historically distinct, sometimes contradictory representations. In this case, those representations have been categorized as narratives of salvage and revival. And, as becomes apparent in the films discussed here, the struggle for survival also entails a struggle to control or determine the possible readings of the potlatch; in other words, it entails a struggle to repossess a particular sign in addition to the objects in which it is physically embodied and symbolized.

The potlatch, which had been notably absent in films of the late salvage period, dominates the iconography of contemporary films. It is central in such films as *Potlatch* (1976) and *Potlatch People*, and plays a lesser but still significant role in others, including *Crooked Beak of Heaven* (1975) and *Those Born at Masset* (1977). In all of these films, the potlatch is a symbolic anchor for the representation of coastal cultures, a meeting ground of audience expectation and directorial intention. Within individual films, the potlatch is also a mnemonic device, whose mention invariably triggers personal remembrance, historical accounts, or a general invocation of originary authenticity. However, the potlatch of these newer films is somewhat different from that of the written ethnography in the preceding period, where it was the object of exclusively historical speculation and explanation. For the potlatch *did* resume on the Northwest Coast; the ban was lifted and thus the "post-potlatch" era described by Helen Codere (1961), in reference to the Kwakiutl, became not so much an end in the linear continuum of disappearance as a temporary pause in a far more complex set of historical processes.

It will be remembered from the last chapter that written ethnography of the 1940s and 1950s postulated an identity between potlatching and a generic Northwest Coast culture through the procedures of synecdoche. Functionalism and structural-functionalism, which originally promised to liberate anthropology from the crude reductions of cultural materialism, ended up contributing to the same reifications through their inability to account for historical processes and the heterogeneity of culture that history produced. By now, of course, the historicist critique of functionalist and structural-functionalist analysis is all too familiar. The waters separating our former "islands of history" are now traversed by myriad vessels bearing goods, knowledge, and the forces of domination, as well as ceaseless transformation (Sahlins 1985; Comaroff and Comaroff 1992). But for this very reason, it is necessary to question what appears to be the resurrection of structural-functionalist assumptions—particularly as they were elaborated in relation to the potlatch—in contemporary ethnographic film, including that of Native filmmakers. Most contemporary film wants to reject the reifications of older representations at the level of content only. The result is often a deep ambiguity of connotation, and an awkward relationship between narrative voices and the visual imageries against which they are juxtaposed. This ambiguity is perhaps most evident in the representation of time, an issue to which I turn once again in the following pages.

Time and Time Again: Ritual and Temporality

If, as Johannes Fabian (1983) argues, processes of cultural objectification are inextricably linked to the ways in which time is accommodated and represented, then the recurrent images of potlatching require that we consider the relationships between the potlatch and the various concepts of historical and ritual time in which it has been embedded. For the potlatch was most frequently linked to that ultimate reification, the representation of the Other as deceased, as specter. I want to suggest that salvage anthropology's conceptualization of the potlatch interlaced two distinct temporalities. Here, it is important to remember that an almost obsessive interest in potlatching emerged at the same time that Native artifacts were being rehabilitated for the Euro–North American public. The concurrent growth in the literature on shamanism and on Northwest Coast spirituality, which defined artifacts primarily in terms of their sacred significations (Jonaitis 1981), buttressed that tendency in post-Kantian thought to unite the sacred and the aesthetic in a single domain. And, in general, anthropology was marked by a widespread concern with—some would say fetishism of—the ritual domain.

This topical focus had broader implications for the representation of time and history; the emphasis on ritual and aesthetics entailed particular visions of temporality, which was itself the measure of radical difference. Maurice Bloch (1976) points out this relationship in his analysis of anthropological studies of "Other" time, and of their privileging of nondurational time. Bloch contends that the argument for a nondurational experience of time in other cultures is really a function of the valorization of ritual in anthropological studies of time. He points out that in all of the ethnographic accounts of such societies, Geertz's work most notable among them, the claim to a nondurational conceptualization of time is, in fact, a claim for the relative predominance of nonlinear time in contexts that also include linear time. Seductive though it may be, there are problems with this approach. To begin with, Bloch's argument never fully undermines the Bergsonian (Western post-Reformation) assumption that time is fundamentally dichotomous, consisting of both static and durational dimensions (Munn 1992:14). Bloch terms the former, which he associates with ritual and sociality, "the presence of the past in the present" (1976:287) and contrasts this with the linear time of agricultural activity and daily life. Though he wants to eschew the esoteric and idealist bias of Geertzian analysis, Bloch's own treatment is intellectualist in nature. His leanings are most explicitly directed in the neat statement that "*cognition* of society, like that of time, is double" (Bloch 1976:287, my emphasis). However, as Nancy Munn (1992:15) so cogently reminds us, this kind of dualism "cannot take account of the problem that people are 'in' cultural time, not just conceiving or perceiving it." I do not mean to single out Bloch's argument for special opprobrium, nor to support its conclusions. Rather, I use it here because it so neatly summarizes— and then reproduces—much of the anthropological thought about time and culture.

Well taken, nonetheless, is Bloch's attempt to overcome the habit of using time to recast older dualisms by which modern and nonmodern worlds are opposed. For in rejecting this opposition, Bloch draws out the tendency in studies of ritual to reproduce the supposed timelessness of sacred activity in the representation of those cultures whose identity is somehow conflated with certain "key" rituals or, more generally, symbolic activity. As was argued in the previous chapter, such a conflation of key rituals with cultural identity was extremely common in the written ethnography of the Northwest Coast, where potlatching and coastal cultural personality or pattern became virtually synonymous. When analyses are conducted *in terms of* the ritual domain, as those of potlatching cultures have been, and when they are construed within the framework of structural-functionalism, the dehistoricization of an entire culture seems to follow all too easily. In the case of Northwest Coast ethnography, the end result of this representational strategy—by which art and ritual were accorded primacy and social time was subsumed by pure reproduction—was that the potlatch itself, banned and suspended, became the most common signifier of death and extinction.

Box of Treasures addresses this history of reification directly; from the first set of running titles onward, we are aware of the film's intention to rehabilitate the potlatch as a valid and a viable ritual practice in ongoing and changing historical circumstances. This rehabilitation takes place on two levels. The legitimation of the potlatch becomes essential for the repatriation of potlatch artifacts while, at the same time, these very objects are construed as the prerequisites of a revitalized ritual tradition. Artifacts, from carved masks to the coppers, are themselves seen as repositories of cultural knowledge, and their repossession becomes essential for the relearning of cultural practice, especially artistic practice. Hence the emphasis on the re-creation— the absolute repetition—of design forms: "Once again artists create traditional masks and poles following designs that are centuries old." Although the situation is changing, the Kwakiutl of Alert Bay have perhaps been more vigilant in this pursuit of aesthetic continuity than have other Bands. In general, Git'ksan and Haida artists have been more free in their interpretations of older forms. Git'ksan two-dimensional art has become widely renowned for its innovative style, most especially for its use of negative space—which was historically avoided in almost all Northwest Coast design. Similarly, Haida sculpture, led by the work of Bill Reid, has developed significant variations and, in a major departure from the arts of adornment and masking, sculpture has moved toward more free-standing forms. But regardless of local variations, the attempt to re-create culture through the reproduction of plastic arts has been a powerful force in all Northwest Coast revival movements. Of course, this is not a purely nor simply material process. Groups of committed artists become the centers of broader networks and communicate their rediscovered knowledge in a variety of ways, only one of which includes the structures of consumption in which artifacts are purchased and used.[1]

In all of this, the relationship between artifacts and potlatching is crucial, as *Box of Treasures* constantly reminds its viewers. With a certain amount of pathos, this fact is acknowledged in the acts of confiscation that followed Dan Cranmer's potlatch, described idealistically in the film as the most powerful *symbol* of loss. What *Box of Treasures* points out, again and again, is that such objects are the material embodiments of vast sets of social relations: the actual objectifications of personal and social identities, power hierarchies, cognition, belief, and affect. In a language of pragmatic politics and nostalgic recollection, *Box of Treasures* recognizes the importance of the artifact "as the form of natural materials whose nature we continually experience through practices, and also as the form through which we continually experience the very particular nature of our cultural order" (Miller 1987:105). In this regard, the film seems to go far beyond the simplistic economism of material culture studies, which underlay salvage ethnography and its films. Indeed, the U'mista Cultural Center seems to demand a radical rethinking of the processes of cultural objectification.

Accordingly, we might expect the film to recognize itself as an exercise in intentional self-objectification, as an artifact like any other, which materializes and evokes the particular cultural values of its makers. But *Box of Treasures* stops short of this extreme self-awareness—as it must in order to appeal to mainstream viewers. While the film clearly expresses a sense of how complex and multifaceted are cultural artifacts, the artifact as a category remains restricted to artistic and technological production, whose primary context is the potlatch. With regard to the question of film itself, *Box of Treasures* retreats into the assumption of transparency and objectivity that grounded salvage ethnographic film of the earlier eras and continues to form the basis of virtually all documentary. Neither the transparency of film nor the priority of the potlatch is questioned here. This is not surprising given the collusion of older anthropological claims to objectivity and film's claim to transparency in ethnographic film. Of particular interest, however, is the fact that the reconceptualization of artifacts did not undermine the reductionist claims about key symbols, dominant rituals, or cultural patterns. It did not lead the film's producers and directors to reject the written accounts of salvage ethnography but, instead, allowed them to reinstitute important parts of those narratives into the new film. It is for this reason that repatriation becomes—in *Box of Treasures* but also in other films of the period—the main vehicle of a continued synecdochic reduction; the potlatch is, as the film tells us, a "link with the past," and potlatching objects (recall here that almost any commodity could be "given" in a potlatch) are the symbols of that temporarily "lost link." In many senses, then, recollection is a doubled term.

However, this duality is not merely indicative of ambivalence; it is tactical. Structural-functionalist ethnography of the 1940s and 1950s began its analysis of the potlatch with the presumption that it was a ritual institution that had religious significance for its participants. The reproduction of the social structure was imagined as a by-product of ritual activity and, at the same time, as its motivating force. The intentions of individual subjects were thus brought in line with a (problematic) collective intentionality, which existed at the structural level. Many Native exegetes retain this fundamentally dualist reading and give it a normative bias. However, in films like *Box of Treasures,* it is the functional dimensions rather than the affective and cognitive meaning of the potlatch that have greatest rhetorical utility in the film's implicit argument against the State. Without wanting to privilege individual intentionality over the power of ideology, one must recognize here the degree to which these new films are determined by the audience to which they address themselves. Thus, inversion of structural-functionalist tropes is carried out inside of that language, and, accordingly, resistance must always be carried out under, or even behind, the banner of the reigning vision.

For this reason I am skeptical about readings that want to see in these new films the mere reinstanciation, the perfect internalization, of the dominant culture's ideology. *Box of Treasures* differs from its salvage precursors in terms of more than just the actual identities of the film's speakers and producers. Indeed, the representations of potlatching in salvage ethnography centered on the fact that the potlatch had ceased and that, as a result, there was no longer an adequate ritual superstructure to reproduce the social organization. The written ethnography began with ritual practice and ended with function. And the filmmaking of the era was left to depict the skeletal remains of the coastal bodies politic. Logically, contemporary filmic ethnography begins with social structure and the necessity of reproduction, and ends with ritual practice in a politically motivated challenge to earlier representations. In simplified form, the narratives of salvage and revival ethnography can be opposed in terms of their normative biases. Tacitly, salvage ethnography says, "Here is a highly ritualized culture in which a central ritual institution functioned to reproduce highly stratified social relations. The discontinuation of the potlatch therefore entailed the dissolution of cultural integrity." The ethnography of revival counters, "The potlatch is a necessary ritual institution for the maintenance and perpetuation of the society. The survival or revival of the society is therefore dependent upon the continuation of potlatching." If both of these statements refer to the structural functions of the ritual, they do so in subtly but importantly different ways. The first statement claims to be a "model *of*" society, whereas the second admits to being a "model *for*" society (Geertz 1973a:93). Revival narratives are explicitly programmatic, refusing the evolutionists' *telos* of disappearance and insisting instead upon the necessity for intervention. The ideology of disappearance and of evolution is therefore overturned with the tools and the building blocks of a previous, quite incompatible vision.

The Nativist productions about the potlatch do not, however, address the problem raised by Codere, Cannizzo, and Goldman—namely, the relatively recent emergence of the potlatch as a dominant institution. In many ways, they naturalize the textual invention of Northwest Coast cultures that ethnographers inscribed in the 1940s and 1950s. And here it becomes apparent that the narrative of revival is only a partial refutation of earlier anthropology's totalizing constructions. Dennis Cole (1985) has observed the irony in recent revival movements, during which Native peoples have sought to reclaim a "captured heritage" through recourse to those institutions that were themselves its captors: anthropology and its museums. Efforts to reinvent tradition, as Eric Hobsbawm and Terence Ranger (1983) term this process, are undoubtedly carried out within particular political projects (Linnekin 1983:250), but this endeavor is neither so simple nor so direct as the language of invention seems to suggest. Native people are not simply concocting identities for themselves in a laboratory of political expediency, though clearly a fear of precisely this kind of activity is motivating a number of juries in American land-claim cases (see Clifford 1988a). The process is far more complex than that, and it should not be assumed that the social constitution of identities occurs with any greater or more Machiavellian intentionality among Native communities than in inner-city neighborhoods or among the cultures of corporate elites. The point of constructivist interventions has been to show how cultures are continually created and at the same time naturalized. If the subject matter of such criticisms has tended to be cultures other than those of the writer (and often the reader), this detail should not be extrapolated to suggest that "Other" cultures are somehow more contingent than those of their inscribers. More important, it is history itself that defines the limits for revival and provides the constraints within which individuals and groups may work out their respective projects (Appadurai 1981:201). Tacitly agreed-upon rules of priority, credibility, and continuity all apply, and although traditions and customs (Hobsbawm and Ranger's distinction notwithstanding) possess a certain plasticity, they are nonetheless restricted by the need for systematicity and for an appearance of naturalness. In this light, the place of the potlatch is fraught with contradiction and the possession of the potlatch as sign (in Bakhtin's sense) becomes a key arena of representational contest. The question then becomes, On what level can the critique of salvage ethnography intervene? How far can one go in deconstructing the representation of the potlatch without effacing all of its meaning for both Native and Euro–North American audiences, all of whom operate within a single, if differentiated, representational domain?

When *Box of Treasures* states that the potlatch was the "key to each family's identity, status and . . . link with the past," it effectively repeats salvage ethnography's identification of one brief period in Kwakiutl history as the real expression of essential Kwakiutl culture. That period in which potlatching was only one among many social institutions involving feasting, dancing, and the exchanges of goods vanishes completely from contemporary filmic narratives. *Potlatch . . . a strict law bids us dance* and *Box of Treasures* are extreme in the repetition of salvage ethnography's obsessive elevation of potlatching. But this time, there is a twist; this time, the potlatch is to be construed not as an index of disappearance but as a symbol of continuity.

Crisis: Salmon and the Land

Recent films develop their narratives around the problem of cultural survival in the face of possible disappearance—not, as earlier films had, around the fact of physical survival concurrent with cultural death, or around the very fact of cultural extinction. Given the emphasis on continued existence, however, the period that earlier ethnographers had identified as a cultural vanishing point must be reconstructed as one of transition.

Yet in almost all contemporary film, there is a sense of caution, a "but" following the affirmation of survival. This "but" has to do with the current political struggles in which most Northwest Coast Bands are now engaged, primarily struggles over land-title and access to fishing territories. Films such as *Bella Bella, On Native Land, The Land Is the Culture, Salmon People,* and *The Nishgas: A Struggle for Survival* (as well as the U'mista Cultural Center productions) directly assert a new danger, a new threat to existence. This is the lack of control over basic economic resources—the means of production—which, on the Northwest Coast, include both fish and land. Native people are not prophesying their own demise; rather, in the imagination of the present moment as a period of crisis, they are constructing their futures around a narrative of conflict, analogous to that of the salvage era. The primary difference is that whereas the narratives of salvage ethnography assumed eventual extinction and the victory, in the sense of domination and incorporation, by Euro–North American culture, these new narratives foresee victory for aboriginal cultures through resistance and cultural regeneration. *Box of Treasures* ends with Gloria Cranmer-Webster asserting that the Kwakiutl will "always be here."

Deploying the motif of possible destruction and invoking the logic of tragedy, contemporary ethnographic films exemplify the doubled nature of representation, whose aesthetics are always political and whose politics must inevitably be given aesthetic form. The normative element in these films, which states that control over fishing and land resources is both necessary and justified by historical tradition, attempts to persuade the viewer of the validity of the Bands' position in their challenge to British Columbian and Canadian federal legislation and legal judgments. Where the potlatch is deemed integral to the ideological reproduction of culture—or to the re-creation of social structure—salmon and the land are defined as the main means of production on which Northwest Coast cultures rest. Because disputes between Northwest Coast Bands and the provincial or federal governments have been mediated by the judicial system, with its emphasis on precedence, claims to (collective) ownership have to be made in terms of historical continuity. That is, Natives have to prove that they should be heir to those resources wrongfully or unfairly taken in earlier times.

In the case of the Kwakiutl, the argument for historical continuity requires a demonstration that the contemporary Kwakiutl are the same Kwakiutl as those who were oppressed by missionaries and State representatives. An onerous task, the proof of continuity is required in all legal actions aimed at the reclamation of land-title or the repatriation of objects. In the United States, such proof is attempted in separate proceedings as the prerequisite for courtroom litigation (see James Clifford's [1988a] account of the Mashpee case), but in Canada the issue of identity is addressed within the larger dispute over title. We now know that the Kwakiutl of the late nineteenth century are the Kwakiutl of the great potlatch and that it was this culture of vigorous ritual exchange that worried federal legislators. If the contemporary Kwakiutl are to establish the legitimacy of the claims for repatriation, then, they must represent themselves as being *identical* with that earlier cultural moment, the one divested of ceremonial objects. Thus, the filmic representation of the Kwakiutl—and this applies to other groups, though in slightly different terms—is an exercise in iconicity, in the search for specific resemblances between the past and the present (Herzfeld 1986). Not just any past will do; the past itself must be differentiated and certain moments emphasized, or selected in a narrative that, as Hayden White (1980) reminds us, necessarily omits some things in favor of others. Of course, these claims are made within limited circles—indeed, within national boundaries. To my knowledge, there has been no attempt to have the objects of Bands now in Canadian territory repatriated from institutions in the United States.

In any case, the Kwakiutl productions (both *Box of Treasures* and *Potlatch ... a strict law bids us dance*) establish two consecutive synchronic states. Between them is a single historical event: the banning of the potlatch and its enforcement. In this respect the potlatch assumes the role of an "epitomizing event" (the term is derived from Fogelson 1985, and elaborated by Harkin 1988), a symbol that mediates and conjoins two distinct states and/ or temporal planes. Epitomizing events are culturally selected according to the needs and the sentiments of the present and then become points of orientation, the demarcators of an experiential before and after. It seems safe to say that, for the Kwakiutl, the enforcement of a ban on potlatching is as significant an event as first contact. For the Nishga, as depicted in *The Nishgas: A Struggle for Survival* and *Nishga: Guardians of a Sacred Valley*, the expropriation of title by the Crown and resultant loss of access to land constitute a similar epitomizing event. Thus, the filmic remembrance of the potlatch, like the cinematic narration of land-claim disputes, is a kind of repetition, a way of making the past present again. As Michael Harkin (1988:102) argues, such symbolic repetitions provide the means through which "historical events become part of a common 'destiny,' meaningful for those living afterward."

The Other Side of Development: Assimilation and Cultural Authenticity Among the Bella Bella

A further qualification is necessary here. The repetition enacted by Chick Olin, Gloria Cranmer-Webster, and the participants in *Box of Treasures* is repetitive insofar as it revives or reconstitutes the historical possibilities that existed prior to the banning of the potlatch. It encompasses the image of assimilation within the narrative of revival as a means of motivating future-oriented action. In this and almost all independent productions, survival is a signifier for authenticity. And purity is a primary, perhaps *the* primary value. Hence Cranmer-Webster's agonizing over the possibility of young people going to the mainland and taking on the ways of the dominant culture.

However, National Film Board productions are far more ambivalent about the nature of survival, particularly in films that recount the struggle for economic autonomy. The degree to which aboriginal cultures can retain authenticity in the context of economic development (primarily capitalist development, sometimes mitigated by trade unionism) is often posed as the narrative's central problem. This is the case in *Bella Bella,* an NFB production about the Heiltsuk-speaking peoples of British Columbia. In the following pages, I consider *Bella Bella* as an example of state-funded but non-museum-based documentary. The film raises for us the thorny problems of authenticity and heterogeneity, and I use it here to raise questions that are being asked, in different ways, in a number of important and surprisingly related domains, from poststructuralist theory to international Native rights organizations.

Synopsis: *Bella Bella* (1975)

The film opens with low aerial shots of the coast, moving from tree-covered mountains to water. A woman's voice describes the scene as the B.C. coast about three hundred miles north of Vancouver—"the ancestral home of the Heiltsuk Indians."

The narrator informs us that there are two explanations for the name "Bella Bella": one that attributes it to the Spanish and the other that accounts for it in terms of a Heiltsuk word meaning "point of land." The scene is now a beach where a man and a woman are gutting fish.

The present community, claims the narrator, is located three miles south of the original Hudson's Bay trading post, where the Heiltsuk moved in about 1870. We see images of the fish and roe. Following are shots of the woman cleaning a basket in the water.

"It's October, the fishing season is almost over. The men are returning from the sea. Fogs close in on the villages." We are told that people are preparing fish for the winter.

The scene shifts to the town: In long-shot we see a street occupied by cars and people. "For a town of 1,200 people, it's quiet along the main street." Next, there are shots of a marina, and the narrator remarks, "Bella Bella has always been a fishing community. In the early days people hunted and fished for what they needed." We see an old woman mending nets. "There was a time for digging clams and a place for gathering seaweed. The men went fishing and the women made the nets." The camera now reveals men assisting the old woman with her nets. Cut to the marina and then to the water seen from the stern of a boat from which nets are being let out.

The skipper of the boat is shown and identified as Ed, a man who owns his own boat. He is contrasted with others who work for the "big company outfits." The narrator tells us that, until recently, men and women have worked at a cannery some thirty miles from Bella Bella. Its foreclosure has led to unemployment and "so Bella Bella are planning to build their own cannery and fish plant."

In mid-range, we are shown a meeting in which non-Natives are speaking to a group of Heiltsuk men assembled at a table. One of the non-Natives is explaining the risks of various locations for the cannery. The narrator speaks: "For each new project the Band council hires a team of consultants to help them in the initial stages, but policy and control are always in the hands of the Band."

Shots of nets are accompanied by remarks about the fishing industry: "Fishing is big business now . . . government has placed restrictions on fishing. This year it was two days a week for salmon." A Heiltsuk-accented man's voice is heard as shots of the nets, full of fish, are being pulled on board the boat. "Two days a week in which to make a living is too limited, so that the joy of being a fisherman, the excitement . . . is relegated to a very secondary position. It's a shaky business proposition."

We see Ed in a portrait shot. He describes the virtues of Band-owned projects whereby profits go back into the reserve and job opportunities can be generated.

Subsequently we see shots of a crane lifting crates from a barge, a forklift moving the boxes, and men loading goods into a truck. The narrator remarks that Thursdays are boat days and describes the isolation of the village, which depends upon imports from without.

Interior shots of a grocery store are voiced over: "The old general store was owned by a White man. Now their own general store is doing a roaring business." In close-up, money changes hands. Then the narrator describes plans for a new complex in which bank, barber shop, and showers are to be housed, as well as plans to build a hotel and bar on the ocean front.

"Bella Bella people have always wanted to be self-sufficient, but it was not until Cecil Reid came home that things got moving." We are shown the bridge of a boat from which Cecil Reid looks to the water. The narrator explains that Reid left a teaching job in Vancouver six years ago to return to his home. From behind his desk, Reid reminisces: "The kind of life that I thought was minimal as far as the standard of living is concerned in White society was not present here."

We are told that Cecil was elected chief councillor. The scene changes to an interior where men are seated around a table, at the head of which sits Cecil. The narrator says that the Band council has attended to basic services—heat, light, garbage disposal, roads, ship-building—and that it is now applying for a logging license. Cecil Reid is heard explaining the Band's "live and let live" arrangement with the provincial New Democratic Party government.[2]

A street scene follows and we see two elderly men walking toward us (the camera). The narrator remarks that the elderly sometimes feel left out and that, at such times, the council seems a long way from "the people." One of the elders remarks, "There's no young people interested to listen to old people today." He expresses distress at not having been invited to the council meeting, at which point Cecil Reid is shown and heard admitting to inadequate participation of the community in its own political affairs: "Yeah, we're not successful yet in involving all our people." A middle-aged man himself, he claims that he does not have the answer to the problem of intergenerational tensions.

A young Heiltsuk woman comments on the council's priorities, saying, "Council has strived for economic development and leaving out the social business, so most of the people don't know what's going on." She describes her own role as part of the effort to inform people and "keep up with the council."

A young man, seated in the doorway of a half-built house, describes the Bella Bella council as slightly more aggressive than others, but he justifies this assertion in terms of the magnitude of problems facing Bella Bella.

A street is shown in which several boys are playing road hockey. Men in work clothes, lunch boxes in hand, approach them from behind. Cecil Reid's voice is heard describing the problems of demographics. He says that the population needs to be stabilized between 1,200 and 1,500 in order for development to be successful, but projections for the village have it doubling this number in about fifteen years.

Ed is seen in interview. He complains about outside interference: "I think we know our own problems better than anyone else." The narrator intervenes and the scene shifts again to the housing project where several men are working on construction, walking on scaffolding and hammering nails into sheets of plywood. The community housing project, funded with government assistance, has, we are told, provided sixty new houses in five years, and in the previous summer, participants painted twenty-three old houses. Still, we are told, "there is a backlog of fifty houses and a need for more government help."

The young man seen earlier, seated in the doorway of an unfinished house, is shown again; now he comments on the importance of owning a house and of the necessity of building it on one's own. The elder previously shown is heard speaking about the housing project: "This is good for the young people, but in the olden days, my time, there was no government help." He describes having spent all his money on his house, which he built himself.

Cut to totem poles, decaying or in disrepair. The narrator remarks, "The Bella Bella were always fine carvers and craftsmen, but with the coming of the White men, most of the old artifacts disappeared, and with them the skills." We see a young man carving and a woman threading beads. "Now, they're trying to revive their ancient culture."

The carver argues for patience, for a slowing down of development: "We have to slow down and get our culture together before going any further . . . 'cause everyone is forgetting what we have as Indians. . . . There's still old people that can help us along." He attributes his knowledge of the language to practice with the elders.

There follows a sequence in a kitchen where two elderly men and a woman are seated, speaking to one another in Heiltsuk. The exterior of the house is shown, and one of the men is seen leaving, cane in hand, and stepping around a motorcycle that is parked on the front porch. The narrator voices over: "Everything changes nowadays."

The narrator describes the tradition of the "old days" when hereditary chiefs provided leadership and wisdom, a role now occupied by young people. Angus (the elderly man we have seen in previous sequences) "still has an important role to play." This is the role of informant to the Dutch linguist who is currently working with the community in an effort to write the first Heiltsuk dictionary. Optimistically, the linguist talks about the possibility of a television station featuring completely Heiltsuk programming.

Cut to a river bed where young boys are fishing. Following this sequence are a series of shots in a classroom where elder women and young children are seen dancing in white blanket capes. "The children are learning their Native dances."

Shots of an explosion, of bulldozers and drills being used on rock, are accompanied by the narrator's description of the construction of a new junior high school and cultural center, planned by the educational committee. We see a group of people (the committee) around a table discussing educational issues, particularly the need to screen teachers who are going to be involved with Heiltsuk children. Their desire to control curriculum and course content is expressed, and the narrator notes that such plans will require the help of "the White man" in the early stages but will eventually be completely taken over by the Bella Bella.

The carver is seen walking on the beach and speaks about the changes in Bella Bella: the development of a logging industry, and the increasing sense in which Bella Bella is no longer isolated. Of the changes, he says, "I don't want to be spoiled. If you're going to keep your culture from going away, you're certainly not going to do it by living like the way the White people live."

In interview, Cecil Reid comments, "I think at the base of every Indian, he is sorry that the total fabric of our existence is no longer available to our young people, but surely there can be a combination of the two worlds so that we have the best of both."

The film cuts back to the young man still seated in the doorway of his house. He remarks, "We can't be backward all our life," and describes the community's present activities as a possibility for fulfillment.

Again the scene returns to the beach, this time in front of houses. Here Angus and his wife are hanging salmon over sticks for smoking and placing them around the fire. They speak Heiltsuk with each other.

Ed and a member of the educational committee both speak about territory, the young woman stating that she does not want Bella Bella to become another small town such as those she spent her childhood in. Ed describes the community as his own home, a place from which he will never move.

The film ends with more shots of Angus dancing around the fire while his wife, still unnamed, claps rhythmically. The two of them are in front of their modest house as the sun is setting on a clear day, the first of the film, whose setting has been almost uniformly grey and overcast. Angus's wife smiles and teasingly prods Angus to dance. They share looks of apparent contentment, then both break into laughter as the film closes.

Other Sides: Power and Ambivalence in the Narratives of Revival

Bella Bella takes the form of documentary pastiche, with an aura of investigative journalism permeating the entire film. Interviews are juxtaposed so as to draw out the latent or intentionally submerged conflicts between community members. These are stitched together with location shots as well as images from staged meetings intended to generate for the viewer a sense of having observed a slice of Bella Bella life sufficiently representative as to allow for an assessment of the total situation. It is not surprising, then, that the opening shots are so reminiscent of Norrish's mapping devices, with aerial photography providing the bird's-eye view so essential to objectivist representation. The subsequent descent into Bella Bella, a literal dropping from the sky onto the treed shore, positions us as viewers within the paradigm of Archimedean perspective, and from those first sequences on, the film claims the authority of pure inscription. The transition between the personal narratives of elderly Heiltsuk and the younger, development-oriented men, themselves at odds with many of the female speakers, then provides an ongoing pendular movement that encourages viewers to interpret the film as "balanced."

Bella Bella shares with *Box of Treasures* a basic narrative line. It tells the tale of a group of Native people, bound by language and history, as they struggle to survive in the contemporary Euro-Canadian context. Its centerpiece is the community's increasing control over social, cultural, and economic processes, all of which, until recently, have been almost entirely determined by federal and provincial policy. The film sets up a set of oppositions between Native and Euro-Canadian cultures, and between a semimythic pre-contact era and the post-contact period. The "epitomizing event," the moment of rupture, in that movement between temporal planes is not legislative, as it is for the Kwakiutl, but consists in the very arrival of Whites. It is contact that initiates the degenerative process for the Bella Bella, which carries the possibility of absolute loss: loss of material culture, knowledge, and skills. Accordingly, current revivalist endeavors are direct repudiations of external involvement, except at the level of resource allocation. Although potlatching is not central to this narrative—and indeed potlatching was not a highly developed ritual complex in the Heiltsuk culture of the immediate post-contact years—there are scenes of children learning to dance that resonate well with those in *Box of Treasures*. Similarly, the indigenous school programs and the cooperative efforts to produce a Heiltsuk dictionary are directly parallel to those depicted in the Kwakiutl productions.

The most obvious differences between *Bella Bella* and the Center-produced films is the degree to which the former admits to cultural deterioration, and the extent to which it problematizes cultural authenticity. Cecil Reid's claim that every Indian regrets the loss "of the total fabric of our existence" is the most extreme statement of this kind. But the tensions between elders and youths, the carver's admonition to other Band members about proceeding too quickly with development, the obvious and seemingly gendered frictions between education activists and local government officials—all point out the deep pain and unevenness of transition. The narrative of *Bella Bella* is torn between what are, for the modernist viewer, two contradictory realities: the fact of a revival that is being pursued via economic policies aimed at self-sufficiency, and the fact that this revival may entail the assumption of new forms of social organization, some of them inimical to traditionalist visions of Native communality. The contradictions between older and newer practice are most visible in the process of government itself, where historically prior forms of leadership, including inherited titles and patterns of usufruct, appear at odds with the elected councils that must negotiate with external governments for resources and basic services.

However, like virtually all films of this period, *Bella Bella* accepts the necessity of acknowledging and even corroborating historical continuity. It must thus extract from these battling factions and contradictory images a single source of narrative continuity, something that binds both the fractious individuals of this economically depressed community and the many generations that have passed before. This Arachnean thread takes the form of an essential moral position, a universal value transcending the changes from a "nomadic" existence to a sedentary life, from subsistence to commercial fishing—namely, the desire for self-sufficiency, which also entails the power to encompass external forces. In some sense, then, the tradition of the Heiltsuk becomes a tradition of centeredness.

The structure of the film's narrative is telling in this regard. Opening with a scene on the beach where two elderly Heiltsuk (Angus and his wife) are gutting fish and laying them out to dry, it closes with them dancing "traditional" dances, literally embodying Heiltsuk practical history in their every act. The film returns to these two throughout the narrative and constructs their voices as the legitimate critics of all that is happening in Bella Bella. To the extent that an appearance of objectivity is important, it is significant that the legitimacy of the elderly couple is generated by and through other people/characters within the film itself, and that the artist, rather than the narrator, actually voices the film's position, though the two converge perfectly on this point. For, insofar as the film is concerned, it is Angus and his wife whom the carver invokes when he says, "There's still old people that can help us along." Present in the end and in the beginning, Angus and his wife are the human frame for the film's long and sometimes awkward narration. They are the personifications of Heiltsuk tradition, that which transcends the narrative of development on every level. And Angus's remonstrations about the need to build one's own house with one's own labor express that ethic of autonomy which the film posits as the essential core of Heiltsuk identity.

Implicitly, Angus disapproves of the community's reliance on government assistance: federally funded housing projects, government guaranteed loans for mechanized and commercialized fishing projects, external expertise in planning, and so forth. Yet for the male youths of the film, these things are precisely the vehicles of revival. The contradiction is integral, as these conflicts between the elders' perspective and the young men's vision are manifestations of the opposition between "tradition" and "modernity" that orients the ideology of Western modernist culture. *Bella Bella* attempts to mediate that opposition in the terms that Heiltsuk culture provides for understanding self-other relations. There remain questions about the level at which this simulated Heiltsuk perspective is being carried out, but the affinities between Heiltsuk cosmology and the film's point of view are both striking and instructive.

According to recent ethnography, Heiltsuk cosmology is articulated in an elaborate set of myths and ritual practices having to do with giving and receiving. The logic that operates within this universe of exchange is one in which the Heiltsuk people encounter potential enemies and nullify their power by making others the recipients of gifts, because receiving always entails a position of inferiority. The obligation of such gifts—their implicit but inescapable debt—is, of course, not unique to the Heiltsuk; and Marcel Mauss's *The Gift* was but the first of many attempts to theorize the logic of gift-giving on a universal plane. In any case, the Heiltsuk construe these exchange relations as ones in which the Heiltsuk partake of the power of others in a process of inversion, whereby outsiders are consumed through the giving of gifts whose return they necessitate (Harkin 1989). The Heilt-suk share this set of symbols and concepts of self-other relations with other groups on the Northwest Coast, and ethnographic accounts indicate that these particular notions of consumption are as integral to potlatching as they are to the winter cannibal dances of different Bands. Nonetheless, there seem to be important differences both in the historical traditions of intercultural relations and in contemporary political practice. The Kwakiutl featured in *Box of Treasures* see Euro-Canadian outsiders as a powerful threat that must be evaded and opposed. To the extent possible, the Kwakiutl (at least those at Alert Bay) eschew—literally spit out—foreign cultural forces that have already invaded the body politic through enforced consumption during periods of missionization and State schooling. In contrast, the younger Heiltsuk of *Bella Bella* differentiate between spiritual and sociological outsiders, attributing far less power to the latter. Rather than opposition through distanciation, they raise the possibility of resistance through consumption and inversion.

Even so, the tendency to see all of Northwest Coast culture in terms of a single condensing symbol, consumption, needs to be mitigated by a recognition that relations between different groups, as well as those between people and an extrahuman world, are also understood along the axes of movement and stasis, insubstantiality and solidity, malleability and sameness, and so on—not all of which are comprehensible in the idiom of consumption. Nonetheless, much ethnography and much Native self-representation accept the centrality of ritual consumption in Northwest Coast cultures. We therefore need to recognize the degree to which all of these representations are mediated by other representations in virtually endless sequences of invocation and connotation. Oppositions between the filmic representations produced by non-Native ethnographers and efforts at Native self-representation must always confront the fact of mutual inscription and the processes by which people naturalize, as their own, the images that more powerful others have projected onto them. And it is in such an intertextual context that this film's play on consumption must be understood.

For the people of Bella Bella (of *Bella Bella*) to see the present relations with non-Native people as a source of power, they must conceive of themselves not as recipients of aid or gifts but as donors. Thus, the Canadian State's usurpation of aboriginal territory and fishing rights is invoked in the redefinition of Native/non-Native relations as ones in which the debtor is the State and not the Band. Confiscation itself becomes a receipt of goods, if not of gifts, and the debt of repayment is therefore still outstanding. Loss here is not the irretrievable loss of salvage ethnography's linear continuum but, rather, a kind of interregnum between the moment of loss (i.e., of giving) and the moment of repayment.

In abstracted terms, this is the position expressed by the young men of Bella Bella, and the film gives these voices considerable time to articulate that view. Angus's claim to moral superiority stems from the fact that he has received little from government agencies, but the young men are still heirs to the debt owed by the State and, as such, can still claim an ethically grounded power. Ultimately, it is Cecil Reid, the successful bureaucrat who has lived inside and outside of the Band's world, who seems to present the film with its most pressing dilemmas. Insofar as the film is concerned—and this view is echoed in a number of the women's comments—Reid's embrace of capitalist development, his willingness to negotiate with State representatives, his aggressive ambition for modernity, all threaten to undermine his Nativeness. He is far more difficult to judge within the terms of Heiltsuk cosmology, because he himself asks to be judged in terms of the dominant Euro-Canadian society. Coupled with his obvious power within this community, these factors make him a source of conflict and the object of a certain resentment that is tempered, but not completely mitigated, by respect. We are then left with a sense of deep strain, a sense of a community rent by disagreement but bound by desire, trying to hold together despite unemployment, poor infrastructure, and horrific poverty.

Conflict as Truth-Value:
The Possibilities of Polyphony

It might be tempting to differentiate between films like *Bella Bella* and *Box of Treasures* on the basis of candidness, explaining tensions and ambivalence through reference to the subject-position of the films' producers and directors. The conflicts of *Bella Bella* and the film's refusal to valorize all of the Band's individual efforts as part of a common project would then be dissolved in the fact of the filmmakers' distance from the community. But this would require a blatantly essentialist vision of cultural selves and others, a complete naturalization of Native/non-Native categories, and the expunging of all difference within them. In other words, we would have to complete the representational moves of colonial discourse, effacing class, gender, personal history, and ethnic affinity in race. This is a strategy that I find philosophically untenable—and politically immobilizing. Yet the assertion of difference should not lead to an assumption that conflict itself is a sign of the real. And this assumption is exactly what realist documentary film has tended to promote. We assume that the appearance of conflict or contradiction between voices is an index of candidness, proof that things have not been scripted. Too much order, too perfect a corroboration, suggests falsification to most viewers. Watching *Box of Treasures*, with its melodious repetition, leaves no doubt that the film was largely scripted, that interviews were filmed repeatedly, and that scenes were staged (though none of these factors necessarily diminishes the validity of what is actually communicated). But *Bella Bella* wants its viewers to believe that the filmmakers are presenting an unmediated slice of Band life, with all its rough edges and intimate irritations visible. The fact of these blemishes is itself supposed to be indicative of the film's purity.

However, direct-address narration, the town meetings, and the implicit interview format of the narration all mark *Bella Bella* as a carefully constructed film. It is no more immediate than *Box of Treasures*, although the question of mediation should not be confused with veracity; indeed, the film's relative accuracy is still open to question and confirmation. The narrator of *Bella Bella* cannot or does not claim an experiential authority as does the narrator of *Box of Treasures*. She defers to Native exegetes and, somewhat ironically, has her authority as an objective observer returned to her when (and because) Native voices clash. In *Box of Treasures* the narrator's authority is buttressed in a different way, through the corroborating or demonstrative voicings of other people. In both films, a literal polyphony is at work; in *Box of Treasures* that polyphony is harmonious, but in *Bella Bella* it is a source of discord. However, in neither case does the fact of polyphony undermine the authority of the narrator's "I," nor does it signal anything specific about that narrator's (and the filmmakers') subject-position. Indeed, the euphoric expectations of polyphony as a politically empowering representational strategy are quietly but pointedly betrayed—or at least reined in—by these two films.

Within poststructuralist anthropological theory, there has been a tendency to assume that the inscription of differing voices within a single text will destabilize and thereby democratize the representational process. But the problem of the author—the author's authority—is not so easily dealt with. The formalism that animates so much poststructuralist theory is abundantly clear here, and until the question of staging is dealt with, until the author's agency in juxtaposition is confronted in its substantive implications, the discourse of ethnographic poetics will remain severed from representation's other side—namely, its politics. This entails, of course, critically acknowledging the institutional and economic contexts in which academics operate. If a film like *Bella Bella* succeeds in representing, which is to say evoking, the sociopolitical realities of life in a particular coastal community, it does so through careful mediation and not through an escape from mediation. There is no possibility for a pure and total presence of the world here.

The Legitimacy of Memory

It is instructive to realize that, for all their differences of narrational strategy, and despite the very different institutional circumstances of their production, these films are directly parallel in their deployment of memory and tradition as the vehicles of legitimation. Remembrance is central to the revival process not merely as a measure of difference or, indeed, of deterioration, but as source of legitimacy for present political practice. Both *Box of Treasures* and *Bella Bella* are overtly concerned with "tradition," and with the ways in which it is transmitted, encoded, and preserved. There is great ambivalence here, for the films speak to a textually oriented audience and employ the standards of verification and textual citation that govern literate discourses in the university industries of cultural production. At the same time, however, they reject the inscriptions of cultural outsiders in favor of aurally transmitted lore and the recollections of Band elders. The actual speech of elders then becomes the ultimate vehicle of tradition: voice conveying an embodied history that must yet be textualized (on audiovisual tapes, and in books) if it is to survive. Perhaps most ironically, the elders being interviewed in these films are themselves the products of the most intensive missionization and State schooling processes. Thus, in many cases, they are being asked to recall other people's—their parents' and grandparents'—memories. They are presented as the repositories of that history which ethnographers, historians, and roguish travelers elided, and to which they themselves were denied practical access. But their memories, unlike those of their parents and their grandparents, are completely internalized, having been supplemented by none of the material *aides de mémoire*—the artifacts—that supplemented the recollections of those before. When in *Box of Treasures* the elders are brought together in the context of the new museum and surrounded by the newly repatriated objects of ritual practice— the masks and potlatching goods, photographs and objects of daily existence—the alienation of social memory and the objects in which it is embedded are finally overcome. The tales told before a video camera become materially real on a new level, both for the elders, to whom objects return like bearers of a past that they recall almost vicariously, and for those watching (whether at the opening ceremony or in the auditoriums where the film is being screened).

The recording of elders' remembrances, and the rendering of these recollections as collective memories, is part of the enactment of revival. But revival here is not a unilinear narrative. It contains and maintains the possibility of extinction as a motivating force, for which the remembrance of cultural near-destruction is exemplary in every sense of the word. There is no unequivocally happy ending but merely the desire to achieve victory in the face of great odds. Both regeneration and degeneration are scripted into revival's narrative, which is less a "future history" than a series of potential scenarios. Thus, if one says that Native revival movements have succeeded in creating a counterhistory, on the basis of a countermemory, it is in this sense of multiply directed but still limited "future histories."

Since ethnography, like history, entails the inscription of a generalized if not unitary memory from diverse individual recollections, the efforts to re-tell Native (Kwakiutl, Nishga, Git'ksan, Tsimshian, Tlingit, etc.) history from Native perspectives are basically efforts to generate a countermemory: in effect, a counterhegemony. This countermemory may actually entail a dif-ferent temporality than that of the dominant narrative; or it may be com-posed of several different temporalities or be oriented around different points of origin and differentiation. In analyzing the *Annales* school, Nathan Wachtel (1986) has observed the degree to which historiography itself has changed in its conception of history as various oppressed groups have emerged to oppose official histories during the twentieth century. Wachtel claims that the *Annales* school reconstrued history, redefining lin-earity and chronology as problem and thus opening up the possibility that history itself—the history narrativized as linearity—would be understood as something composed of many distinct, perhaps even conflicting temporali-ties (1986:218). Wachtel had in mind working-class and French provincial or ethnic groups, but his comments are germane to the Northwest Coast as well. In the past two decades, ethnography has reiterated Wachtel's asser-tion: that representations are always mediations and that dominant represen-tations inevitably elide differences of experience (not yet a prediscursive ex-perience, as discussed in Chapter 2), including the lived experience of time and history, which are themselves structured by relations of power and placement. Now, Native groups are commanding the apparatus of represen-tation in order to objectify those memories that, until recently, had re-mained in the recesses of individual consciousnesses. Totalitarian regimes have always recognized that it is remembrance of this sort that ultimately threatens their power. Accordingly, they frequently attempt to realign calen-drical time, to create new moments of historical epitomization, and to con-trol historical representation in all of its manifestations (Munn 1992:33). Similarly, counterhegemonic movements can legitimate and consolidate themselves by organizing their own self-narrations around different epito-mizing moments, by valorizing objects with specifically charged historical value, or by reenacting modes of temporality that have been relinquished or denied for various reasons. This is, I think, what is entailed by the revivals of different aesthetic and ritual practices. Not only are objects reclaimed and reproduced, but because those objects are the externalizations of particular temporal orientations and, indeed, the vehicles by which those orientations are produced and inhabited, repatriation literally restores an other time (cf. Munn 1983, 1992; Miller 1987).

This process is explicitly dramatized in *Box of Treasures* in the scene where an elder woman is actually speaking her mind in front of a video camera, which will "preserve" her memories and stories for future generations. Here the videotape becomes analogous to the storage box after which the film is titled: a receptacle for memory, as the woman herself has been these many hungry years. Because, as Walter Benjamin wrote, "*memory* creates the chain of tradition which passes a happening from generation to generation" (1969b:98; original emphasis), the video and, indeed, *Box of Treasures, Bella Bella*, and other such films are part of the process of transmitting, some would say "inventing" (Hobsbawm and Ranger 1983), tradition.

Within these films, certain concepts and images serve an evocative purpose, and because they circulate in whole chains of signification, a single image can carry within itself an entire historical scenario. This is not the interiorized and alienated remembrance of a Proust, for whom subjective experiences of sensual delight or repulsion are the only vehicles of recollection, but a highly collectivized imagery (visual and aural) of associative recall. Such collective remembrance need not imply a reified social consciousness, and individual appropriations of, and responses to, particular images will inevitably vary. Rather, as Roger Bastide (1970, cited in Wachtel 1986:215) argues, collective memory is "a system of interrelating individual memories" whose parameters are those of the social group, and whose instruments are public images or shared objects.

In the contemporary films about various Northwest Coast Bands, the potlatch, salmon fishing, and the land are not merely loci of social practice, nor focal points for social organization, though they are all of these things as well. They are mnemonic devices, signposts for the remembrance of a time when these things were locally controlled. Nor is it incidental that many of these films—perhaps most notably *The Land Is the Culture*—posit land, or fishing territories, as the foundation of identity. The importance of territory includes but also exceeds its importance as the means of production in a hunting and gathering economy. It is the iconic ground on which memory is spatialized and embedded. The landscape itself is a signifier of history and lived time.

In *Blunden Harbour* (discussed in Chapter 4), an introductory creation story recalls how a "supernatural" being assumes human identity through settlement at a particular location. This mythological identification of humanness with territorial attachment is typical throughout the Northwest Coast (and in many other areas as well) and hence the current struggle over land-title is a fight both for living space and for cultural survival. As Joanne Richardson (1982) says of Bella Coola origin myths, this embedding of history in space is a magical and performative act whereby "the miracle is to make it solid." Gloria Cranmer-Webster expresses a similar conception of identity when she describes assimilation as departure from the island community. For anthropologists now battling the image of the island, which has long been the very symbol of ahistoricity, Cranmer-Webster's description must appear vexingly ironic. But it is no less poignant for all that; adopting Euro-Canadian ways is for her a kind of "going away" from Kwakiutl history. But the Kwakiutl vision is not unique in this respect; indeed, it is the shared concern with territory that permitted the multi-Band "Union of B.C. Chiefs" to collaborate in the 1975 production of *The Land Is the Culture*.

In his ground-breaking treatise on social memory, *La mémoire collective* (1968), Maurice Halbwachs describes the dialectic between place and identity as a means of projecting identity onto a place and then reforming identity in response to the limits of space. He writes, "Once a group fits into a part of space, it remakes it in its own image, but at the same time it bends and adapts to physical things that resist it" (1968:118). In this manner, the imbuing of landscape with historical significance is as much a projection from the present as is the future, and the landscape (and other *aides de mémoire*) then becomes a vehicle for constructing a relationship to past and future histories (Munn 1992:43–44). Wachtel suggests, as have many others, that those exiled from their own place carry with them images of that place, either in texts or in photographs, culturally specific maps, or other tokens—and that these then serve the function of a symbolic space (Wachtel 1986:212). There can be no doubt that the reservation system constitutes a kind of exile, an exile without wandering. In this context, films become special kinds of collective images. Like the texts of exiles, they are also the means to recall space, and hence the time, of former residence. But unlike other inscriptions, films claim to be immediate presentations of that place. And their claim to immediacy also allows them to present the spectral shadows of objects that are held elsewhere (often in museums thousands of miles away) as being, in some sense, the real things. Thus, films that are composed of iconic and symbolic image systems often seem to offer the most perfect vehicle of remembrance. Their assertion of pure presence and their narratives of renewal bind a remembered past presence and a present absence with the possibility of reconstruction through repossession.

Like the phantasmic memory palaces of which Frances Yates writes in *The Art of Memory* (1966), films provide—literally project—spatial images that anchor more complex narrative (memorial) constructions. Some of these, such as land or fishing territories and museums or cultural centers, are literally spatial, whereas others, such as the potlatch, are symbolically spatial in that they constitute a context for action. According to Yates, the art of Western European memory had its origins during or before the period of classical oratory and rested on the principles of the mnemonic (Mnemosyne, the rememberer, was mother of the Muses). In its classical formulation, mnemonics worked by "imprint[ing] on the memory a series of *loci* or places" (1966:13). As Frances Yates points out, by the medieval period "the art of memory was a creator of imagery" (1966:91). Although she notes the distinction between externalized representations and mental pictures, she also suggests that since the Middle Ages, imagery has served didactic purposes through its association with memorization, whereby memorization is a kind of *imagination* (Yates 1966). Clearly, this is a history of Western modes of consciousness, but Native peoples are not immune to the developments in Euro–North American thought and practice. Indeed, they have been rigorously schooled in them, and hence we can trace resonances between Halbwachs's universalist notions of the spatialization of memory and the mnemonic localization of memory that Yates describes with respect to our own consideration of Native Northwest Coast revival.

In all of the films discussed here, space and place (a strip of rain forest, a beach front, a museum in which "past and present are blended") are mnemonic devices as well as projected remembrances of cultural origin. Their invocation is the invocation of a past that legitimates present practice. In all cases, the physical location of a community and its spatial separation from non-Native villages are important and cultural revival is phrased as a kind of return, a going home in which time is spatialized and space temporalized. This is equally true of the Heiltsuk of Bella Bella, who understand resistance as a kind of relation with outsiders, as it is of the Kwakiutl, who cling to the islandness of their community.

It is important, of course, to recognize that the space and time of film does not, or need not, correspond to that of experiential reality. As Hugo Munsterberg (1916) argued, film is able to overcome the dimensions of space and time through the construction of an independent narrative space and time.[3] Indeed, the ethnographic films of the Northwest Coast, and almost all films, use one to evoke the other, while surreptitiously collapsing the two in order to buttress the films' very power of evocation. Recognizing the degree to which the *durée* of film differs from the *durée* of lived time, itself a malleable and differentiated continuum, is crucial for an understanding of film as mediation. If any doubt remains as to the rhetorical nature of film's transparency, the divergence between lived and filmed time should put an end to such doubt.

Concluding Remarks: In Praise of Real "Talkies"

The temporalization of space in these films is a product of recollection and narrative, both of which are appropriately condensed in the Kwakwala term "u'mista" (as discussed above). Whereas films of the later salvage period

were concerned with memory as a relationship to a fixed past, recent films
are concerned with a kind of remembering, in the sense of putting back
together or gathering up again. Thus, contemporary filmmaking reflects
and is analogous to broader social processes in which the repatriation
of artifacts and the reclamation of land are the centers of political emancipation.

Teresa de Lauretis has argued that, in a general sense, film is inherently
narrative and that this narrativity is organized around Western European
principles of remembrance and desire. De Lauretis herself is not intent upon
theorizing these processes in culturally specific ways, but, qualified in this
way, her insights do provide a means of comprehending the workings of
cinema in contemporary Western cultures. She writes that "the operations of
narrativity construct a full and unified visual space in which events take place
as a drama of vision and a *memory spectacle*. The film *remembers* (fragments
and makes whole again) the object of vision for the spectator" (1984:67, my
emphasis). In an important respect, the concepts of memory spectacle and
remembrance can entail different orientations toward the past. Spectacle
clearly implies and necessitates alienation, and is the proper locus and object
of voyeurism. Not surprisingly, then, theories of cinema that posit film as
spectacle emphasize the viewer's impotent desire and the tendency toward
a reifying, often sexually fetishizing gaze (Cowie 1990; Mulvey 1975; Friedberg 1990). Although de Lauretis is interested in theorizing cinema as a
social technology, her understanding of the memory spectacle seems to me
to capture the heart of salvage ethnography's representations, and much of
the ethnographic documentary now being produced for television (witness
the swashbuckling antics and lurid savagery of *Ring of Fire* [1988] or the
self-acknowledged salvage ethos of Granada's *Disappearing World*). With its
fabulous exotica and its endlessly essentializing reifications, salvage ethnography functions to maintain distance between its audience and its subject
(object). Its condition of possibility is the curious, often desirous gaze of a
self in search of its Other. But recent Northwest Coast filmmaking, and
much other documentary of the contemporary era, differs in being part of a
performative re-creation. We therefore need to acknowledge the degree to
which films can be part of a process of enactment and not merely of voyeuristic consumption (Schechner 1985). This means comprehending the
viewing context not merely as the momentary period of actual screening but
as something co-extensive with the social and historical relationships within
which viewing is possible. And just as theories of consumption must include
a consideration of production if they are to deconstruct the fetishism of exchange that Marx so brilliantly demonstrated, so theories of cinema (ethnographic cinema, Hollywood, and the avant garde included), must also attend to this total process of what Stephen Heath and de Lauretis (1980)

have rightly called a "social technology." Only in this broader sense of the viewing situation can we understand revival film as part of political practice, rather than as the pure reflection of an ontologically privileged—that is, a "more real"—activity.

However, one must further ask how the historical transformation of filmic narratives relates to the anthropology of the same period. For if it is true, as I have argued, that institutional contexts, restructured financing, and technological advances permitted stylistic diversification in documentary cinema generally, it is still necessary to ask why ethnographic film had the trajectory that it did. Throughout this book, I have attempted to show how film styles manifested certain aspects of the social and political milieu in which they were produced. But, as stated in Chapter 2, this effort should not be interpreted as a statement about film's reflectionist nature. Rather, I have been arguing that both film and other modes of representation are part of a single discursive formation, and that they share the same ideological ground. Again, a discursive formation is not a homogeneous thing, and however successful a hegemony may be, there are always traces of other remembrances, counterhegemonic images, and alterior visions. Whether they become organized as they have been on the Northwest Coast is quite another question. But anthropology of the past two decades has given us ample reason for concluding that there is no perfectly totalized society, nor any homogeneous social consciousness.

Yet, if this is so, and if ethnography managed to deny the fact of heterogeneity for so long, one wants to ask what factors could have precipitated the surrender (still a very partial surrender) of the seamless and teleologically oriented narratives of modernist totality. In part, the answer to this question lies in ethnography's own methodological tradition, in its fieldwork imperative, and in its Cartesian privileging of the subject as a locus of knowing. In considering the status of ethnographic representations (filmic or otherwise), the issue is not whether representations ever partake of any absolute reality beyond or outside the frames of mediation—clearly they cannot—but to what degree they are founded upon a supposed immediate experience. Anthropologists are expected to go to "the field" and to see for themselves, experience for themselves, what life is like at a given moment in a given community's history. They reconstruct these encounters and experiences in textual form, according to some vaguely statistical criterion of accuracy or truth. But the mediated nature of experience itself is rarely questioned to the extent that it necessitates an alternative methodology. Experience remains central as the locus of ethnographic knowing, and the authority of the observational subject finds its apotheosis here in the ethnographer's assumption of a vantage point that is at once historically unique and uniquely objective (externality being conflated here with objectivity).[4]

Ultimately, however, the valorization of subjective knowledge must cede to its own logic and grant informants the same authority that ethnographers, invoking subjective experience, use to assert their special position. Ethnographers who have relied on the participant side of participant-observation to ground their claims to (power/)knowledge must now defer to other participants, other subjects. As much as anything else, it is this fact that explains anthropology's recent concern with the inscription of other voices, with the dialogics of anthropology, and with Native ethnography (see, for example, Bruner 1986; Clifford 1986a; Crapanzano 1980; Dwyer 1987; Marcus and Fischer 1986). This concern has, however, been accompanied by a simultaneous reclamation of "objectivity" (in the sense of externality) as a cardinal value in fieldwork, the more so as the former argument gains ground. Much contemporary ethnographic film is marked by this unraveling of ethnographic authority. What we see in films like *Bella Bella* is, of course, achieved with much greater sophistication in a film like David Marshall's *N!ai: Story of a !Kung Woman 1952–1978* (1980), where the pains of social transformation are heard in the many conflicting voices and often cruel antagonisms between characters. But *N!ai* is not a revival film, and there is a far more cynical tone to it than to *Bella Bella,* where the use of polyphonics is always constrained by the exigencies of a particular political project. The implications of ethnography, however, are laid bare in different ways by either film. *N!ai* implicates the viewer in the history of degradation to which the film's characters have been subject. And in the section about the making of *The Gods Must Be Crazy* (which is never announced as such) every viewer is forced to confront, in visceral terms, the objectifications and mortifications entailed by primitivist cinema. Such explicit demands are not made upon viewers watching *Bella Bella,* but *Box of Treasures* assaults every museum patron with accusations of complicity.

This is dialogics with a vengeance. In the case of Northwest Coast ethnography, the very fact of speaking is a refutation of ethnographic representations prophesying doom. Moreover, the entrance of Native ethnographers and filmmakers into the ethnographic arena is a major factor in the development of alternative film strategy, even in those films being produced outside of the Native North American context. Earlier I discussed Marshall and Blue's *Kenya Boran* (1974) as one instance of film in which voices other than that of the narrator can be heard, and the same strategy can be seen in all of the Northwest Coast films discussed in this chapter. More radical formal experimentations, such as Yvonne Rainer's feminist tour de force *Film About a Woman Who . . .* or Robert Gardner's ambiguously beautiful production, *Forest of Bliss* (1985), have generally been absent from Nativist ethnographic productions. The primary objectives of the latter have been communicative, and, accordingly, the films tend to accept the discursive traditions of dominant ethnographic cinema in order to explore its rhetorical (practical) possibilities in immediate battles with the State.

Whether this assertion of "Other" voices finally escapes the binarisms of salvage ethnography is a separate issue and, as I have already pointed out, it would be naive to assume that contemporary ethnographic film, including that produced by or for Native communities, is exempt from the problems of cultural essentialism. Many Nativist films set their problem against an assumed Native identity, but for the most part their narratives are more specific than that, focusing on a particular community in a particular linguistic tradition. They do not completely reject the structural oppositions of salvage ethnography so much as mitigate them. And, as was suggested in reference to the images of the potlatch, the ironies of ethnography are such that many of the endeavors at self-representation are naturalizations of salvage ethnography's most blatant reifications. Many of the recent films valorize a singular difference rather than multiple and conflicting differences, and slip from a critique of salvage ethnography to a positive or inverted revaluation of salvage ethnography's imagery. The deployment of old Curtis photographs is but one example of this kind of irony, and one sees it again in the repetition of certain tropes, especially those concerned with aesthetic production and ritual activity.

But essentialism is often a strategic move, a self-conscious strategy by which other essentialisms can be engaged. Angela Carter takes up this issue with zeal in her provocative book *The Sadeian Woman and the Ideology of Pornography* (1978). In an implicit attack on Laura Mulvey's (1975) demand for an end to visual pleasure, Carter argues that reifying objectifications cannot be overcome through a retreat from objectification, for such is the condition of all language and all representation. Rather, they must be confronted through aggressively self-conscious self-objectifications in which the object is, in some senses, a projection of a subjectivity. Accordingly, this subjectivity resists being reduced to and by the viewer's gaze. Without completely accepting Carter's claim of autonomy for the self-objectifying subject, I suggest that Nativist cinema's reproduction of salvage ethnographic images must not be dismissed so much as questioned and then judged on individual bases. Recent filmmaking efforts have injected ethnographic cinema with other perspectives, with a much-needed sense of historical heterogeneity and representational accountability. One can speak here of a new insistence upon responsibility, in the dual sense that filmmakers are being asked to respond directly to other subjects, and that they then accept the political and ethical burden of representation. Nor, however, should one underestimate the historicity of cinema and the kinds of intertextual determinations that underlie it.

As John Berger so cogently reminds us, we are speaking of "ways of seeing" and these always entail "ways of looking" (Berger and Mohr 1982). This book, from the beginning, has been an attempt to explicate the social and historical forces that determine the ways of looking at Northwest Coast people. Deconstructing the claims to transparency and absolute authority that documentary film has made, and exploring the relationships between images and their contexts of production, I have tried to reveal the specific historicity of ethnographic cinema, while limiting discussion to a relatively small body of material. In the end, I am unprepared to grant any ultimate authority to any of these representations. However, this is not a relinquishing of judgment. The films dicussed here are not of equal value and do not all have the same significance for anthropology or for practical politics. And, insofar as it escapes the trite but dangerous simplifications and reifications of Northwest Coast and other Native cultures, Nativist ethnographic cinema succeeds in improving on its predecessors. Remembering, it creates "new worlds from fragments."

Notes

1. Much of my sense of how these new artists' communities arose grows out of my experiences as a resident of Vancouver, which is a center for such activity. I have also learned much about that process through personal friendships with carvers and jewelers.

2. At the time the film was shot, the New Democratic Party (NDP), a democratic socialist organization and one of Canada's three main political parties at both the provincial and federal levels, was in power. The party's tenure was short-lived, however, and throughout the 1980s, the right-wing Social Credit Party held office with little contest, except for a brief period in 1983, when strikes by a coalition of labor, women's organizations, Natives' groups, and educational workers threatened to topple it. In 1991, the NDP was returned to power in B.C.'s Legislative Assembly.

3. Munsterberg assumed the universality and absolute reality of time. His blindness to the cultural relativity of lived time need not, however, undermine the claim that filmic time differs from lived time. In fact, the disparities between Western filmic time and other cultural times, and the implications of those disparities for film viewing and cultural practice in different places, are subjects in need of further research. But Munsterberg's essential observations stand uncontested, and I am grateful to Ian Jarvie for drawing my attention to this historically significant but sadly neglected text.

4. See Renato Rosaldo (1986) for a discussion of this epistemological positioning and its inscription into ethnographic texts through the image of the tent.

6

Wider Angles:
Toward a Conclusion

Vision undergoes re-vision; intention, symbol, reality are the factors that undergo
constant change in the appearance of any art form.
—Stan Vanderbeek

Toward a Theoretical Conclusion

IN SILENT FILMS, those oddly literary productions of cinema's infancy, closure was announced in a blunt title that proclaimed the end of a fantasy.
Concluding a book about film is a somewhat more complicated endeavor,
particularly with a book like the present one, which ranges over so much
time, covers so many films, and tries to trace the connections between seemingly disparate phenomena. This book has been an attempt to explore the
historical relationships between specific representational strategies and the
institutional contexts of their production. Accordingly, I have looked at particular cinematic texts in terms of the ideological narratives that they tacitly
embodied, as well as the structural and ideological milieux from which they
emerged. Believing that ethnographic film is at once related to and distinguished from other forms of inscription, but that the differences between
them are to be found in the history rather than the ontology of film, I have
argued for a historicist genre analysis of ethnographic cinema.

I want now to pose questions that were asked of individual films in a
broader arena, where the images of ethnographic film circulate and interact
with those of Hollywood and the international news media to form part of a
public culture. In many regards, this desire to open up the book's theoretical project to issues beyond the realm of purely academic interest is part
of a quest to understand the effectivity or, to use Michel Foucault's (1980)
term, the "productivity" of anthropology and its imageries. It is an effort to

understand how scholarly discourses are involved in the creation of popular culture and how they inform the consciousness of an era. Before doing so, however, I want to review some of the main arguments and discussions of the preceding chapters.

Earlier, I asked how meaning enters the image. And perhaps as much as any other question, this one lays the foundation for a critical visual anthropology. For in the moment that one acknowledges the constructedness of images and the relativity of their realism (Roemer 1971), in the moment that one admits film to be something other than what Stanley Cavell (1973) calls the "world viewed," it becomes necessary to ask what ideological project is being encoded or instilled into cinematic and other pictorial texts. This is particularly true of documentary images, which succeed precisely to the extent that they are able to deny their own status as fabrications or mediations. Yet, as the phenomenologists (from Schutz to Geertz) remind us, to speak about the mediations of any cultural system, one must necessarily speak about double mediations, for "the world" is really multiple and always already coded. As Angela Carter (1978) says of the body, it comes to us through history. Not merely a social construction (Berger and Luckmann 1966), it is a set of discursive representations and productions that both evolve and compete for ideological hegemony. That hegemony is, in essence, the appearance of reality, and in stating as much, we immediately confront the broader issue of seeing in general.

A consideration of ethnographic film history has both permitted and demanded that we explore the historicity of vision itself. Because realism entails—first and foremost—assumptions about the *appearance of reality,* a critical consideration of realist aesthetics is always about more than the style and content of a particular representation. It is also about the perceptual consciousness of viewers, viewers who will validate or reject the image's claims to truth on the basis of a supposed correspondence between it and the *ordered world.* As Stan Vanderbeek has remarked, "[S]eeing is the real illusion" (1971:227). We might say that the realist aesthetic is mimetically linked to the reigning forms of looking and apprehension in a given era, although this other dimension of realism is often neglected in the criticism of ethnographic or other inscriptions. Nonetheless, an anthropological critique of realism must ultimately challenge both representational aesthetics and the tacit dimensions of vision itself.

Such an understanding of anthropological purpose owes much to surrealism and, more especially, to its recent rehabilitation by contemporary anthropologists (Clifford 1988b; Marcus and Fischer 1986:122–125). Although this approach has many detractors, I agree with those critics who see the surrealist impulse of ironic and decentering juxtaposition as an integral component of the ethnographic project. Surrealism refuses us the tempting but tautological recourse to prediscursive or precultural worlds as a way of surreptitiously legitimating our representations. In so doing, it insists upon epistemological humility but also on the necessity of constant self-criticism at every moment of the perceptual/analytical/representational process.

Readers will recall these issues from an earlier discussion (see Chapter 2) about objectivity and "superobjectivity," and the ambiguous rhetoric of reflexivity in contemporary debates about the status of ethnographic representations. There is no need to repeat that argument here, but it seems to me that the seemingly insatiable desire to corroborate or undermine the authenticity of images, to explain them with reference to the prefilmic moment, or to provide supplementary information about the extrafilmic context is understandable in this context: as an ironic containment by realist aesthetics, which admits of the camera's limitation only to reinscribe the limitless perspective of the interpreter as someone who is able to apprehend the "real world" and then use it to interrogate the "reel world." After all, a realist commitment—and this is the heart of most ethnographic cinema—does not encourage the consideration of reality as being itself a discursive construction. Even in its most sophisticated forms, as in *vérité*, it frequently acknowledges the subjectivity of representation only at the cost of a truly radical reading of culture (that of both filmmaker and subject) as something always in-the-making, as something that is endlessly and creatively being fashioned by both local actors and transnational forces.

Clearly, I have taken my cue from theorists who have been concerned to elaborate an antirealist or discourse-centered analysis of literary texts and visual imagery. Although there are significant philosophical differences among these theorists, a common belief in the historical specificity of representations has bound their works together. In my own attempts to understand how ethnographic film works, I have found a great deal of value in Bill Nichols's (1981) discussion of narrative principles, and I want to reiterate some of the points made earlier to focus the present discussion and to raise the issue of spectatorial audience. In *Ideology and the Image*, Nichols argues that narrative operates through the complex relationships that pertain between expectations and their satisfactions, enigmas and their resolutions. Nichols's analysis underscores the active dimension of reading not merely as something that begins with the textual encounter but as something that has both a personal and a social history. That is, narrative mobilizes the social history of the reader in the act of reading, bringing into play the vast and often unconscious conventions by which phenomenal experiences, concepts, and values are typically evoked, represented, or symbolized. Its awareness of this history grounds its success or failure, even when success takes the form of thwarting expectation. Of course, the reader is always a socially situated being, someone who has matured within the categories and the possibilities of a particular social and linguistic tradition. Hence, in the moment of reading, narrative mobilizes both a personal aesthetic response and the social history of representation. Notions about what constitutes a person or an actor, about forms of speech and address, about the logic of time and its possible evocations, about causality and sequentiality, about the very act of reading and the nature of the text, may all be manipulated by a given narrative.

This dynamic interaction between texts and readers applies to pictorial imagery as well. The history of line and perspective, the principles of color and its translation into monochromatic ranges, notions about proportion and the limits of the visible, the symbolism of form, hue, and density, ideas about positive or negative space—all these are called up in the act of viewing, even when they are not available to the consciousness of the viewer. The matter is a complicated one, however, and, as Pierre Bourdieu (1977) has shown, much of perceptual consciousness is experienced at a level of bodily orientation that eludes articulation or explicitation. Thus, responses to imagery must be understood as the literal embodiments and enactments of representational history. Meaning itself (never a fully conceptual entity) emerges in this culturally confined relationship of response, responsivity, and even responsibility. The additional point to be made here is that, depending on the cultural history in which an image emerges, it will attain its objectives through dramatically different means. One has only to think of the shell and wooden grids of Oceanic map-making, the multiperspectival cartography of eighteenth-century Japan, or the fusion of time and distance on a vertical plane in Chinese landscape painting to understand that the codes for inscribing the real are various indeed. It will perhaps be argued that these are symbolic representations and not indices, that they do not pretend to immediacy or universality in the way that photography does. But such a claim simply begs the question of realism as a mode. It is possible for photography to take the form of abstraction; in fact, photographic and filmic imagery that is not oriented with the human body—a positionally female body (Mulvey 1975; de Lauretis 1984)—as its primary point of reference and scale usually appears as such. The abstract works of Michael Snow or Pat O'Neill provide abundant testimony to this fact. Even in more mainstream works, such as Jane Campion's *Sweetie* or Julie Dash's *Daughters of the Dust,* viewers are often discomforted by a camera that refuses to rest at a distance that reveals post-Renaissance proportionality (with the female form as measure and focal point).

I do not want to blur all of the lines of differentiation between photographs and films. Clearly, films exceed the individual pictorial image in their temporality and, hence, their narrativity. They are the ultimate hybrid, existing not so much between the picture and the narrative text but as the synthesis of the two. And they operate on many different levels to engage the reader/viewer in the processes of signification. This is why it is so important to understand the ethnographic film text as something with a specific audience, a community that shares certain assumptions about how to represent reality, but also about what reality looks like. It is in this space between text and reader that the historical dialogue becomes not only possible but inevitable. Nonetheless, the history that audiences body forth in the act of viewing ethnographic films is one infused by all sorts of discourses, and not merely the history of film or anthropology. Thus, when one asks how the meaning implanted in anthropological images is refracted outward and how it then interacts with other forms of knowledge and inscription, one is also asking how those images and ideas enter into anthropology. These relationships must be understood in terms of dialogue, reciprocity, reinforcement, and circularity, as much as contradiction and resistance. It would be a mistake to seek links of absolute priority or causality between academic discourses and popular culture. What an analysis of ethnographic films reveals is that anthropological representations emerge in the same discursive formations as do other kinds of representations, sharing with them many of the same tropes and commitments, even when there are other points of conflict.

Recollecting the History of Ethnographic Films and Museums

We are left, then, with a visual anthropology that is both films *in* anthropology and an anthropology *of* films. In recounting the history of visual anthropology on the Northwest Coast, I have pointed to the ongoing assessment, critique, and displacement of ethnographic narratives as a process whereby different representations are constantly in conflict with one another and with the histories to which they ambivalently refer. The various and successive narratives of Native history discussed in the previous three chapters were distinguished by their differing temporal orientations, their narrational strategies, and their positioning vis-à-vis Native and non-Native audiences. The poles of this differentiation, defined in both temporal and categorical terms, are homogeneity and differentiation, disappearance and continuity. Nor is it coincidental that these oppositions are also the limiting terms of poststructuralist debate and the extreme moments of Western history (retroactively conceived) in which poststructuralist theory emerges. If modernity is the loss of difference, then poststructuralism—postmodernity's brainchild—is an attempt to recover lost alterity. The ethnographic film of the Northwest Coast also manifests this trajectory, with the narratives of disappearance gradually being supplanted by those of revival, the latter coming into being through new strategies of representation, new methods of voicing, and new demands for dialogue. These strategies respond to the exigencies of representational politics, most visible in legal contests over land rights, the repatriation of artifacts, the battles against poverty, and the effort to recover indigenous languages.

It cannot be said too often that the institutional loci of film production have been of central importance in this history. In Canada, the predominance of the museum as a context for anthropology, and especially for visual anthropology, has been enormously significant. But this does not mean that the museum or its productions have been unchanging. They have not. In my discussions about the logic and practice of collecting (so long synonymous with ethnography), I have tried to show that the nature of the museum itself has been radically reformed over the past thirty or so years. In some cases, Native museums have localized the institution of collecting in such a way as to completely realign the epistemological structures of looking and knowing upon which traditional ethnographic museums have rested.

By now, of course, the topic of ethnographic inscription and its relationship to the ideology of vision has been widely explored by cultural critics. Whether in studies of literary (Fabian 1983; Rosaldo 1986) or visual (Edwards 1992) anthropology, there is general agreement that the tropes of seeing have been instrumental in the construction and the inscription of both ethnographic objectivity and cultural otherness. Yet, there is a tendency to flatten out the history of vision and to assume that Western perspectival representation has been uniform across the centuries. Often this tendency takes the form of assertions that Western social science, or even Western culture in general, is dominated by optical metaphors. The most powerful recent articulation of that position probably comes from Frederic Jameson, who introduces his collection of essays, *Signatures of the Visible* (1992), with the audacious (but seductive) assertion that an ontology of the modern world "would have to be an ontology of the visual, of being as the visible first and foremost, with the other senses draining off it" (1992:1). But in visual anthropology, as in the literary criticism enacted by Jameson and others, the demand for a history of vision's predominance has not yet been accompanied by a deconstruction or differentiation of vision itself. Too few critics have attended to the history of sight itself, to the varieties of seeing and looking that have emerged in post-Renaissance cultures. If it is true that the modern episteme is one in which the eye reigns supreme, it is equally true that vision's horizons have been constantly extended and redefined by technology and ideology, and that with each new move toward expanded visibility there also emerges a new domain of the invisible that simultaneously marks the limits of vision and calls up its transcendence (Crary 1990; Foucault 1973). And with each new cartography of possible insight comes a new mode of looking, an utterly new logic of the eye and of opticality. Visual processes in the era of the first telescope were undoubtedly organized and structured quite differently from those of the X ray, magnetic resonance imaging, and interactive video technology of today. To say that all of these modalities of looking assume a penetrative logic is to radically underestimate the fact that we are speaking not simply of deeper insight into a given world but about the production of new sites, dimensions, and objects of vision and visibility.

In important ways, new Native museums remind us of this fact by constantly insisting upon the possibility of alternative conceptions and practices of seeing and/or viewing. Redefining the museological space, many Native museums are organized around a temporal dimension absent in other forms of metonymic display. They provide a performative context in which the viewer is encompassed by an indigenous logic of witnessing that casts the visitor in a role of witness/participant quite distinct from that of mere spectator. These exteriorized memory palaces mitigate the reifying gaze of foreign and ethnographic observers. In other words, they undermine the authority of the surveying eye and offer in its place an eye situated amid other senses whose orientations are not purely spatial or architectural, nor Archimedean in aspiration, but also temporal and contextually responsive.

Yet insofar as film is concerned, one must caution against the desire to see such radical museology as being simply or univocally related to the filmmaking that occurs within these institutions. The factors involved in this relationship are numerous and extremely complex. And it is this complexity that accounts for the sometimes unsettling fact that the anthropology of museums and the anthropology inherent in ethnographic films are occasionally at odds with each other. Certainly this is the case with films produced by or for many Nativist museums. Despite the radicalism of their display and their profound restructuration of the viewing experience, many films associated with new museums are deeply conservative in their formal strategies. Their aesthetic traditionalism cannot but seem ironic.

In the discussions of earlier films, it was apparent that the rhetorical devices of realism buttressed the authority of ethnographic interlocutors. The photograph's claim to indexicality itself was employed in this process, even as photographers staged their images and retouched already fabricated scenes. Coalescing around apocalyptic narratives, which State representatives were both recounting and effecting, the ethnographic films of the early years narrated an impending disappearance and legitimated themselves as tools for future remembrance. Later, under the influence of functionalism and cultural anthropology's fetishism of the potlatch, salvage ethnography assumed a symbolically archaeological role, becoming a kind of "museum without walls" in which the screen replaced the glass case and cultures became traces of object forms. It is important to recognize here that the emerging disjuncture between cinematic and textual anthropologies also coincided with a growing distrust of photographic records. The more that social anthropology shifted away from its initial natural-history orientation and the more dominant the culture concept became, the less useful seemed photography. Precisely because photographic inscription was deemed to be indexical but only in relation to the material realm, it seemed inadequate to the task of representing culture when this latter was understood as something systematic and composed of abstract or symbolic meanings. Had ethnographic film—perhaps in opposition to anthropological photographs—been understood as a more complex and hybrid kind of representation that was fully capable of abstraction, it might not have been assigned the banal task of image collection. But it was some time, several decades in fact, before an awareness of its potential could generate a more properly social problematic for ethnographic film.

To understand the ironies of recent filmmaking, then, one must attend to two dimensions or processes by which the visual anthropology of the Northwest Coast has been reformed. On the one hand, there is the unexpected (from the point of view of salvage ethnography) stabilization of Native populations and the assertion of local identities through revival movements that transcend the Band in contests with the State, but that do not completely resolve local differences into a pan-cultural unity. Individual Bands have mobilized around land and fishing rights as well as around the repatriation of artifacts, at once allying with other Bands and maintaining highly local control over political processes, social programs, and educational activities. This revival has had political, economic, and aesthetic dimensions and, at various points, has been allied (somewhat precariously) with different environmentalist and progressive political organizations.

On the other hand, one finds a diffusion of primitivism beyond the art world, the growth of tourism with its related commodification of culture and its fetishism of authenticity, as well as the development of national multicultural policies. These factors have reinforced and promoted—directly and indirectly—the revival that Native groups have themselves been pursuing from within. Nor have Native-based movements been exempt from self-commodification and self-aestheticization. At times, they appear to have been virtually encompassed by ethnographic representations, aspiring to a distorted and historically unprecedented purity that originates in the romantic desires of early ethnographers as much as in Native cultures and histories. As was apparent in films like *Bella Bella* or in more widely distributed American productions, such as Michael Apted's *Incident at Oglala* (1991), many communities are themselves rent by conflicts over what constitutes traditionalism and modernization, and what separates self-preservation from self-commodification. In visual anthropology, these developments and conflicts are most clearly visible in the gradual emergence, one should perhaps say the growing audibility, of speaking Native subjects. For with the assertion of individual subjectivities, the legitimacy of a totalized and artificially unified Native consciousness—an essentialized Nativeness—is undermined.

This emergence corresponds directly to the displacement of authoritarian voice-over narration, thought attribution, and the trivializing translations that filled early films. Nonetheless, the conflict with older representations has generally been carried out within the parameters of realist documentary cinema. There are exceptions to this generality, of course. I can think of nothing on the Northwest Coast that approaches Trinh Minh-ha's cinematic *écriture*, but Jan-Marie Martel's recent production about a Salishan healer, *Bowl of Bone* (1992), does attempt to explore the virtues of expressionism and montage for a reflexive ethnographic cinema. However, films like *Bowl of Bone* are a rarity, and it must be acknowledged that most of the films discussed in this book are part of an ongoing political practice already limited in scope; they address—they must address—audiences steeped in the realist tradition. It is not spurious to note the fact that Native Bands and their filmmakers are producing films not in order to dislodge cinematic conventions but to awaken political consciousness and to effect change in the ways they are treated by the State. Hence their pastiche of tactics and imageries, their extreme eclecticism and their frequent recourse to a prediscursive "reality."

In considering this eclecticism, the juxtapositions that often place the same tired functionalism or the yellowed photographs of another era next to dialogic confrontations or more expressive forms, one is struck again by Franz Boas's remarks about fragmentation and reconstruction. On several levels—levels that Boas almost certainly did not entertain—contemporary ethnographic films reproduce the phenomenon of mythic bricolage. Each film constructs a world unto itself, a world composed of fragmentary imagery and exposition that mediates the given in the guise of transparency. Ethnographic films structure these images in narratives organized around specific principles of time and history, person and culture, self and other—none of which directly correspond with any such processes in the lived world. Thus do films become their own mythic universes, naturalizing fabricated worlds, while claiming to partake of an absolute and originary Being. This is why what Roland Barthes (1972:142) says of myths is equally applicable to films—whether those films are made in Hollywood or in ethnographic museums: They naturalize historical intention.

Can there then be a reflexive and self-critical ethnographic cinema? If films are always and inevitably products of their times, what are the possibilities for sustained autocritique? The need for new ways of representing seems urgent (Howes 1989:23). Although my purpose here is not really programmatic, it seems to me that any such revolution will require, first and foremost, that the erroneous assumptions about film's supposedly unmediated relationship with the world be relinquished. What does this entail? To begin with, it must mean more than the rhetorical flourishes of self-conscious self-presence, such as one finds in the trembling of a hand-held camera or in the prefacing remarks in which a filmmaker describes the circumstances of filming. Indeed, such stylistic devices are now as common in television sitcoms and hyperreal dramas of police investigation as they are in documentary cinema, and their capacity to *signify* reality has been correspondingly negated in the process. But perhaps this is Bertolt Brecht's lesson. Reality changes, and so must our modes of representing it. One might refocus Brecht's aphoristic aesthetics and say instead that realism changes and hence our strategies for disrupting or challenging it must also change.

Still Life with Vanishing Natives

At various points in this book, I have called for an exploration of anthropology's relationship to public culture, and for a critique of its imbrication in the history of representational othering. I have called for a plumbing of conscience and an investigation of the role played by ethnographic museums and films in the processes of cultural dispossession and repossession. Finally, I have called for a consideration of the discipline's contemporary history, its involvement in cultural commodification, and its participation in the discourses of desire that now afflict transnational consciousness in the form of nostalgia. Let me then close this book with a return to the issues of Chapter 1, and with a perusal of that phenomenon we now observe in the marketplaces of loss and acquisition—namely, the traffic in authenticity.

As I write the conclusion to this book, I am overwhelmed by the sheer quantity of Nativist memorabilia that circulates in our society. And observing these new curiosities, the coveted objects of desire in the era of the supertourist, I am struck again by Walter Benjamin's perspicacity and by his prescience (Buck-Morss 1989). Benjamin argued that the sense of historical loss that emerged in the whirlwind of European capitalization fueled a fetishism of the old and the authentic. But it could do so only in the aftermath of an equally powerful fetishism of the new (Buck-Morss 1989:82). These two tendencies imply each other, and it was mechanical reproduction—in all its forms—that rendered new things accessible to the degree that old, manually produced objects could be discarded by the middle classes and then desired by the upper classes as things inscribed with the signature of originality. In an economy of scarcity and under the influence of commodity fetishism, such objects soon appeared inherently valuable. In an ironic way, this transformation entailed the commodification of authenticity even as the commodity economy entailed the loss of authenticity. All of this occurred in a symbolic economy where a consciousness of historical rupture marked and evidenced the emergence of alienated labor. For if nostalgia implies anything, it is alienation: the alienation of personhood through commodification, the alienation of authenticity through rationalization, and the alienation of what Benjamin called the aura of the original through the technologies of reproduction. This process of alienation occurred at the very height of Europe's imperial power (imperialism having facilitated capitalism), and as it did so, other cultures acquired the power of representation for Western Europeans and North Americans. Let us remind ourselves once again that the moment of salvage ethnography's birth was also the moment in which "Other" cultures became something other than themselves: when they became representations of loss. Supposedly vanishing peoples became stand-ins for a historical and cultural organicism from which Western postindustrial cultures felt they had been cut off. It was in this sense that I spoke of the contemporary market of Native memorabilia as a pursuit of proxy authenticity on the part of non-Native and, occasionally, Native consumers.

In the antique galleries of posh shopping arcades in North American cities, reprints of the Curtis portfolio sell for hundreds of dollars. Postcard racks abound with sepia-toned images of pristine Natives taken from the archives of major museums. International news magazines feature cover stories about disappearing peoples and advertising agencies have adopted the imagery of neoprimitivism—in the form of costumed models—to market everything from long-distance telephone services to casual wear and environmentally friendly cosmetics. Hollywood too has discovered that films with "Native themes" are a highly marketable commodity. Among the most lucrative studio productions of the past three years, *Dances with Wolves* and *Last of the Mohicans* attest to this fact. Even in places that seem remote from the centers of Euro–North American power—such as certain border towns in Northern Thailand!—the imagery of North American Natives is sold as something with almost talismanic power over the increasingly banal world of infinitely available and reproducible commodities.

So we live unregenerately in the age of the still-vanishing Indian, where the image of "the Native Other" is not so much an embodiment of disappearing primitiveness as a *sign* of longed-for authenticity. Of course, the representation of cultural otherness is no longer a realm under anthropology's jurisdiction. Popular ideas about life in pre-contact Native North America are as likely to come from Hollywood as they are from ethnographies. Eugene Linden, the author of *Time*'s apocalyptic tale about cultural homogenization, was perhaps less prophetic than descriptive when he imagined Native cultures as inherently marketable entities. Indeed, the interlocutor has been displaced by the middleman. Yet, even if displaced in this manner, anthropology can return here to help us understand precisely how such marketing operates. In fact, I would argue that one of the discipline's primary imperatives is now the analysis of how market desire operates in the symbolic economies by which cultures are produced, commodified, and/or consumed for their authenticity value.

At base, one must bear in mind that only what is alien can be desired. Ovid's lesson in the tale of Narcissus and Echo is indeed that the consummation of desire (consumption) requires difference as its prerequisite. Although consumption may result in the final encompassment of an entity, it requires the prior alienation and objectification of the thing-to-be-consumed. And thus the use of Native authenticity as an instrument of desire—in advertising or Hollywood film—marks the consciousness of Western consumers as one afflicted by the sensation of lack. Here, as in the introductory chapter of this book, I want to stress that the trope of the vanishing Native and the concomitant discourses of preservation are less about a feared loss of absolute difference (cultural death) than about an experiential sense of self-loss and historical rupture. In other words, preservation holds out the possibility of maintaining a proxy past in the present. This proxy past can then be consumed, if only voyeuristically, in ways that never exhaust the object's capacity to signify the lack that it both evidences and satisfies. For if postindustrial Western cultures are divorced from their own authentic roots, then other (usually aboriginal) cultures can enact the drama of indigenous purity and provide a substitute for that which modernity and/or postmodernity feels it lacks. This cultivation of alterior authenticity, this staging and even trafficking in pure otherness, is what Benjamin observed in the Paris arcades, and what he identified as the most significant indicator of modern consciousness. Although he was primarily concerned with historical otherness, it is not coincidental that the antique gallery is now one of the most prominent sites of cultural commodification. It is not merely the past but cultural foreignness that sells in galleries. As Johannes Fabian (1983) has reminded us time and again, the axes of distance are at once temporal and spatial, historical and cultural. Nor can these dimensions be separated in analyses of distanciation.

How awkward and contradictory, then, is the position of Native people who must negotiate the politics of survival, the necessity of a historical consciousness in which to ground identity, and the more dangerous reifications that nostalgia entails. These tensions are often the bases of overt political cleavages within individual Bands, and they provide the terms in which so-called traditionalists and progovernment Natives disagree with each other. And it is extremely important to recognize the degree of difference and political argumentation that does take place within Native communities. Some indication of those contradictions was apparent in the NFB production *Bella Bella,* and in Chapter 5 I stressed how that film differed from others produced by and for particular Bands, such that the need to present a unified front in opposition to the State seemed to overwhelm the possibility of addressing internal conflict. Having said as much, however, I find it that much more important to recognize films, such as Michael Apted's *Incident at Oglala* (1991) and *Thunderheart* (1992), that are simultaneously concerned with denouncing State abuses and with exposing the ways in which the State manipulates local conflict and exacerbates already tendentious situations. It is also important that we maintain critical distinctions between films like *Thunderheart* and more popular epics like Kevin Costner's *Dances with Wolves,* although both films can appear to be "Native friendly" when compared to other, more baldly ethnocentric works. To understand where and how these films differ is to understand both the best and the worst that anthropology can be when it takes popular forms. We are also enabled to perceive the ideological linkages between sites that are, as often as not, analyzed and staged in opposition to each other. For this reason, I want to briefly consider these two films in their relationship to the problem of history, contemporary anthropology's central problematic, for they adopt profoundly different stances toward both the past and the future.

An analysis of *Dances with Wolves* allows us to comprehend how the rhetoric and narrative strategies of the "period piece" can actually dislodge a moment in the past from history itself, effecting that shock of discontinuity that John Berger identified with the photograph in particular and with the nostalgic impulse in general. *Dances with Wolves* is an instructive example for ethnographic filmmakers because it shows us how films "about" history— even well-intentioned ones—can render an event part of the eternal/ethnographic present, at once denying the agency of historical individuals and stranding them on an island-of-no-history for which the future is an impossibility. We have seen similar scenarios in ethnographic films, particularly *Blunden Harbour* and the neosalvage pieces of the postwar years. But just as the NFB and U'mista Cultural Center productions offered an alternative to ethnographic presentism, so narrative cinema has its own versions of historicist drama. In contrast to *Dances with Wolves, Thunderheart* evokes a world that is not torn from time and its various power relations but, rather, is deeply embedded in a changing and constantly negotiated set of social and political relations.

I do not intend to summarize the plots of either film at this point. Both are widely available to audiences through video distributors. However, in keeping with the conclusions of Chapter 5, I do want to examine their respective approaches to the problems of Native subjectivity and self-representation. I do so because their respective answers to the question that Bill Nichols places at the heart of documentary—namely, "What to do with people?"—is also, fundamentally, an answer to the question of what to do with history. Both *Dances with Wolves* and *Thunderheart* exist firmly within the realist tradition; both use the rhetoric of documentation as a means of self-authorization, framing their narratives with an exposition that points to the extrafilmic world and employing indigenous languages to signify the veracity of narrative content. Nonetheless, they do so in radically different ways, assuming and interpolating quite different kinds of viewers.

The most obvious point of differentiation between the two revolves around the identity of either film's hero, his function, and his relationship to the assumed audience. Both films force the viewer to identify with a male protagonist who is initially external to a "Native" culture and history.

Indeed, these protagonists act as points of visual and psychic entry. In *Thunderheart*, our point of view is constructed through a young "Native" man, Ray Levoi, who is so alienated from his cultural roots that he knows neither the words nor the gestures appropriate for the most mundane social occasions. More important, he rejects those traditions as being outmoded and irrelevant. However, when Levoi is drawn back into the Sioux fold through his relationship with an aging healer and his own inexplicable visions of the massacre at Wounded Knee, we go with him. The journey is a conflicted one, but the endless confrontation with otherness becomes less an obstacle to transcend than a point of articulation and contestation in which identity is forged through choice and self-affirmation. As is not the case with *Dances with Wolves*, where an unseen translator gives us entry into Sioux culture through subtitling, the viewer of *Thunderheart* remains as befuddled and marginalized as does the hero when indigenous language is used. Like him, we are forced to confront the irreducible opacity of Sioux culture; language marks the point at which the will to power through knowledge is thwarted. Brought face to face with this untranslatability, we must also acknowledge the autonomy and the integrity of both language and culture, although the latter is never reduced to a singular or unified set of historical possibilities.

Consider, in contrast, the linguistic heroics of Lieutenant John J. Dunbar in Kevin Costner's romantic epic. Few Hollywood films have received more praise for their careful use of indigenous language than has *Dances with Wolves*. Costner's decision to use actual Lakota speech and to provide subtitles marks it as a film apart from those earlier productions in which a babel of supposedly mimetic but otherwise meaningless sounds evoked pure otherness for English-speaking audiences. The film's refusal to infantilize Native languages with bastard translations is a laudable gesture toward linguistic parity, although other films, notably *Windwalker*, had attempted the same thing a decade before. Yet this semblance of equality is ultimately undermined by the fact that it is only the allies of the exiled colonial officer who are granted intelligibility. The film's antagonistic Natives, the Pawnee, remain utterly incomprehensible to the main character, and hence to viewers, their linguistic otherness marking their political undesirability and indeed their inhumanity. Where the Sioux are concerned, though, language is both the marker of distance and the measure of its transcendence. Although Dunbar must struggle to acquire rudimentary skills in Lakota Sioux, the audience is never denied access to Sioux consciousness and the titles achieve what Costner's character cannot: the traversal and translation of cultural difference. Regarding the dramatic plot of *Dances with Wolves*, difference is overcome through the female character "Stands with a Fist," who retains a truncated memory of her murdered parents' English. She is the one who ultimately provides Dunbar with the object and the means of cultural transcendence, her own liminal identity acting as a bridge between otherwise separate universes. In this manner, she plays the archetypical role of obstacle in a cinematic narrative that uses the woman as the vehicle for male subject formation (de Lauretis 1984:119). Significantly, though, the film has us believe that her ability to provide such linkage stems not from the fact that she is the product of a colonial family at the vanguard of colonial expansion but, rather, from the fact that she has been brutally victimized by the scalping Pawnee. Here, *Dances with Wolves* surreptitiously inverts the structure of colonial domination. And following this initial tableau, which provides the context for Dunbar's personal and romantic quest, the Sioux act rather like an operatic chorus, mirroring and refracting the woman's character, while providing yet another instrument for the formation of that perfect colonial character: the man who crosses over into otherness as a means of expanded selfhood.

In the end, *Dances with Wolves* is not really about the Sioux, certainly not in the sense of Sioux subjectivity. They are objects in a fundamentally antimiscegenist drama (the White officer is instinctively drawn to the White woman). The film's ending, which reminds audiences of the pathos that lay in store for the Sioux and other Native groups, attempts to seduce viewers into believing that this—the story of the Sioux and their violent subjugation—is really the film's heart. And in that moment, the film cuts history off from the present, forever deferring questions about how Sioux individuals might have negotiated their own relationships to history. The tacit implications of those last titles can be nothing if not an assertion of the irrevocability of history, which is carried exclusively by the agents of Western culture. Here is memory spectacle in its purest form. The question of identity and, more important, of Sioux subjectivity remains unasked, and in this way the film specularizes both Native cultures and their disappearance.

In contrast, *Thunderheart* refuses this strategy of enchantment and attends instead to the problem of identity in moral and political terms. In addition to being a denunciation of U.S. governmental policy and treatment of Native peoples, it addresses the issues of identity from the perspective of a "Native" man who is deeply ambivalent about what his biography implies and entails. Not only does Ray Levoi refuse the easy assumption of Native authenticity that blood would confer, but he shuns it in an effort to play the part of the ultimate American hero, the CIA officer. In terms of the debates now engaging Native ethnographers and activists, the film's value lies in its refusal to treat the question of being Native on the facile level of mere legal status or blood ancestry. Unlike much Nativist work, though not completely without contradiction, *Thunderheart* defines contemporary Native identity as something that pivots around the relationships that individuals *choose* to pursue with their own and their families' traditions and histories, these being both multiple and historically contingent. That is, it gives Native characters the full range of ethical and political decisionmaking that

Hollywood viewers demand for other (usually White and male) persons. In this schema, the possibility of historical transformation remains open and subject to negotiation and partial control.

Two films. Two narratives. Two different approaches to the problem of subjectivity. Two kinds of history. And yet this juxtaposition of films may seem somewhat unfair, given the different subject matter that drives each narrative. It may even seem that I have staged an impossible contest in which films about contemporary conflict are automatically privileged as being historically aware in ways that those about the past cannot be. But this is not my intended conclusion. Rather, I have chosen to discuss these films as exemplars of different approaches to the problem of subjectivity and historicity and, even more, to the problem of their interrelationship.

Thunderheart is no less about a historical moment than is *Dances with Wolves.* The question of history is not a question of chronological placement but, instead, has to do with the kinds of agency that we attribute to the inhabitants of various eras, and with the kinds of consciousness that we, as interlocutors or artists, permit our represented subjects/objects. What defines *Dances with Wolves* as a nostalgic and antihistoricist piece is not the temporal distance of its story/event from our own moment. Rather, the film's nostalgia lies in the way it abstracts other cultures into ideal types and renders individuals as the mere enactments of a predetermined History and a unified Culture. What saves *Thunderheart* from a similar fate (though the film is not without romanticism) is the fact that it assigns historical agency to Native individuals and recognizes not just conflict but choice. In *Dances with Wolves,* one is a Sioux or a Pawnee by birth and no Native character is given the range (unquestioned for Dunbar) to choose in what manner he or she will be Sioux or Pawnee. But that existential question is the very soul of *Thunderheart,* and it marks that film as an important intervention into the field of mainstream cultural representation.

Some clarification is perhaps necessary here. I do not mean to elevate the radical individualism of modernist fiction to a position of preeminence in historicist cinema. The question of identity is always a social one, but it might be fruitful here for us to attend to the other half of Marx's dictum about history and agency. We may not make history in the manner that would please us most, but we do make history. Part of the recognition of other subjectivities requires an acknowledgment of this creative capacity in others. All representations entail objectification, but that need not imply the erasure of subjectivity and, more specifically, of historical subjectivity. This is, I think, the lesson of *Thunderheart.* And it is a lesson with momentous implications, for it would inevitably mean that "Other" cultures could no longer serve as stand-ins for the lost or rejected past of Euro–North American culture.

Last Words

Let me then conclude with history. And with History. In his exquisite but maddening meditation on photography and the meaning of memory, Roland Barthes remarks that the nineteenth century discovered both History and Photography (1980:93). Needless to say, the nineteenth century did not discover the past, or even nostalgia, but it did give both of these things a particular conceptual structure, an order, and an aesthetic form. On the verge of his own death, Barthes was led by this realization into a revery on the difference between history, "a memory fabricated according to positive formulas," and the photograph that he describes as a "certain but fugitive testimony" to that which has always disappeared (1980:93). *Camera Lucida* is a romantic but strangely positivist (in the context of Barthes's later writings) account of photography, but its central insight, that history and photography are highly specific modes of remembrance, is an instructive one with immediate and, I hope, obvious relevance for my own consideration of ethnographic cinema.

In order to understand how photography and cinematography can be harnessed to the project of cultural representation, we must first ask what role remembrance plays in that process. We must then inquire, "What and how do photographs and films testify?" What testimony can photographs and films give in the service of a directed memory? For Barthes, history, a fabricated memory, stands *in opposition* to the photograph, the proof that what we recall actually existed in another time. But in the many accounts of films and photographs provided here, we have seen how fabulous a thing an image is, even when it is rooted in processes of photochemical transference. Above all, we have seen that indexicality is a complex phenomenon, one that entails questions of iconicity, resemblance, and artificiality at the levels of meaning and interpretation. We have also seen that the impossible claim to indexicality has sustained ethnographic film, while veiling its rhetorical and ideological content (Nichols 1981:283). Ethnographic films, like Barthes's photographs, *do* tell us that a thing imaged has existed in the world, but the nature of that thing—its social and historical meaning—is implanted in the image through fantastically elaborate processes of rhetoric and narrative. These processes are both the products and the constituents of ideological traditions that exceed any individual text or reader.

These are far-reaching conclusions for a book that is mainly about the neglected history of Northwest Coast visual anthropology. Yet, in confining my inquiries to such a narrow field, I have tried to write a historical account that demonstrates how representational traditions work, how notions of culture and culture area define and focus a particular gaze, how that gaze consolidates itself, and how changes in the horizon of vision emerge. The writing of this book was driven by a desire to argue against the naive reflectionism that afflicts so much ethnographic film theory, but it was also motivated by a need to comprehend the ways in which film and other representational forms emerge out of concrete historical circumstances, and then reenter history as constituent parts.

An analysis of the ways of ethnographic looking immediately demands a recognition of how the field of anthropology (and the anthropology of "the field") ramifies outward into endless and intertextually linked circles that traverse a multitude of discourses and media. This "effectivity" is apparent whether one is considering the genealogy of the potlatch concept from salvage ethnography to poststructuralist theory and Kwakiutl revival, or the role of Curtis photographs in the popular media's imaginings of Native authenticity. From *Time* to Hollywood, from Coca Cola commercials to Michael Jackson videos, the images of neoprimitivism move forward faster and faster. To take hold of those images, to reappropriate and redefine them, to imbue them with different significations and the significations of difference: This has been the task of much recent filmmaking. And if visual anthropology has, historically, been a prime site of cultural othering, of reification and fetishization in the service of intellectual colonialism, it might still prove useful in a battle against the current renewal of exoticism. But it will do so only by addressing itself to the culture of image-making, by cultivating a scrupulous and historically attuned awareness of its own poetics, and by problematizing the very processes of objectification upon which it and all representation rests. It would perhaps be easier to throw in the towel, or to reject the history from which ethnographic cinema emerges altogether—and there are many who advocate such silence. In the end, though, it is the refusal of silence that will provide the ground for a new cinema. From the ruins of our museums we may yet build new worlds.

References

Abu-Lughod, Lila. 1986. *Veiled Sentiments: Honor and Poetry in a Bedouin Society.* Berkeley: University of California Press.

Adams, John W. 1981. Recent Ethnology of the Northwest Coast. *Annual Review of Anthropology* 10:361–392.

Adorno, Theodor W. 1981. Transparencies on Film. Trans. Thomas Y. Levin. *New German Critique,* pp. 24–35.

Allen, Rosemary. 1981. The Potlatch and Social Equilibrium. In *Northwest Anthropological Research Notes: A Reprint of the Entire Davidson Journal of Anthropology, 1955, 1956, 1957.* Fall/Spring 21(1/2):233–244.

Ames, Michael. 1986. *Museums, the Public and Anthropology: A Study in the Anthropology of Anthropology.* Vancouver: University of British Columbia Press.

Anderson, Joseph, and Barbara Anderson. 1980. Motion Perception in Motion Pictures. In *The Cinematic Apparatus.* Eds. Teresa de Lauretis and Stephen Heath. New York: St. Martin's, pp. 76–95.

Appadurai, Arjun. 1981. The Past as a Scarce Resource. *Man* 16:201–219.

Appiah, Kwame Anthony. 1991. Is the Post- in Postmodernism the Post- in Postcolonial? *Critical Inquiry* 17:336–357.

Arnheim, Rudolf. 1958. *Film as Art.* Berkeley: University of California Press.

Asad, Talal (ed.). 1973. *Anthropology and the Colonial Encounter.* London: Ithaca Press.

Asch, Timothy, and Patsy Asch. 1988. Film in Anthropological Research. In *Cinematographic Theory and New Dimensions in Ethnographic Film.* Eds. Paul Hockings and Yasuhiro Omori. Osaka: National Museum of Ethnology, pp. 165–187.

Bakhtin, Mikhail. 1981. Discourse in the Novel. In *The Dialogic Imagination.* Trans. Caryl Emerson and Michael Holquist, pp. 259–422.

Balikci, Asen. 1975. Reconstructing Cultures on Film. In *Principles of Visual Anthropology.* Ed. Paul Hockins. The Hague: Mouton.

———. 1983. Visual Anthropology in Canada. In *Methodology in Anthropological Filmmaking: Papers of the IUAES Intercongress, Amsterdam, 1981.* Ed. Nico C. R. Bogaart and Henk W.E.R. Ketelaar. Gottingen: Editions Herodot.

Banks, Marcus. 1988. The Non-transparency of Ethnographic Film. *Anthropology Today* 4(5):2–3.

Barthes, Roland. 1972. *Mythologies.* Trans. Annette Lavers. London: Paladin. (Originally published in 1957.)

———. 1980. Where to Begin. In *New Critical Essays.* Trans. Richard Howard. New York: Hill and Wang. (Originally published in 1970.)

———. 1982. *Camera Lucida.* Trans. Richard Howard. London: Jonathon Cape.

———. 1985. Rhetoric of the Image. In *Semiotics, An Introductory Anthology.* Ed. Robert E. Innes. Bloomington: Indiana University Press.

Bass, Warren. 1982. Filmic Objectivity and Visual Style. In *Film/Culture: Explorations of Cinema in Its Social Context.* Ed. Sari Thomas. London: Scarecrow Press.

Bastide, Roger. 1970. Mémoire collective et sociologie du bricolage. *L'Année sociologique* 21:45–108.

Bataille, Georges. 1967. *La Part maudite précedé par "La notion de dépense."* Introduction by Jean Piel. Paris: Minuit.

———. 1985. *Visions of Excess: Selected Writings 1927–39.* Trans. Allan Stoekl, Carl Lovett, and Donald Leslie. Manchester: Manchester University Press.

Batalle, G. M., and C. L. Silet (eds.). 1980. *The Pretend Indians: Images of Native Americans in the Movies.* Ames: Iowa State University Press.

Baudrillard, J. 1975. *The Mirror of Production.* Trans. Mark Poster. St. Louis: Telos Press. (Originally published in 1973.)

———. 1983. *L'Echange symbolique et la mort.* Paris: Gallimard.

Baudry, Jean-Louis. 1974–1975. Ideological Effects of the Basic Ideological Apparatus. *Film Quarterly,* Volumes 7–8.

Bazin, André. 1967. *What Is Cinema?* Berkeley: University of California Press.

Benedict, Ruth. 1959. *Patterns of Culture.* Cambridge, Mass.: Riverside Press. (Originally published in 1934.)

Benjamin, Walter. 1969. The Storyteller: Reflections on the Work of Nikolai Leskov. In *Reflections.* Ed. Harry Zohn. New York: Schocken Books, pp. 80–100.

———. 1973. The Work of Art in the Age of Mechanical Reproduction. In *Illuminations.* Trans. Hannah Arendt. New York: Schocken, pp. 219–253.

———. 1977. *The Origin of German Tragic Drama.* London: New Left Books. (Originally published in 1928.)

Berger, John, and Jean Mohr. 1982. *Another Way of Telling.* New York: Pantheon.

Berger, Peter L., and Thomas Luckmann. 1966. *The Social Construction of Reality.* Garden City, N.Y.: Doubleday.

Berkhofer, R. F., Jr. 1965. *Salvation and the Savage: An Analysis of Protestant Missions and American Indian Response, 1787–1862.* Lexington: University of Kentucky Press.

———. 1978. *The White Man's Indian.* New York: Alfred A. Knopf.

Bhabha, Homi. 1983. The Other Question. *Screen* 24(6):24–36.

Bidney, David. 1953. *Theoretical Anthropology.* New York: Columbia University Press.

Blau, Herbert. 1990. The Surpassing Body. *The Drama Review* 35(2):74–96.

Bloch, Maurice. 1976. The Past and the Present in the Present. *Man* 12:278–292.

Boas, Franz. 1898. Introduction. In *Traditions of the Thompson River Indians.* James Teit. Memoirs of the American Folklore Society No. 6.

———. 1923. The Aims of Anthropological Research. Reprinted in *Race, Language and Culture.* New York: MacMillan, pp. 243–259.

———. 1940. *Race, Language and Culture.* New York: Macmillan.

———. 1966. The Potlatch. In *Indians of the North Pacific Coast.* Ed. Tom McFeat. Toronto: McLelland and Steward, pp. 72–80. (Originally published in 1895.)

Boon, James. 1972. *From Symbolism to Structuralism.* London: Basil Blackwell.

———. 1982. *Other Tribes, Other Scribes: Symbolic Anthropology in the Comparative Study of Cultures, Histories, Religions, and Texts.* Cambridge: Cambridge University Press.

Bourdieu, Pierre. 1977. *Outline of a Theory of Practice.* Cambridge: Cambridge University Press.

———. 1984. *Distinction: A Social Critique of the Judgement of Taste.* London: Routledge and Kegan Paul.

Brantlinger, Patrick. 1985. Victorians and Africans: The Genealogy of the Myth of the Dark Continent. *Critical Inquiry* 12:166–203.

Browne, Colin. 1979. *Motion Picture Production in British Columbia: 1898–1940.* Heritage Record No. 6. Victoria: Ministry of the Provincial Secretary and Government Services.

Bruner, Edward. 1986. Ethnography as Narrative. In *The Anthropology of Experience.* Eds. Victor Turner and Edward M. Bruner. Urbana and Chicago: University of Illinois Press, pp. 139–155.

Brunette, Peter. 1988. Towards a Deconstructive Theory of Film. In *The Cinema as Text.* Ed. R. Barton Palmer. New York: AMS Press, pp. 215–236.

Buck-Morss, Susan. 1989. *The Dialectics of Seeing: Walter Benjamin and the Arcades Project.* Cambridge, Mass.: MIT Press.

Cannizzo, Jeanne. 1983. George Hunt and the Invention of Kwakiutl Culture. *Canadian Review of Sociology and Anthropology* 20(1):44–58.

Carter, Angela. 1978. *The Sadeian Woman and the Ideology of Pornography.* New York: Pantheon.

Cavell, Stanley. 1973. *The World Viewed: Reflections on the Ontology of Film.* New York: Viking.

Caws, Mary Ann. 1981. *The Eye in the Text.* Princeton, N.J.: Princeton University Press.

Clastres, Pierre. 1980. *La Société contre l'état.* Paris: Minuit.

Clifford, James. 1986a. Introduction: Partial Truths. In *Writing Culture: The Poetics and Politics of Ethnography.* Eds. James Clifford and George E. Marcus. Berkeley: University of California Press, pp. 1–26.

———. 1986b. On Ethnographic Allegory. In *Writing Culture.* Eds. James Clifford and George E. Marcus. Berkeley: University of California Press, pp. 98–121.

———. 1988a. Identity in Mashpee. In *The Predicament of Culture: Twentieth Century Ethnography, Literature, Art.* Cambridge; Mass.: Harvard University Press, pp. 277–346.

———. 1988b. On Collecting Art and Culture. In *The Predicament of Culture.* Cambridge, Mass.: Harvard University Press, pp. 215–251.

Clifford, James, and George E. Marcus (eds.). 1986. *Writing Culture: The Poetics and Politics of Ethnography.* Berkeley: University of California Press.

Codere, Helen. 1950. *Fighting with Property: A Study of Kwakiutl Potlatching and Warfare, 1792–1930.* Monographs of the American Ethnological Society, Vol. 18.

———. 1961. Kwakiutl. In *Perspectives in American Indian Culture Change.* Ed. Edward Spicer. Chicago: University of Chicago Press.

Cole, Douglas. 1985. *Captured Heritage: The Scramble for Northwest Coast Artifacts.* Seattle: University of Washington Press.

Collins, Richard. 1976. Genre: A Reply to Ed Buscomb. In *Movies and Methods.* Ed. Bill Nichols. Berkeley: University of California Press, pp. 157–164.

Comaroff, Jean. 1985. *Body of Power, Spirit of Resistance: The Culture and History of a South African People.* Chicago: University of Chicago Press.

Comaroff, Jean, and John L. Comaroff. 1991. *Of Revelation and Revolution: Christianity, Colonialism, and Consciousness in South Africa*, Vol. 1. Chicago: University of Chicago Press.

Comaroff, John L., and Jean Comaroff. 1992. *Ethnography and the Historical Imagination*. Chicago: University of Chicago Press.

Cowie, Elizabeth. 1990. Woman as Sign. In *The Woman in Question*. Eds. Parveen Adams and Elizabeth Cowie. Cambridge, Mass.: MIT Press, pp. 117–133. (Originally published in 1978.)

Crapanzano, Vincent. 1980. *Tuhami: Portrait of a Moroccan*. Chicago: University of Chicago Press.

———. 1985. *Waiting: The Whites of South Africa*. New York: Random House.

Crary, Jonathon. 1990. *Techniques of the Observer: On Vision and Modernity in the Nineteenth Century*. Cambridge, Mass.: MIT Press.

de Brigarde, E. 1975. The History of Ethnographic Film. In *Principles of Visual Anthropology*. Ed. Paul Hockings. The Hague: Mouton, pp. 13–43.

de Certeau, Michel. 1986. *Heterologies: Discourse on the Other*. Minneapolis: University of Minnesota Press.

———. 1988. *The Writing of History*. Trans. T. Conley. New York: Columbia University Press.

de Lauretis, Teresa. 1984. *Alice Doesn't: Feminism, Semiotics, Cinema*. Bloomington: Indiana University Press.

de Lauretis, Teresa, and Stephen Heath (eds.). 1980. *The Cinematic Apparatus*. New York: St. Martin's.

Doane, Mary Ann. 1990. Remembering Women: Psychical and Historical Constructions in Film Theory. In *Psychoanalysis and Cinema*. Ed. E. Ann Kaplan. London: Routledge, pp. 46–63.

Donato, Eugenio. 1979. The Museum's Furnace: Notes Toward a Contextual Reading of *Bouvard and Pécuchet*. In *Textual Strategies: Perspectives in Poststructuralist Criticism*. Ed. Josué V. Harari. London: Methuen, pp. 213–238.

Drucker, Philip. 1955. *Indians of the Northwest Coast*. American Museum of Natural History, Anthropological Handbook No. 10.

Duffy, Dennis J. 1986. *Camera West. British Columbia on Film: 1941–65*. Victoria: Ministry of Provincial Secretary and Government Services.

Dwyer, Kevin. 1987. The Dialogic of Anthropology. *Dialectical Anthropology* 2:143–151.

Eco, Umberto. 1976. *A Theory of Semiotics*. Bloomington: Indiana University Press.

Edwards, Elizabeth (ed.). 1992. *Anthropology and Photography, 1860–1920*. New Haven, Conn.: Yale University Press, with the Royal Anthropological Institute.

Eisenstein, Sergei. 1949. *Film Form*. Ed. and trans. Jay Leyda. New York: Harcourt Brace Jovanovich.

Fabian, Johannes. 1983. *Time and the Other: How Anthropology Makes Its Object*. New York: Columbia University Press.

Fischer, Michael M. J., and Mehdi Abedi. 1990. *Debating Muslims: Cultural Dialogues in Postmodernity and Tradition*. Madison: University of Wisconsin Press.

Fogelson, Raymond D. 1985. Interpretations of the American Indian Psyche: Some Historical Notes. In *Social Contexts of American Ethnology, 1840–1984*. Washington, D.C.: American Anthropological Association, pp. 4–27.

Foucault, Michel. 1973. *The Order of Things: An Archaeology of the Human Sciences.* New York: Vintage. (Originally published in 1966.)

———. 1975. *The Birth of the Clinic: An Archaeology of Medical Perception.* Trans. A. M. Sheridan Smith. New York: Vintage.

———. 1980. *Power/Knowledge: Selected Interviews and Other Writings, 1972–1977.* Ed. C. Gordon. Trans. C. Gordon et al. New York: Pantheon.

Friedberg, Anne. 1990. A Denial of Difference: Theories of Cinematic Identification. In *Psychoanalysis and Cinema.* Ed. E. Ann Kaplan. London: Routledge, pp. 36–45.

Garfield, V. 1939. *Tsimshian Clan and Society.* University of Washington Publications in Anthropology 7(3):167–349.

Gates, Henry Louis, Jr. (ed.). 1986. *"Race," Writing and Difference.* Chicago: University of Chicago Press.

Geertz, Clifford. 1973a. Religion as a Cultural System. In *The Interpretation of Cultures.* New York: Basic Books, pp. 87–125.

———. 1973b. Thick Description: Toward an Interpretive Theory of Ethnography. In *The Interpretation of Cultures.* New York: Basic Books, pp. 3–30.

———. 1983. "From the Native's Point of View": On the Nature of Anthropological Understanding. In *Local Knowledge: Further Essays in Interpretive Anthropology.* New York: Basic Books, pp. 55–70.

Geffroy, Yannick. 1989. Comments on "Filming Ritual." (Edited transcript of round-table discussion.) Ed. Paul Henley. *Society for Visual Anthropology Newsletter* 5(1):19–23.

Genette, Gerard. 1982. Frontiers of Narrative. In *Figures of Literary Discourse.* Trans. Alan Sheridan. New York: Columbia University Press, pp. 127–144.

Gilman, Sander. 1985. Black Bodies, White Bodies: Toward an Iconography of Female Sexuality in Late Nineteenth Century Art, Medicine, Literature. *Critical Inquiry* 12:204–242.

Ginsburg, Faye. 1988. Ethnographies on the Airwaves: The Presentation of Anthropology on American, British and Japanese Television. In *Cinematographic Theory and New Dimensions in Ethnographic Film.* Senri Ethnological Series No. 24. Eds. Paul Hockings and Yasuhiro Omori. Osaka: National Museum of Ethnology, pp. 31–66.

Goldman, I. 1975. *The Mouth of Heaven.* New York: John Wiley and Sons.

Gramsci, Antonio. 1971. *Selections from Prison Notebooks.* Trans. Quintin Hoare and Geoffery Nowell Smith. New York: International Publishers.

Halbwachs, Maurice. 1968. *La mémoire collective.* Ed. Jean Duvignaud. Paris: Presses Universitaires de France. (English translation, 1980. *The Collective Memory.* New York: Harper and Row.)

———. 1980. *The Collective Memory.* New York: Harper and Row.

Harkin, Michael. 1988. History, Narrative and Temporality: Examples from the Northwest Coast. *Ethnohistory* 35(2):99–130.

———. 1989. The Symbolic History of the Heiltsuk Indians. Unpublished paper, presented to the Department of Anthropology, York University.

Heath, Stephen. 1981. *Questions of Cinema.* Bloomington: University of Indiana Press.

———. 1987. Body, Voice. In *Questions of Cinema.* Bloomington: Indiana University Press, pp. 176–193.

Heider, Karl. 1976. *Ethnographic Film*. Austin: University of Texas Press.

Henderson, Brian. 1976. Two Types of Film Theory. In *Movies and Methods*. Ed. Bill Nichols. Berkeley: University of California Press, pp. 126–135.

Herzfield, Michael. 1986. Of Definitions and Boundaries: The Status of Culture in the Culture of the State. In *Discourse and the Social Life of Meaning*. Ed. Phyllis Pease Chock and June R. Wyman. Washington, D.C.: Smithsonian, pp. 75–93.

Hobsbawm, Eric, and Terence Ranger. 1983. *The Invention of Tradition*. Cambridge: Cambridge University Press.

Hockings, Paul. 1988. Ethnographic Filming and the Development of Anthropological Theory. In *Cinematographic Theory and New Dimensions in Ethnographic Film*. Ed. Paul Hockings and Yasuhiro Omori. Osaka: National Museum of Ethnology.

Holm, W., and G. Quimby. 1980. *Edward S. Curtis in the Land of the War Canoes*. Vancouver: Douglas and MacIntyre.

Howes, Arthur. 1989. Comments on "Filming Ritual." (Edited transcript of roundtable discussion.) *Society for Visual Anthropology Newsletter* 5(1):19–23.

Indian and Inuit Affairs Program (Canada). 1985. *Multi-Media on Indians and Inuit of North America, 1965–80*. Ottawa: Public Communications and Parliamentary Relations Branch.

Jacknis, Ira. 1988. The Picturesque and the Scientific: Franz Boas's Plan for Anthropological Filmmaking. *Visual Anthropology* 1(1):59–64.

Jameson, Fredric. 1971. *Marxism and Form: Twentieth Century Dialectical Theories of Literature*. Princeton, N.J.: Princeton University Press.

———. 1984. Postmodernism, the Cultural Logic of Late Capitalism. *New Left Review* 146:53–92.

———. 1992. *Signatures of the Visible*. New York: Routledge.

Jarvie, Ian. 1987. *Philosophy of the Film*. London: Routledge and Kegan Paul.

Jonaitis, Aldona. 1981. Creations of Mystics and Philosophers: The White Man's Perceptions of Northwest Coast Indian Art from the 1930s to the Present. *American Indian Culture and Research Journal* 5(1):1–45.

Jorgenson, J. G. 1980. *Western Indians: Comparative Environments, Languages and Cultures of 172 Western American Indian Tribes*. San Francisco: Freeman.

Krupat, Arnold. 1985. *For Those Who Came After: A Study of Native American Autobiography*. Berkeley: University of California Press.

Leab, Daniel. 1976. *From Sambo to Superspade*. New York: Houghton Mifflin.

Leaf, Murray J. 1979. *Man, Mind and Science: A History of Anthropology*. New York: Columbia University Press.

Lellis, George. 1982. *Bertolt Brecht: "Cahiers du Cinema" and Contemporary Film Theory*. Ann Arbor, Mich.: UMI Research Press.

Lesser, Alexander. 1985. Franz Boas and the Modernization of Anthropology. In *History, Evolution and the Concept of Culture*. Ed. Sidney Mintz. Cambridge: Cambridge University Press.

Levi-Strauss, Claude. 1955. The Structural Study of Myth. *Journal of American Folklore* 68(270).

———. 1963. *Totemism*. Trans. Rodney Needham. Boston: Beacon.

———. 1969. *The Raw and the Cooked*. New York: Harper and Row.

————. 1984. *Tristes Tropiques.* Trans. John Weightman and Doreen Weightman. New York: Atheneum.

Linden, Eugene. 1991. Lost Tribes, Lost Knowledge. *Time* 138(12):40–48.

Linnekin, Jocelyn C. 1983. Defining Tradition: Variations on the Hawaiian Identity. *American Ethnologist* 10(2):241–252.

Lyell, Charles. 1830. *Principles of Geology.* London.

Lyman, Christopher. 1982. *The Vanishing Race and Other Illusions: Photographs of Indians by Edward Curtis.* New York: Pantheon.

Lyotard, Jean-Francois. 1984. *The Post-Modern Condition: A Report on Knowledge.* Trans. Geoffery Bennington and Brian Massumi. Minneapolis: University of Minnesota Press.

MacCannell, Dean. 1989. *The Tourist: A New Theory of the Leisure Class.* New York: Schocken Books.

McDonald, Henry. 1986. *The Normative Basis of Culture: A Philosophical Inquiry.* Baton Rouge: Louisiana State University.

MacDougall, David. 1976. Prospects of the Ethnographic Film. In *Movies and Methods.* Ed. Bill Nichols. Berkeley: University of California Press, pp. 135–150.

————. 1978. Ethnographic Film: Failures and Promise. In *Annual Review of Anthropology* 7:405–425.

McFeat, Tom. 1966. Introduction. In *Indians of the North Pacific Coast.* Toronto: McLelland and Stewart.

————. 1976. The National Museum of Canadian Anthropology. In *Contributions to the Canadian Ethnology Society.* Ottawa: National Museum of Man, Mercury Series.

McLuhan, T. C. 1972. Curtis: His Life. Introduction to Edward S. Curtis. In *Portraits from North American Indian Life.* Toronto: Newpress, pp. viii–xii.

Malinowski, Bronislaw. 1961. *Argonauts of the Western Pacific.* New York: Dutton. (Originally published in 1922.)

————. 1984. *Argonauts of the Western Pacific.* Prospect Heights, Ill.: Waveland Press. (Originally published in 1922.)

Malraux, André. 1953. *The Voices of Silence.* Trans. Stuart Gilbert. New York: Doubleday.

Marazzi, Antonio. 1988. Ethnological and Anthropological Film: Production, Distribution and Consumption. In *Cinematographic Theory and New Dimensions in Ethnographic Film.* Senri Ethnological Series No. 24. Eds. Paul Hockings and Yasuhiro Omori. Osaka: National Museum of Ethnology, pp. 111–132.

Marcus, George E., and Dick Cushman. 1982. Ethnographies as Texts. *Annual Review of Anthropology* 11:25–69.

Marcus, George E., and Michael M. J. Fischer. 1986. *Anthropology as Cultural Critique: An Experimental Moment in the Human Sciences.* Chicago: University of Chicago Press.

Mauss, Marcel. 1954. *The Gift.* London: Cohen and West.

Metz, Christian. 1982. *The Imaginary Signifier: Psychoanalysis and the Cinema.* London: Macmillan.

Michelson, Annette. 1984. On the Eve of the Future: The Reasonable Facsimile and the Philosophical Toy. *October* 29.

Miller, Daniel. 1987. *Material Culture and Mass Consumption*. Oxford: Basil Blackwell.

Mitchell, W.J.T. 1986. *Iconology: Image, Text, Ideology*. Chicago: University of Chicago Press.

Morson, Gary Saul, and Caryl Emerson. 1990. *Mikhail Bakhtin: Creation of a Prosaics*. Stanford, Calif.: Stanford University Press.

Mulvey, Laura. 1975. Visual Pleasure and Narrative Cinema. In *Screen* 16(3):6–18.

Munn, Nancy. 1977. Spatiotemporal Transformations of Gawa Canoes. *Journal de la Société des Océanistes* 33:39–52.

———. 1983. Gawan Kula: Spatiotemporal Control and the Symbolism of Influence. In *The Kula: New Perspectives on Massim Exchange*. Eds. J. Leach and E. Leach. Cambridge: Cambridge University Press.

———. 1992. The Cultural Anthropology of Time. *The Annual Review of Anthropology* 21:93–123.

Munsterberg, Hugo. 1916. *The Photoplay: A Psychological Study*. New York: D. Appleton.

Murdoch, G. P. 1936. *Rank and Potlatch Among the Haida*. Yale University Publications in Anthropology 13:1–20. New Haven, Conn.: Yale University Press.

Nichols, Bill (ed.). 1976. *Movies and Methods*. Berkeley: University of California Press.

———. 1981. *Ideology and the Image: Social Representations in the Cinema and Other Media*. Bloomington: Indiana University Press.

———. 1983. The Voice of Documentary. In *Film Form* 36(3).

Oberg, K. 1934. Crime and Punishment in Tlingit Society. *American Anthropologist* 36:145–156.

Pearce, Roy Harvey. 1965. *Savagism and Civilization: A Study of the Indian and the American Mind*. Berkeley: University of California Press.

Pefanis, Julian. 1991. *Heterology and the Postmodern: Bataille, Baudrillard and Lyotard*. Durham, N.C.: Duke University Press.

Phillips, Christopher. 1991. Between Pictures. *Art in America* (November), pp. 104–116.

Philp, K. 1977. *John Collier's Crusade for Indian Reform, 1920–54.* Tucson: University of Arizona Press.

Piault, Marc. 1989. Comments on "Filming Ritual." (Edited transcript of roundtable discussion.) Ed. Paul Henley. *Society for Visual Anthropology Newsletter* 5(1):19–23.

Piddocke, Stuart. 1965. The Potlatch System of the Southern Kwakiutl: A New Perspective. *Southwestern Journal of Anthropology* 21:244–264.

Pierce, Charles S. 1977. *Semiotics and Significs: The Correspondence Between Charles S. Pierce and Victoria Lady Welby*. Bloomington and London: Indiana University Press.

Pleynet, Marcelin. 1978. Economical-Ideological-Formal. In *May '68 and Film Culture*. Ed. Sylvia Harvey. London: British Film Institute.

Ponting, J. Rick. 1986. *Arduous Journey: Canadian Indians and Decolonization*. Toronto: McLelland and Stewart.

Pratt, Mary Louise. 1986. Fieldwork in Common Places. In *Writing Culture*. Eds. James Clifford and George E. Marcus. Berkeley: University of California Press.

Pryluck, Calvin. 1988. Ultimately We Are All Outsiders: The Ethics of Documentary Filming. In *New Challenges for Documentary.* Ed. Alan Rosenthal. Berkeley: University of California Press, pp. 255–268.

Rabinow, Paul. 1985. Discourse and Power: On the Limits of Ethnographic Texts. *Dialectical Anthropology* 1:1–17.

Radhakrishnan, R. 1987. Ethnic Identity and Post-Structuralist Difference. *Cultural Critique* 6:199–220.

Ray, Verne. 1966. Boas and the Neglect of Commoners. In *Indians of the North Pacific Coast.* Ed. Tom McFeat. Ottawa: Macmillan, pp. 159–165.

Richardson, Joanne. 1982. The Miracle Is to Make It Solid. M.A. thesis, University of British Columbia.

Rilke, Rainer Maria. 1991. *Letters on Cézanne.* Ed. Clara Rilke. Trans. Joel Agee. London: Vintage.

Roemer, Michael. 1971. The Surfaces of Reality. In *Perspectives in the Study of Film.* Ed. John Stuart Katz. Boston: Little, Brown and Co., pp. 98–109.

Rosaldo, Renato. 1986. From the Door of His Tent: The Fieldworker and the Inquisitor. In *Writing Culture.* Eds. James Clifford and George E. Marcus. Berkeley: University of California Press.

Rosenthal, Alan (ed.). 1988. *New Challenges for Documentary.* Berkeley: University of California Press.

Rouch, Jean. 1988. Our Totemic Ancestors and Crazed Masters. In *Cinematographic Theory and New Dimensions of Ethnographic Film.* Eds. Paul Hockings and Yasuhiro Omori. Osaka: National Museum of Ethnology, pp. 225–238.

Ruby, Jay. 1982. Ethnography as Tromp l'Oeil: Film and Anthropology. In *A Crack in the Mirror: Reflexive Perspectives in Anthropology.* Philadelphia: University of Pennsylvania Press, pp. 121–132.

———. 1983. An Early Attempt at Studying Human Behavior with a Camera: Franz Boas and the Kwakiutl—1930. In *Methodology in Anthropological Filmmaking: Papers of the IUAES Intercongress, Amsterdam, 1981.* Gottingen: Editions Herodot.

———. 1988. The Image Mirrored: Reflexivity in the Documentary Film. In *New Challenges for Documentary.* Ed. Alan Rosenthal. Berkeley: University of California Press, pp. 48–77.

Sahlins, Marshall. 1976. *Culture and Practical Reason.* Chicago: University of Chicago Press.

———. 1985. *Islands of History.* Chicago: University of Chicago Press.

Said, Edward. 1978. *Orientalism.* New York: Pantheon Books.

———. 1989. Representing the Colonized: Anthropology's Interlocutors. *Critical Inquiry* 15:205–225.

Sarris, Andrew. 1976. Towards a Theory of Film History. In *Movies and Methods.* Ed. Bill Nichols. Berkeley: University of California Press, pp. 237–250.

Schechner, Richard. 1985. Restoration of Behavior. In *Between Theatre and Anthropology.* Philadelphia: University of Pennsylvania Press, pp. 34–116.

Scholte, Bob. 1986. The Literary Turn in Contemporary Anthropology. *Dialectical Anthropology* 7(1):33–47.

Scott, James. 1985. *Weapons of the Weak: Everyday Forms of Peasant Resistance.* New Haven, Conn.: Yale University Press.

Seguin, Margaret. 1985. *Interpretive Contexts for Traditional and Current Coast Tsimshian Feasts.* Ottawa: National Museum of Man, Canadian Ethnology Society Paper No. 98.

Sontag, Susan. 1966. The Anthropologist as Hero. In *Claude Levi-Strauss: The Anthropologist as Hero.* Eds. E. Nelson Hayes and Tanya Hayes. Cambridge, Mass.: MIT Press, pp. 184–196.

———. 1977. *On Photography.* New York: Farrar, Strauss and Giroux.

Stam, Robert, and Louise Spence. 1983. Colonialism, Racism and Representation— An Introduction. *Screen* 24(2):2–20.

Stewart, Susan. 1984. *On Longing: Narratives of the Miniature, the Gigantic, the Souvenir, the Collection.* Baltimore: Johns Hopkins University Press.

Stocking, George (ed.). 1968. *Race, Culture and Evolution.* New York: Free Press.

———. 1974. *The Shaping of American Anthropology: A Franz Boas Reader.* New York: Basic Books.

———. 1985. Philanthropists and Vanishing Culture: Rockefeller Funding and the End of the Museum Era in Anglo-American Anthropology. In *Objects and Others: Essays in Museums and Material Culture.* Madison: University of Wisconsin Press, pp. 112–145.

———. 1987. *Victorian Anthropology.* New York: Free Press.

Strathern, Marilyn. 1987. Out of Context: The Persuasive Fictions of Anthropology. *Current Anthropology* 19:673–701.

Suttles, Wayne. 1987. *Coast Salish Essays.* Vancouver: Talonbooks.

Swanton, J. R. 1909. *Contributions to the Ethnology of the Haida.* Memoirs of the American Museum of Natural History, Vol. 8, pp. 1–300.

Szathmary, E.J.E., and N. S. Ossenberg. 1978. Are the Biological Differences Between North American Indians Truly Profound? *Current Anthropology* 19: 673–701.

Tagg, John. 1988. *The Burden of Representation: Essays on Photographies and Histories.* London: MacMillan.

Teit, James. 1898. *Traditions of the Thompson River Indians.* American Folklore Society, Memoir No. 6.

Tepper, Leslie. 1987. *The Interior Salish Tribes of British Columbia: A Photographic Collection.* Ottawa: Canadian Museum of Civilization, Mercury Series No. 111.

Terdiman, Richard. 1985. Deconstructing Memory: On Representing the Past and Theorizing Culture in France Since the Revolution. *Diacritics* (Winter), pp. 13–37.

Thomas, Sari. 1979. Basil Wright on Art, Anthropology and the Documentary. *Quarterly Review of Film Studies* (Fall 1979), pp. 465–481.

Thompson, Richard. 1976. Meep Meep. In *Movies and Methods.* Ed. Bill Nichols. Berkeley: University of California Press, pp. 126–134.

Torgovnick, Marianna. 1990. *Gone Primitive: Savage Intellectuals, Modern Lives.* Chicago: University of Chicago Press.

Tudor, Andrew. 1976. Genre and Critical Methodology. In *Movies and Methods.* Ed. Bill Nichols. Berkeley: University of California Press, pp. 118–125.

Turin, Maureen Cheryn. 1985. *Abstraction in Avant-Garde Films.* Ann Arbor: University of Michigan Imprints Press.

Turner, Victor. 1977. Process, System and Symbol: A New Anthropological Synthesis. *Daedalus* 196(3).

Tyler, Stephen. 1987. *The Unspeakable: Discourse, Dialogue, and Rhetoric in the Postmodern World.* Madison: University of Wisconsin Press.

Vanderbeek, Stan. 1971. Re-vision. In *Perspectives on the Study of Film.* Ed. John Stuart Katz. Boston: Little, Brown and Co., pp. 227–233.

van Gennep, Arnold. 1960. *Rites of Passage.* London: Routledge and Kegan Paul. (Originally published in 1908.)

Vizenor, Gerald. 1987. Socioacupuncture: Mythic Reversal and the Strip-Tease in Four Scenes. In *The American Indian and the Problem of History.* Ed. Calvin Martin. New York: Oxford University Press.

Wachtel, Nathan. 1986. Introduction. In *History and Anthropology* 2:307–334.

White, Hayden. 1980. The Value of Narrativity in the Representation of Reality. In *On Narrative.* Ed. W.J.T. Mitchell. Chicago and London: University of Chicago Press.

Williams, Elizabeth. 1985. Art and Artifact at the Trocadero. In *Objects and Others.* Ed. George Stocking. Madison: University of Wisconsin Press, pp. 145–166.

Williams, Raymond. 1973. *The Country and the City.* Oxford: Oxford University Press.

Wolf, Eric. 1982. *Europe and the People Without History.* Berkeley: University of California Press.

Wollen, Peter. 1976. Cinema and Semiology: Some Points of Contact. In *Movies and Methods.* Ed. Bill Nichols. Berkeley: University of California Press, pp. 481–492.

Worth, Sol. 1969. The Development of a Semiotic of Film. *Semiotica* 1:282–321.

———. 1972. Toward the Development of a Semiotic of Ethnographic Film. *PIEF Newsletter* 3(3):8–12.

Yates, Frances. 1966. *The Art of Memory.* Chicago: University of Chicago Press.

Young, Colin. 1989. Documentary and Fiction, Distortion and Belief. In *Cinematographic Theory and New Dimensions in Ethnographic Film.* Senri Ethnological Studies No. 24. Eds. Paul Hockings and Yasuhiro Omori. Osaka: National Museum of Ethnology, pp. 7–30.

Zavarzadeh, Mas'ud. 1991. *Seeing Films Politically.* Albany: SUNY Press.

Zimmerly, David W. 1974. *Museocinematography: Ethnographic Film Programs of the National Museum of Man, 1912–1973.* Ottawa: National Museum of Man, Mercury Series No. 11.

Selected Filmography

THE ABBREVIATIONS USED in this filmography are as follows: D = director, DP = director of photography or camera, NARR = narrator, PC = production company, and SCR = scriptwriter.

Bella Bella. 1975. PC: National Film Board of Canada. D: Barbara Green. 16 mm, col., 27 mins.

Blunden Harbour. 1951. PC: Orbit Films. D/SCR: Robert Gardner. DP: W. H. Heick, P. Jacquemin. NARR: Richard Selig. 16mm, b&w, 20 mins.

Box of Treasures. 1983. PC: U'Mista Cultural Society. D: Dennis Wheeler. NARR: Gloria Cranmer-Webster. 16mm, col., 16 mins.

Dances with Wolves. 1990. PC: TIG Productions. D: Kevin Costner. DP: Dean Semler. SCR: Michael Blake. 35mm, col., 181 mins.

Incident at Oglala. 1991. PC: Miramax films/Spanish Fork Motion Picture Company. D: Michael Apted. DP: Maryse Alberti. NARR: Robert Redford. 16mm, col., 90 mins.

In the Land of the War Canoes. 1914. PC: originally Edward Curtis; now Burke Museum, University of Washington. D: Edward Curtis. DP: Edward Curtis. 16mm and 35mm, b&w, 47 mins.

Potlatch . . . a strict law bids us dance. 1975. PC: U'mista Cultural Society and Chuck Olin Associates. D: Chuck Olin. DP: Chuck Olin and Tony Westman. 16mm, col., 55 mins.

Saving the Sagas. 1927. PC: Associated Screen News. D/DP: J. S. Watson. 35mm, b&w, 1 reel.

The Silent Ones. 1961. PC: British Columbia Department of Recreation and Conservation. D/DP: Bernard H. Atkins. SCR: Harry P. McKeever. NARR: Peter Elkington. 16mm, col., 25 mins.

The Tsimshian Indians of the Skeena River of British Columbia. 1925–1927. PC: National Museum of Canada. D/DP: Harlan I. Smith. 16mm and 35mm, b&w, 10 mins.

Thunderheart. 1992. PC: TriStar Pictures. D: Michael Apted. SCR: John Fusco. 35mm, col., 118 mins.

Totem. 1959. PC: Canadian Broadcasting Corporation. DP: Kelly Duncan. SCR/NARR: Bill Reid. 16mm, b&w, 24 mins.

About the Book and Author

BRINGING TOGETHER the insights of literary criticism, film theory, history, and anthropology, this book explores the tradition of ethnographic film on the Northwest Coast and its relationship to the ethnography of the area. Rosalind Morris takes account of these films, organizing her discussions around a series of detailed readings and viewings that treat questions of form and content in broadly historical terms. Asking why the films took the direction they did, each with a distinct representational strategy, and how the written and filmic ethnographies of the area have differed from each other, she points out the complex relationships between particular epistemological positions, aesthetic strategies, and institutional politics.

The book explores both the ethnographic imagination of the Northwest Coast and the place of that particular image in the discipline's representation of non-Western "others." The introductory and concluding chapters extend the discussions beyond the Northwest Coast, directly addressing the politics of anthropological poetics through an analysis of the discipline's relationship to the Western mass media's imaging of non-Western peoples. Morris works toward a radically historicized film theory, one that refuses the empiricism of documentary realism while confronting its own aesthetic traditions in order to re-envision them.

Rosalind C. Morris is a doctoral candidate in anthropology at The University of Chicago. She conducted research on ritual theater and cultural politics in Northern Thailand and is currently writing her dissertation. A graduate of the New York Film Academy, she lives in New York.

Index